University of Hertfordshire

Learning and Information Services

College Lane, Hatfield, Hertfordshire, AL10 9AB

For renewal of Standard and One Week Loans,
please visit the website: http://www.voyager.herts.ac.uk

This item must be returned or the loan renewed by the due date.
The University reserves the right to recall items from loan at any time.
A fine will be charged for the late return of items.

4827/KM/DS

Healthy living in the Alps

Manchester University Press

STUDIES IN POPULAR CULTURE

General editor: Professor Jeffrey Richards

Healthy living in the Alps

The origins of winter tourism in Switzerland, 1860–1914

SUSAN BARTON

Manchester University Press
Manchester and New York

distributed exclusively in the USA by Palgrave Macmillan

Published by Manchester University Press
Oxford Road, Manchester M13 9NR, UK
and Room 400, 175 Fifth Avenue, New York, NY 10010, USA
www.manchesteruniversitypress.co.uk

Distributed exclusively in the USA by
Palgrave Macmillan, 175 Fifth Avenue, New York,
NY 10010, USA

Distributed exclusively in Canada by
UBC Press, University of British Columbia, 2029 West Mall,
Vancouver, BC, Canada V6T 1Z2

British Library Cataloguing-in-Publication Data
A catalogue record for this book is available from the British Library

Library of Congress Cataloging-in-Publication Data applied for

ISBN 978 0 7190 7843 9 *hardback*

First published 2008

17 16 15 14 13 12 11 10 09 08   10 9 8 7 6 5 4 3 2 1

Typeset in Adobe Garamond with Gill Sans display by
Koinonia, Manchester
Printed in Great Britain
by Biddles Ltd, King's Lynn

STUDIES IN POPULAR CULTURE

There has in recent years been an explosion of interest in culture and cultural studies. The impetus has come from two directions and out of two different traditions. On the one hand, cultural history has grown out of social history to become a distinct and identifiable school of historical investigation. On the other hand, cultural studies has grown out of English literature and has concerned itself to a large extent with contemporary issues. Nevertheless, there is a shared project, its aim, to elucidate the meanings and values implicit and explicit in the art, literature, learning, institutions and everyday behaviour within a given society. Both the cultural historian and the cultural studies scholar seek to explore the ways in which a culture is imagined, represented and received, how it interacts with social processes, how it contributes to individual and collective identities and world views, to stability and change, to social, political and economic activities and programmes. This series aims to provide an arena for the cross-fertilisation of the discipline, so that the work of the cultural historian can take advantage of the most useful and illuminating of the theoretical developments and the cultural studies scholars can extend the purely historical underpinnings of their investigations. The ultimate objective of the series is to provide a range of books which will explain in a readable and accessible way where we are now socially and culturally and how we got to where we are. This should enable people to be better informed, promote an interdisciplinary approach to cultural issues and encourage deeper thought about the issues, attitudes and institutions of popular culture.

Jeffrey Richards

Contents

Illustrations

General editor's foreword

Mountains were integral to the ideology of Romanticism as an embodiment of the sublime. They represented freedom, elemental purity, escape from an increasingly complex urban world and the chance to commune with Nature or the Almighty. But in the nineteenth century the Alps came to offer practical as well as spiritual fulfilment. Switzerland evolved a dual identity, attracting seekers after health and seekers after sport. This twin appeal informs Su Barton's fascinating analysis of the development of the Swiss resorts of Davos, St Moritz, Arosa, Leysin and Grindelwald, whose transformation into tourist destinations she compares and contrasts. That characteristic curse of the nineteenth century – consumption – drove people to Switzerland as a variety of medical experts recommended the air and the atmosphere and sanatoria were created with a strict regime of diet, rest and fresh air. Alongside health, there was a development of winter sports – ice-skating, climbing, tobogganing and skiing, though Su Barton points out that skiing developed slowly and was initially seen as a pastime for an eccentric minority. She shows how tourism stimulated technological developments (railways, cable cars, trams, telegraphy, hydroelectric schemes), not to mention alpine sportswear and Swiss chocolate. She analyses the class background and professions of the tourists and discovers that alongside the celebrities who did so much to make Switzerland fashionable (Arthur Conan Doyle, Saki, E.F. Benson, John Addington Symonds, Erskine Childers), middle- and upper-middle-class visitors predominated, with clergymen particularly prominent. As a result, the public school ethos was pervasive and informed the codes drawn up to govern alpine sports. Su Barton's meticulous and wide-ranging research is brought to life by the sympathetic insight she brings to the subject, born of her personal experience of being sent to a Swiss sanatorium for her health in the 1960s. Her vivid personal memoir prefaces the book, which is a captivating study of an important and neglected aspect of tourism history.

Jeffrey Richards

Acknowledgements

Thanks to the British Academy, Heidi Reisz at Switzerland Tourism and the many individuals who have assisted and supported me with this work in so many ways: Maurice André (Leysin); Jacob Bracher (Grindelwald); Ernst Lichtenhahn (Arosa); Ruth Schaeuble (Arosa); Veronique Bernard (Leysin); Corina Huber (DB St Moritz); Timothy Nelson (DB Davos); Prof. Laurent Tissot (University of Neuchatel); Prof. Richard Holt (de Montfort University); Prof. Pierre Lanfranchi (de Montfort University) Grahame Carter; Marie Weston and Max Barton for feeding the cats.

Introduction

Those who are born and bred among the mountains accept with composure their heritage of beauty, and those who never see the hills do not realise all that they are missing. But the child whose early life is divided between London and the Alps pays for his few weeks in Paradise with moments of poignant despair, and with months of gnawing home-sickness for the hills.[1]

My own homesickness began in 1968 when I left my home and family and travelled to Switzerland for the first time in the company of complete strangers. We were a band of fifteen children and young people between the ages five and fifteen years old accompanied by a female teacher from England on a journey not just to the Alps but into life and adventure for the first time. We were on the way to Arosa in the eastern part of the country in the canton of Grisons or Graubunden, as it is in German, to stay for a whole term from September to Christmas in a place called *Prasura* that styled itself a *Kinderkurhaus*. It turned out to be a cross between a school, a hospital and a children's home. All the young people staying there were mostly seeking relief from asthma or in my case, the odd one out, a skinny, frail eleven-year-old constantly vulnerable to infection and illness. A charity called *Alpine Sun for British Children* had paid for us all to go to Switzerland where the climate would give us strength and some respite, if not a cure, from our ailments. There were two dormitories, one for boys and one for the five girls. Two younger boys stayed upstairs in the *Kindergarten*. The first night there we all felt the pain of homesickness, not for the mountains which surrounded us but for our houses and families in England. How I cried that night, hoping that if I made enough fuss I'd be sent home.

The first morning in Arosa was so strange. We were woken by a young woman in knee-length socks opening the blinds to wake us up. She was called Fraulein Heidi, which is just what we had expected a Swiss girl to be called.

What was a surprise was that she had to take our temperatures with what she called a 'temmomater' under our armpits. Having to keep our arms still and clamped to our sides for several minutes was our first experience of the discipline imposed on those following the regime of a sanatorium. This routine was repeated twice every day.

The surprise of the thermometer, each with a child's name on it, was soon overcome by the shock of breakfast. A gong was carried by a child up the central stairs, bonged all the way up and down, to call us four times every day to our meals. The breakfast was a large cup of hot milk, crusty bread and jam. Perhaps the staff had forgotten we were coming and would obtain the necessary food for English children ready for the next day. But this turned out to be our staple, twice a day, morning and afternoon. On Sunday we had a change, cheese replaced jam and cocoa was substituted for warm milk. We also had two cooked meals daily, in the middle of the day and in the evening. In England at that time there seemed to be potatoes with every meal. To our absolute amazement, we were subjected to dinners and suppers without potatoes but accompanied by all sorts of strange things, some more palatable than others. Noodles and ravioli were my favourite although I had no idea what they were called at the time. No one was allowed to leave any food on the plate, everything had to be eaten. How we all dreaded the days when the acrid smell of *sauerkraut* wafted up the stairs to us and we knew we would have to suffer the torture of being forced to eat this cabbage fermented in vinegar.

Some foods were treated with ambivalence and we got used to them, such as *Frankfurters* and what we called 'muckle bangers', after the exclamation of a young Geordie boy when seeing a massive sausage. It wasn't just awareness of foreigners from Switzerland or Germany that we were gaining; we were also becoming familiar with people and accents from regions of England other than our own, such as Tyneside, the West Midlands and Merseyside. There were also several children from other countries there, although the majority of the residents were Swiss and German. I made friends with two American sisters, sent to safety from US Air Force accommodation in Laos, now suffering the affects of the escalating Vietnam War. An Argentinian brother and sister told us about the *gauchos* on their father's vast cattle ranch.

On Sunday the cook had the afternoon off and so we had a cold supper, sandwiches which reinforced our sense of superiority to the 'foreigners' because their makers hadn't realised that they needed to put a second slice of bread on the top to stop the contents falling off! An alternative to open sandwiches was something we ungratefully called a plate of sick. Actually it was *Muesli* which we didn't know until *Alpen* came on the market in Britain. For us though it was served as a warm supper dish on a plate, not as a cold breakfast cereal. Every night we drank a kind of tea which was served without milk and had a strange smell which was universally hated by the English children.

The next thing that was completely unexpected was the afternoon rest period. For two hours every afternoon we lay on reclining wicker chairs, like sun-loungers on a balcony whatever the weather. Each bed was supplied with a thick blanket and if it was cold we could wear our coats, hats and even gloves. We were not allowed to talk on the balcony and if we couldn't sleep we had to read silently, a command difficult for unruly young English people to obey. So many times lines were given as punishment for breaking this rule: 'I must not talk on the balcony' written out a hundred times. One thing that made us all fall instantly into silence was hearing the words 'Frau Doctor's coming!' As Frau Doktor Lichtenhahn was in charge of *Prasura*, we saw her as an authority figure and associated her, probably unjustly, with the sternness of a headmistress. Little did we know that we were following a century-old ritual when we lay on the balcony, a tradition that was rapidly becoming extinct. I don't know whether the tradition survived anywhere else at that time; perhaps we were among the last to follow it.

The third element of the regime we followed was daily exercise. Whatever the weather we went for a walk, beginning with an extremely short stroll on the first day while we acclimatised, extending to long excursions on the mountains. All fifteen of us and the teacher went out every afternoon following our bread-and-jam tea, after the balcony rest period. We also had a shorter walk in the morning after lessons and before lunch. For half the time of our stay we wandered on grassy meadows and rocky tracks. Then came the snow and our excursions became walks in the new winter wonderland that waited to be explored. We slid along icy paths and on a small frozen lake up in the mountains where no one else went. As one of the more adventurous of the group, I hired some skates and took off alone to the deeply frozen Obersee where I taught myself to skate. Soon a few of us clubbed together and hired sledges, an Argentinian boy hired a bobsleigh. What we weren't allowed to do was ski. I don't know why, probably for insurance reasons. However this didn't stop us joining in at the bottom of the ski slope opposite the *Hotel Kulm,* we collected large cardboard boxes, opened them up flat and used these as make shift boards on which we stood to slide down the slope. The more expert riders with stronger legs could crouch and stand up alternately in a single run down.

Life in *Prasura* was not all eat, sleep and play; we had school lessons every morning for a couple of hours before our first walk of the day and once a week two specialist teachers came so we could do craft work, wood carving, pottery and weaving. Once a week we had a bath supervised by our nurse Heidi, who soon left to be replaced by Fraulein Ursula or Ursi.

Switzerland in the 1960s was very different from England, unmistakably foreign and exciting to a young inquisitive mind. We children knew that the Swiss spoke a foreign language but we hadn't realised how differently they would dress. Everyone seemed to wear short-length trousers which fitted into a cuff just below the knee. Outside long thick socks were worn, usually with leather ankle boots. We English wore Wellingtons, with the boys in jeans or grey trousers and the girls in stretch ski pants that had straps under the feet. Swiss school children carried satchels on their backs. These school bags were made of animal skin with the fur left on. In their breeches, socks and boots with these bags on their backs they looked so different from British school children in their uniforms with their satchels slung over their shoulders. Indoors, the Swiss children staying at *Prasura* wore strange footwear, long knitted patterned socks with leather soles attached. The English had slippers which we could kick off and so slide in our stockinged feet down the long, smooth corridor outside our dormitories and rooms to practise our glissading on the ice and slopes outside.

The monotony of the routine is reflected in the diary I kept every day. For almost each entry is written 'had lessons, on balcony, went walk'; or just 'had lessons, went walk'. Living in a closed community caused the children and young people to adapt their behaviour to cope with the situation that alternated between extremes of excitement, boredom and homesickness as well as coping with the illnesses that had sent us out there. For the first time we had an awareness of our Englishness, of being different from the other nationalities around us. Some became rebellious to preserve their sense of autonomy and individuality. We had parties on birthdays, midnight feasts after lights-out and sadly, often fell out with each other and fought. In the very little unsupervised time we had, I sneaked out to wander in the woods or on the mountains alone. One day I had an irresistible urge to climb up a particularly tall pine tree in garden. It was so easy, the branches grew almost parallel and were about nine inches apart, making the ascent like climbing a ladder and I couldn't stop myself going higher and higher until I could look down on our third floor balcony. I wasn't afraid of falling but I was aware I was doing something that wouldn't be allowed and was scared of an adult discovering what I was up to. I made it up and down undetected and couldn't wait to boast to my companions. I was so indignant when no one would believe me, just because I was a girl, I supposed! As an adult reading Thomas Mann's *Magic Mountain*, I felt that my tree- climbing episode was similar in significance to Hans Castorp's skiing experience: a forbidden act of rebellion and an attempt to assert autonomy over my own physicality.

Torn between love of the mountains and longing for home, many children felt cast off by their parents. I was so lucky, my wonderful mother wrote to me everyday but some children heard from home only infrequently. These emotions have never really left me. In England I constantly yearn to be back in the mountains but being in Switzerland where I travel nearly every year makes me love my home more. To pass the time between visits I began work on this volume once I realised the significance of the life I'd experienced in Arosa. The feelings and emotions I remember became even more significant once I realised how many others had gone through similar experiences in sanatoria in the century or so before.

Note

1 Lunn, Arnold, *The mountains of youth,* London, 1925, p. 1.

The quest for health
in the Alps

The contribution of the Alps to health care, and of health seekers to alpine sports is examined in this book through a study of the pursuit of health and the celebration of health as the opposite of illness in the alpine resorts between the latter years of the nineteenth and the early twentieth centuries. Treatments offered the hope of a cure for tuberculosis and the relief of asthma and other ailments affecting the lungs. The therapies in the Alps challenged earlier medical views of how to care for tuberculosis patients. The *Curhaus* (*Kurhaus* or cure-houses) and sanatoria emerged from a blending of the philosophies of romanticism and alternative medicine, later backed up by scientific investigation. The legacy of this philosophy prevails into the present, not necessarily as a cure but as a way of maintaining, restoring or even celebrating health. The location of sanatoria at high altitude, where air was 'thinner', was a vital part of the treatment. Patients were taken from regions blighted by industrialisation and removed from the hot, stuffy rooms of previous treatments to atmospheres uncontaminated by civilisation. Not just respiratory illnesses were offered a respite: the less tangible sickness of heart and spirit or nervous breakdown caused by the stresses of the evolving life of modernity could be healed in the mountains. People came to the Alps to regain health and strength. This echoes the spirit of Romanticism voiced by Rousseau and others which saw the Alps as a retreat where people could live among simple, honest country folk in contact with the beneficial influences of nature. Johanna Spyri's story of *Heidi* can be viewed in this context. Heidi knew the mountains could make her invalid cousin, the offspring of urban, bourgeois parents, well, and they did.[1] Senancour saw men divided into two classes: those of the heights and the multitude who are men of the plains. The man of the heights is as nature intended. If he descends to the plains he breathes with difficulty an atmosphere laden with corruption, hatred and anguish.[2] In the *Magic Mountain*,

Thomas Mann continues Senancour's sentiment within his characters at the Davos *Berghof.* Mann's fictitious assortment of people staying in Davos to cure their respiratory diseases have come to accept that they are different from people of the flatlands and fear that if they leave their mountain sanctuary they will immediately suffer a decline in health once again.[3] It is within this context of the almost mystical concept of the Alps as a place of healing that sanatoria may be placed.

The Romantics were right in their condemnation of urban landscapes as being blighted. Cities were breeding grounds for disease and one of the worst diseases was tuberculosis, characterised by fever, night sweats and coughing up blood (haemoptysis). It was known as consumption as it seemed to consume its victims. As the population grew denser so did incidences of the illness. It was one of the most common causes of death, especially in young people. Another common name given to the disease was 'phthisis'. Through the premature death of poets like John Keats, the disease itself became romanticised. Nevertheless it had a devastating effect on the urban poor who lived in conditions that easily allowed the disease to spread at a time when it was not understood that it was contagious. The sanatoria in Switzerland catered for the affluent who could at least suffer in comfort. It is important to remember that most victims of consumption died at home where they could infect their carers and families or in the Britain of the early twentieth century in one of forty-one public institutions funded by the Poor Law by 1910.[4] However, this book is not the story of tuberculosis in general or how it affected the majority of its victims, the urban poor. Neither is it a study of treatments in Britain. Although these are important topics of study, this work will focus on the experiences of a predominantly wealthy minority and the facilities opened for them in Switzerland and the sporting activities in which they indulged in the winter snows. Until past the middle of the nineteenth century, these people, if they succumbed to the illness, were recommended by their physicians to travel south to the warmer climate of the Mediterranean countries if they hoped to recover. Strangely, cold, snowy Switzerland in winter was soon to become a rival to the established resorts of southern Europe and north Africa.

In the first half of the nineteenth century, spas and climatic resorts were recommended to ease many disorders. Physicians sent their affluent tuberculosis patients to the Mediterranean in the hope of affecting a cure. By the end of the century tuberculosis, the great illness of the Romantics that affected the poor in the growing cities was the principal fatal condition of Europe.[5] In the absence of any effective drug treatments, 'medical climatology', the belief that different climates had different effects on the constitution, was popular. Switzerland already had a reputation as a place of healing owing to its mineral springs around which spas and hotels were erected.[6] In the area of the Grisons there were already spas at St Moritz, Tarasp, Vulpera, Alveneu, Spinabad near Davos and Pfäffers where Paracelsus was the first physician in 1555.[7] According to Dr H. Keller, writing in the 1920s, 'one could count no less than 252 springs in 156 spa towns.[8] Some of these springs had been known since prehistoric times. In Switzerland the Alps had a hundred spas, Jura had twenty-six and there were another thirty in the Swiss Highlands. In the introduction to the booklet from which these statistics were acquired, Switzerland is promoted as having been a meeting point for tourists and sports people as well as those in need of peace and wishing for health. In these spa towns were well-furnished guest-houses and hotels with everything that could be wished for by their guests.[9]

In the middle of the eighteenth century alpine 'milk cures' came into medical fashion. Milk from goats, cows, asses, horses and humans was used therapeutically in ancient medicine, above all in the treatment of tuberculosis and gout. Animals were fed with certain medicinal herbs to make their milk especially effective. As milk could frequently cause digestive problems, it was often thinned with mineral water. In the mountains of Switzerland, milk and its products – butter, cheese, whey and curds – were the main food of farmers and herdsmen. The high pasture lands of alpine cattle were rich in a variety of plants and herbs. Goats' milk was often seen as more effective than cows' milk and could be mixed with herbs, flowers and honey. Butter made from cows' and goats' milk had already been used in medicine for a long time. Goats' butter was used for hair and skin care products and goats' milk used in the treatment of stomach problems. A Glarner speciality, *Ziegerkraut* was used in earlier times as a wormer. Less appetising of the cattle products used as remedies were urine and excrement. These were important components of the so-called 'dirty-apothecary' (*Dreckapotheke*) used in rural areas. Liquid burnt off from cow faeces was drunk to treat yellow fever. For stomach cramps the juice of fresh cowpats was pressed out and given as a drink. Sometimes fresh manure was mixed with wine, pressed through a cloth and the juice given to patients, sometimes mixed with a few spices. Cowpats were sometimes burnt to ashes and a spoonful of it taken – good for dropsy (*Wassersüchtigen*). Ox urine was mixed with myrrh to treat earache.[10]

In 1749 Dr Meyer of Arbon advised his seriously ill brother-in-law who suffered from a disease of the chest to take goats' milk. He was urged to take the goats' milk in Appenzell where the milk was brought down from the Alps daily and where its consumption could be combined with a stay in clean mountain air and in the comfort of a respectable guest-house which could provide a regular and nourishing diet, which at that time was not easy to find. The brother-in-law went to the *Gasthof zum Ochsen* at Gais. Herdsmen carried the still warm milk down to the village daily. After several weeks the man was cured and returned home.[11]

As news of this cure spread around medical circles, other doctors sent their patients to Gais which became a centre for the so-called *Milchkur*. The goats' milk was distributed daily in the village square after being carried for about three hours. The milk was used as a laxative. This combined with good food and moderate activity in the open air made many patients noticeably better. The low cost of this type of cure also contributed to its popularity.[12]

Other milk cure centres opened in the region, in Weissbad, Appenzell and Heinrichsbad near Herisau. The milk cure spread to other mountain regions and also to the lowlands where cows' milk was mostly used. This form of cure brought its own advisers, guides and travel literature. Cures using milk remained popular until the end of the nineteenth century when sanatoria and high-altitude cures became more popular.

Like other tourism initiatives, the milk cure brought infrastructure development with local opposition. After a year of arguments and resistance, a traffic-carrying road was built to Gais, where previously access was only on foot or by pack horse. Also for the comfort and edification of guests, the open, shadowless square where the milk was distributed had lime trees planted in it to provide shade. In Heinrichsbad by the 1830s mineral baths and milk cure were combined and cowshed therapy was also available. North of the bath building was a farm house with cowshed rooms suitable for guests who also drank cows' milk or asses' milk to treat tuberculosis.[13]

In a cowshed the stable air, which included animal breath and body vapour, could be inhaled. There was warmth and the ammonia gases from urine were supposedly a balsam for infected lungs. Also there was a ready supply of warm milk. It is possible that breathing in ammonia could have altered the natural pH value in the lungs, making it harder for bacteria to develop.

In its embryonic days as a resort, cowshed cures were used in Davos in the 1850s. A clergyman and missionary from Basle called Forchhammer moved to Davos under the care of altitude cure pioneer Dr Alexander Spengler. Forchhammer worked as a teacher in the Davos valley, walking miles daily in his work despite being described as seriously ill with lung disease. For a long time he had to sleep in the ammonia-filled cowshed, the main part of his cure programme. He also drank another favourite medicinal drink of that part of Switzerland, Veltliner wine from nearby Italy. Cowshed cures were part of the folk medicine tradition.[14]

Spengler incorporated some aspects of the milk cure when he began to receive patients for high-altitude cures in Davos from the 1860s. In the routine of his *Curhaus,* guests got up at 6 am in the morning. The first thing they did was drink two glasses of cow-warm milk in the *Milchhalle* next to the *Curhaus.* Then they went for a short walk before breakfast after which they had another walk. At 10 am they went back to the *Milchhalle* for the prescribed quantity of milk. Then patients relaxed by reading or writing letters until lunchtime at 1 pm when they ate meat and vegetables, drinking *Veltliner* wine with the meal. After that it was a rest, lying on a balcony or in their room by an open window until 4 pm when cow-warm milk was drunk again. Then the patients went out of doors again until it was time for the evening meal. Milk remained an integral part of the diet in sanatoria throughout their existence.

When the more tightly regulated closed sanatoria opened in the 1880s, a similar regime was imposed, as shown on sanatoria prospectus. Breakfast and afternoon snack was always warm milk with bread and jam, in some places substituted with cocoa and cheese on Sundays.

Dr John Davy in 1842, suggested that a mountain climate was likely to offer the best check to diathesis 'as alpine people rarely had tubercles because of the greater respiratory activity occasioned by a rarefied atmosphere'.[15] Davy's hypothesis was further developed by a Silesian medical student, Hermann Brehmer, who proposed in his doctoral thesis that at its outset tuberculosis was always curable. Attributing to poor circulation, caused by diseased pulmonary tissue, the comparatively small, weak hearts he claimed to have observed in autopsies of tuberculosis sufferers, he concluded that this could be corrected by a healthy, active life at high altitudes.[16] Reduced pressure would ease the pumping action of the heart muscle and improve the body's constitution and its capacity to overcome disease. Brehmer was correct in his assertion that at higher altitudes air was 'thinner'. In fact the pressure is lower and so the air is less compressed. At around 1,560m there is only about 83 per cent of the pressure at sea level. However, this means that higher up there is less oxygen to breath and so breathing is faster and the heart has to work harder to circulate blood around the body.[17] Many people find they cannot exercise as hard at elevations over 1,500m. However, this can have a beneficial effect as the body increases the number of red blood cells and the respiratory and cardio-vascular systems are strengthened.

Though his thesis was not based on experimental evidence, Brehmer's arguments convinced others, possibly because the intellectual legacy of 'mountain mysticism' made them want to believe in the curative properties of pure alpine air. With the support of friends in academic and medical circles, Brehmer set up the first sanatorium for pulmonary tuberculosis in the Bavarian Alps. Patients lived in wooden chalets and followed a regime of carefully graded, mapped-out walks in the forest, coupled with lengthy periods of rest and a nutritious diet. Soon it was noticed that vigorous exercise was actually harmful and so the amount of activity was reduced.[18]

One of Brehmer's patients, Dr Peter Dettweiler, abandoned the small heart theory and created his own sanatorium at Falkenstein in the German Taunus Mountains. Here the rest periods had greatest emphasis and took place on sheltered, open balconies.[19] It was Dettweiler who devised two of the most enduring symbols of sanatorium life. For his consumptive patients to lie on during their rest periods he created the *Liegestuhl*, a reclining wicker chair like a modern sun-lounger. He also developed a pocket flask for coughing into to prevent infected spit, mucus and blood going on the ground, *ein Spucknapf* which in Davos was to become known as *der Blaue Heinrich*, Blue Henry.[20]

The theories of Davy, Brehmer and Dettweiler were further corroborated by a German refugee from the 1848 democratic revolutions in Heidelberg where he had been studying law. Alexander Spengler had fled in fear to Switzerland after the defeat of the radicals. Spengler gave up law and was able to study medicine in Zurich. After qualifying as a doctor, through the support of Hans Hold, a Swiss friend he met at Heidelberg University, he was appointed as *Landschaftsarzt*, physician to the community of Davos and its valley.[21] Serving the high mountain valley people, Spengler noticed that those who had left the area and migrated abroad or to cities to work and had contracted tuberculosis while they were away, soon recovered and were cured of the disease when they returned home.[22] Spengler wrote about his observations and these were published by Dr Meyer-Ahrens in a German medical journal. It was this publicity that contributed to Davos becoming a year-round health resort and the arrival in 1865 of the first two winter visitors desperately seeking relief for respiratory disease.

Other invalids soon followed, one of them the writer John Addington Symonds. His articles in *The Fortnightly Review* helped spread the word about this new kind of treatment for consumption. This helped popularise Davos in the winter and raised awareness of Switzerland generally among a wider population than were actually likely to travel. He dispelled any qualms and fears invalids and their families would undoubtedly have had about the long journey to remote alpine resorts in the cold of winter. 'Accustomed as we are to think that warmth is essential to the satisfactory treatment of pulmonary tuberculosis, it requires no little courage to face the severity of winter in an alpine valley, where the snow lies for seven months, and where the thermometer frequently falls to ten degrees or fifteen degrees Fahrenheit below zero. Nor is it easy, by any stretch of the imagination, to realise the fact that, in spite of this intense cold, the most sensitive invalids can drive in open sledges with impunity, expose themselves without risk to falling snow through hours of exercise, or sit upon their bedroom balconies, basking in a hot sun, with the world all white around them, and a spiky row of icicles above their heads. Yet such is a state of things which a few months spent in Davos renders quite familiar.'[23]

The first establishments for the treatment of tuberculosis using the healing power of the high-altitude atmosphere allowed patients a remarkable amount of freedom. These *Kurhause* or 'cure-houses' were operated under what was later known as the 'open system'. They were run on the lines of hotels and patients were free to choose and employ their own physicians and care staff if required. They were also free to come and go as they pleased and to take part in any activities that appealed to them, even those that involved vigorous exercise. Their cure programme depended on self-discipline rather than a strictly enforced regime. Not everyone was as disciplined as the cure demanded; this is indicated by a joke printed in *The Davos Courier*: Young doctor – 'Well several days of absolute rest will make you all right again, by the way will you give me the first waltz tomorrow night at the ball?'[24] An advertisement in the same newspaper shows this same dichotomy, Tobias Branger advertised folding chairs of every variety in accordance with the instructions of medical men but speciality sport toboggans, Swiss, American and Norwegian systems were also for sale in his shop or could be hired from him.[25]

John Addington Symonds went to Davos because he was ill. He describes the routine of the cure in an open establishment, in his case the *Hotel Buol*.

> The cure method is very simple. After a minute personal examination of the ordinary kind, your physician tells you to give up medicines, and to sit warmly clothed in the sun as long as it is shining, to eat as much as possible, to drink a fair quantity of Veltelline wine and not to take any exercise. He comes first to see you every day, and soon forms a more definite opinion of your capacity and constitution. Then, little by little, he allows you to walk; at first only upon the level, next up-hill, until the daily walks begin to occupy from four to five hours.[26]

In the Taunus Mountains north of Frankfurt a sanatoria opened soon followed by another at Nordrach in the Black Forest founded by Otto Walther in 1876. These institutions were noted for their strict discipline and the restriction of activities patients were allowed to follow.[27] The advent of closed sanatoria in Switzerland from the 1880s, beginning with that of Dr Turban in Davos in the 1880s, meant that patients who stayed in them had no choice but to follow the strict regime imposed if they hoped for a cure. From early in the morning patients could enjoy the fresh air through the open windows of their rooms whilst still in bed. After breakfast they would then sit in the open air on a balcony or verandah. After lunch some exercise, such as walking would be taken. Later in the afternoon patients retired to the balcony again for more rest in the open air. Evenings were also spent in the open air. A typical sanatorium timetable would have been: 7 am get up, shower, first breakfast, walk for a half to one and a half hours, depending on physical strength, then *Liegekur,* lying on the balcony for a couple of hours; 10.30 am there was the second breakfast followed at 11 am by a short walk; 12 pm was another *Liegekur* until 1 pm when lunch was served; in the afternoon was the main *Liegekur* session until about 4 pm when there was another walk for an hour or so followed by yet another *Liegekur* from about 6 pm until it was time for the evening meal at 7 pm. The evening was made up of yet another *Liegekur* between 8 and 9 pm when a drink of milk was provided before bedtime at 10 pm.

Davos offered facilities not just for the sick to get better but career opportunities for carers and medical professionals. English and American patients could engage English nurses by application to the superintendent Miss Crothers at the *Chalet Boner*.[28] Two nurses were staying at the *Hotel Belvedere* in November 1886. They were the only people whose occupations were listed in the guest list. In December 1894 Nurse Morrison gave a well-attended lecture on the 'description, symptoms and management of the most common diseases of the chest'. The object of these frequent lectures was to teach what to do in cases of emergency until the doctor comes.[29]

So important was the prospect of a cure through the benefits of the high alpine air that those lucky enough to experience it themselves wanted to share their good fortune with others. Therefore a fund began in 1888 to support invalids of insufficient means whose money had run out before they were well enough to return home. It was administered by Hugo Richter at the *Hotel Strela*. Its beneficiaries were supported to remain in the sanatoria or *Kurhaus* where they were already staying. The charity ran no separate premises of its own.[30] Nine thousand Swiss francs, about £360, were raised by a bazaar held in aid of the *Poor Invalids' Fund*, as it was called.

In the winter as well as the strict routine there were also other regulations to be adhered to. Cold weather rules in the sanatorium included the warning 'never to omit regular bathing, for unless the skin is in active condition the cold will close the pores and favour congestion and other diseases'. After exercises of any kind patients were warned never to ride in an open carriage or near the window of a car for a moment; it is dangerous to health or even life.[31] Not everyone enjoyed the snowy climate. 'The weather here has been *very* bad', wrote a patient in Leysin. 'It began to snow and "blizzard" Thursday night and has never ceased. Over five foot of snow have already fallen. It's awful!'[32]

In Davos patients needed to feel trust in the quality of their medication. The *Grand Pharmacie International* would prepare English prescriptions strictly according to the *British Pharmocopoeia* by an English qualified chemist so that customers could rely on having their medicines prepared with the same exactitude as in a first-class London pharmacy.[33] Even though they had faith in the Swiss climate, for some English this faith obviously did not extend to the Swiss themselves or their pharmacists.

Arosa developed as a centre for health seekers from the 1880s, influenced by the experience of Davos as a resort for both cures and sports.

A visit to Davos inspired Dr Louis Secretin to create similar facilities in Vaud, a canton in French speaking Switzerland. He chose the area of Feydey, just above the village of Leysin, where the geographical situation was excellent. Any fog lay below the village, at between 1,300 and 1,500m altitude. The promoters of Leysin as a medical centre were reluctant to call their establishments 'sanatoria' and so the most exclusive of them was called the *Grand Hotel*. Construction began in 1890 with completion of the project in 1892. Treatment for the tuberculosis patients in the *station climatérique* of Leysin followed similar programmes to those of Davos and Arosa, offering the hope of a cure to sufferers whilst avoiding the contamination of others. Previously, French-speaking consumptives had gone to traditional hotels on the shores of Lake Geneva, where the healthy and sick with various diseases mixed together, at great risk of contamination.

In Leysin the timetable revolved around the cure and its needs, the environment of the resort was kept calm and quiet, to the extent that during the rest periods everything in the village stopped. The timetable was strict and the meals simple. To allow easy cleaning and disinfecting, rooms in sanatoria were minimally furnished.[34] As the sanatoria in Leysin were founded somewhat later than the cure centres of Davos, after the discovery of the tuberculosis bacillus by Koch in 1882, from the start the centre was aware that the disease was contagious and took precautions. Two systems of treatment could be attempted. The first was to kill the bacillus, the other the more traditional open air cure where the body was strengthened and aided to fight the illness itself. This second treatment was characterised by prolonged stays in the open air. The patients spent most of their days in the open, covered with blankets in winter. Windows were kept open during the night. Food was nutritious and fortifying to complement the treatment. They were served appetising meals to try to tempt them to eat plenty: meat and above all milk were important elements of the diet designed to build up patients.

Some kinds of tuberculosis affected parts of the body other than the lungs. These could sometimes appear as external lesions. In the nineteenth century it was thought these were localised infections that could be cut out like tumours and so they were surgically removed. This form of the condition was therefore wrongly termed 'surgical tuberculosis'. Removal of the infected areas did not cure the disease but could lead to secondary infection, mutilation and scarring. The body was immobilised in a plaster case. Dr Bernhard of Samaden was the first to develop the treatment called *heliotherapy* for external tuberculosis in Switzerland. The theory though had already been applied centuries before by Muslim healers in the Middle East and developed further more recently by surgeons in Lyon.[35] Heliotherapy, as practised by Bernhard, was used as an auxiliary to surgery. After an operation the affected area of the body was immobilised in a plaster cast before the localised area was exposed to the sun. Bernhard opened a clinic in St Moritz which inspired August Rollier to develop this treatment further. For Rollier, the treatment had to be general and not localised. This was so that the sunlight could stimulate the body's natural defences. 'The air and sun bath judiciously applied, stimulates the appetite and digestive functions and renews energy. Rollier emphasised that the mountain environment could increase the number of red corpuscles in the patient's blood.[36] Rollier was keen on the photographic representation of his ideas put into practice. His publications contain before and after pictures of patients treated by *heliotherapy*. They were transformed from pale emaci-ated beings covered in sores with swollen joints to healthy, tanned individuals with athletic physiques.[37] He also used photographs of patients, including children, lying or working in the sun in his marketing materials. At Leysin, Rollier extended the sanatoria treatment to patients beyond the wealthy elite by creating colonies where patients could work as outworkers in light indus-tries and thereby contribute to the cost of their care. At the *International*

1

Children undergoing heliotherapy in Rollier's clinic, Leysin

Clinique Manufacture and at *l'Abeille*, for convalescents, small workshops were provided where patients could work as well as facilities to enable the bedridden to work from their beds while lying in the sun.

In Grindelwald the proposed cure principles of its *Kurhaus* at the *Hotel Adler* were to be modelled on those of the other resorts with high, airy rooms, balconies covered by glass, movement in the open air and baths and showers.[38] Invalids were not inclined to go to Grindelwald because its lower altitude compared to the other resorts meant it could not compete as a health centre offering a high mountain cure.

The aim of this work is not just to tell the story of sanatoria and health seekers in the five resorts in the study. The growth in winter visitors occurred simultaneously with the development of new winter sporting activities imported from abroad. The extent to which the resorts' pre-existence as health centres and summer resorts had on the development of these sports will also be discussed. Transfer of technology was also important in the expansion of resorts. Infrastructure and transport had to be developed using technology and inventions discovered elsewhere in industrialised Europe and America but adapted, implemented and exploited for use in the remote mountains even before they were in full use in cities in the more developed nations. The other and perhaps most important factor in the resorts' development were the visitors from those cities and industrial regions who braved the winter snows to spend months at a time in the mountains either in the hope of relief from illness or just for enjoyment. The background of some British guests whose names were published in visitors' lists in the resorts of Davos and St Moritz in particular will be investigated and analysed to discover what kind of person left their home and pioneered a new kind of tourism – the winter sports holiday.

Notes

1 Spyri, Johanna, *Heidi*, 1880.
2 Senancour, Etienne Pivert de, *Obermann*, Paris, 1804.
3 Mann, Thomas, *The Magic Mountain*, Translated into English in 1927 by Alfred A. Knopf Inc. and published 1928 by Martin Secker & Warburg. Same translation published by Penguin, 1960.
4 Porter, Roy, *The greatest benefit to mankind: a medical history of humanity from antiquity to the present*, London, 1997, p. 422.
5 Desponds, Liliane, *Leysin, histoire et renconversion d'une ville á la montagne*, Yens-sur-Morges, 1993, p. 20.
6 Wyder, Margrit, *Kräute, Kröpfer, Höhenkuren, Alpen in der Medizin – Medezin in der Alpen*, Zurich, 2003.
7 Wyder, p. 53.
8 *Schweizer Badekurorte und ihre Heilquellen*, c. 1920, p. 5.
9 *Schweizer Badekurorte und ihre Heilquellen*, p. 3.
10 Wyder, pp. 75–77.
11 Wyder, p. 85.
12 Wyder, p. 85.
13 Wyder, p. 92.
14 Ferdmann, Jules, *Der Aufstieg von Davos*, Davos, 1945, second edition, 1990, pp. 34–35.
15 Pemble, John, *The Mediterranean passion: Victorians and Edwardians in the South*, Oxford, 1987.
16 Dormandy, Thomas, *The white death – a history of tuberculosis*, London and Rio Grande, 1999.
17 www.altitudephysiology.org.
18 Dubos, Rene and Jean, *The white plague – tuberculosis, man and society*, New Brunswick and London, 1952.
19 Dormandy; Dubos.
20 Schmid, Christian, 'Rund um dem Davoser Liegestuhl', *Davoser Revue*, 79 Jahrgang, Nr 1, Marz 2004, pp. 37–39.
21 Ferdmann.
22 Ferdmann.
23 Symonds, John Addington, *Our life in the Swiss highlands*, 1892; first published in *The Fortnightly Review*, July 1878.
24 *The Davos Courier*, 22 December 1898.

25 *The Davos Courier,* 5 November 1892.

26 Symonds.

27 Porter, p. 422.

28 *The Davos Courier,* 1 November 1886.

29 *The Davos Courier,* 24 November 1894.

30 *The Davos Courier,* 8 November 1888.

31 *The Davos Courier,* 20 December 1888.

32 Jaeger, A.J., Letter to Sir Hubert Parry, 11 March 1906.

33 *The Davos Courier,* 25 January 1901.

34 Desponds, Liliane, *Leysin, histoire et renconversion d'une ville á la montagne,* Yens-sur-Morges, 1993, pp. 54–55.

35 Rollier, Auguste, *The international factory clinic for the treatment by sun and work of indigent cases of 'surgical' tuberculosis,* Lausanne, 1929, p. 4.

36 Rollier, p. 5.

37 Rollier, p. 5.

38 Rubi, Rudolf, *Im Tal von Grindelwald, Bilder aus seiner Geschichte, vom Bergbau-erndorf zum Fremdenort, Gastgewerbe, Alpinusmus, Band II,* Grindelwald, 1986, p. 53.

2

Davos

There had been a spa in the Davos valley since the 1840s, along with milk and cowshed cures for tuberculosis and other diseases, but these attracted only summer health seekers. Most people understandably believed that the cold snowy winters would be harmful. Alpine valleys, like that of Davos and the Engadine, were also extremely remote, inaccessible except over high mountain passes or primitive tracks. Hardly the sort of journey a person in poor health would be advised or feel inclined to undertake, especially in freezing weather, travelling through the snow on a sleigh for hours. Obviously, any popularisation of alpine villages as health centres had to depend on the development of transport and communication infrastructure. Murray's *Handbook to Switzerland, Savoy and Piedmont*, 1856 edition, could only say of Davos that its *Rathaus* served as an inn and had once been decorated with the heads of wolves but that these were no longer there. All that remained was a net that had been used in their capture. This was an enhancement compared to a French guide of the 1830s which just mentioned of Davos that the *Rathaus* (town hall) was the only place to stay in the village. Davos was known by those who passed along the valley of the Landwasser river to the spas at nearby Wiesen, Sertig and Spina. A brochure written in English from the baths at Alvenau, dated 1883, mentions Davos as an excursion destination for its guests, not a resort in its own right, although by this date it was developing as both a winter and summer resort.[1] A distinguishing feature of the local inhabitants which alludes to the good health acquired in the area was their tall stature, strength and good nature.[2] This was despite the obvious health problems in some alpine communities, associated with cretinism and goitre, conditions that were prevalent in some areas of Switzerland owing to mineral deficiencies in the water.[3] With the building of the road along the Prättigau Valley to Klosters in 1859, Davos began to become accessible for slightly less intrepid travellers. On 15 October of that year the first horse-drawn post wagon came into service, converted with sleigh runners for use in the snow. It took six hours between Landquart and Davos Platz and the return journey downhill took four hours.[4]

Looking at Davos' first two winter visitors, we can examine what influence they may have had on the resort's subsequent development as a venue for winter sports tourism. The story goes that to the great astonishment of the people of Davos, on 8 February 1865 a sleigh pulled up in the village centre carrying two sick young German men, doctor of medicine Friederich Unger and book dealer, Hugo Richter. The only place heated and open was the *Rathaus* but its sole room was already occupied. The only alternative accommodation was at the *Pension Strela* opened in 1860, which offered air cures, milk cures and cowshed cures to summer visitors, mostly from Chur. Richter was too weak even to walk the short distance to the hotel. The *Strela*, though, did not open in winter and so Unger and Richter had to persuade the proprietor, Herr Michel, who also worked as a vet and a builder, to let them in. They were not immediately made to feel welcome. The four guest rooms were unheated and there was little food. Supplies had to be brought in from Chur, by no means a popular or simple task in the cold and snow.[5] No wonder these new guests were seen as a bit of a nuisance. The two men, both suffering from tuberculosis, had been treated at Dr Brehmer's sanatorium in Görbersdorf, situated at a height of 560 metres above sea level, with no success. They learnt of Dr Spengler's claims for the health giving properties of Davos, lying at 1,560 metres above sea level, being just as effective in winter as in summer from the work of Spengler and Dr Meyer-Ahrens and in desperation left Görbersdorf and undertook the long, difficult and tiring winter journey to Davos a '*Kur zu machen*'. Unlike at Brehmer's clinic, in Davos there was nowhere to lie for the long rest periods of 'the cure'. The pair improvised by using hay-sleighs covered with planks to lie on in the open air. After a relatively short time, they began to feel well enough to work but decided to remain in Davos. Both of them were to play a major role in the future development of Davos as both a health and a tourist resort.

Dr Unger opened his own medical practice after obtaining recognition of his German qualification by the authorities in Chur. He became a colleague and devoted friend to Spengler and was to stay and work in Davos for twenty years where he introduced daily cold showers as an integral part of the cure.

Hugo Richter married the daughter of Herr Michel and took over the management of the *Pension Strela*, renamed *Hotel Strela*, for a while. He was more interested in the book trade and publishing and helped spread the fame of Davos by publishing literature about the village. He had his own printing press there and produced the local newspapers *Davoser Blätter* and *Davoser Wochenblatt*. Later he was a founder of a secondary school in Davos in 1881, the *Kurverein* (tourist organisation), the local section of the Swiss Alpine Club, and many other clubs and organisations.[6]

Soon after Unger and Richter came to Davos, two more people joined them at the *Strela*, the Charpentier brothers from Russia. The 'cure community' of the village still totalled less than half a dozen people who regularly met to play cards at the *Strela*, the beginning of organised entertainment for guests. In the following summer of 1865 the little community was enlarged by the addition of Nikolaus Kern and the banker Friederich Riggenbach with his sick daughter from Basle. Sadly, the girl died the same year. During the next year the number of sick people grew until there were fifteen of them over the winter of 1866/67.

In May 1867, a wealthy Dutch banker, Willem Jan Holsboer, with his terminally ill, consumptive English wife arrived in Davos. They came on the advice of her doctor in London, Hermann Weber. After his wife's death in October of that year, the grieving Holsboer remained in Davos where he too was to play a major role in the development of Davos as a resort. Spengler had been trying slowly to create his own clinic and accommodation for tuberculosis patients but lacked adequate finance. Holsboer provided the capital to build the *Curhaus* (*Kurhaus* or cure-house), the *Kuranstalt Spengler-Holsboer* which opened in 1868.[7] Holsboer cemented his commitment to Davos by marrying a local woman, the sister of his late first wife's nurse.

This original *Curhaus* was not blessed with longevity and in January 1872 it was destroyed by fire. The cure community recovered from this blow by forming a company of shareholders to create a new *Curhaus*.[8] Friedrich Riggenbach, the banker from Basle, who had remained at the *Curhaus* along with other financier guests were key members of this company which raised the capital to build a completely new *Curhaus*. Riggenbach became company president, a position he held until his life's end in 1904. The new *Curhaus*, which was completed in 1873, was much more spacious than the original and had a number of villas around it for cure guests who wanted to stay in self-contained accommodation with their families. Spengler dedicated himself to the new institution, giving up his position as *Landschaftsarzt* to provide its medical leadership. A couple of years later a large meeting room was added to the *Curhaus* for concerts and entertainment and after a decade a winter-garden was built. Cowsheds and milking parlours were located close-by to provide milk, an integral part of the cure diet, for guests. Alpine milk was proclaimed more nutritious than milk from cows farmed elsewhere because the animals were free to roam and graze on a much wider variety of grasses, plants and herbs.[9] More privately owned villas and chalets grew up around the *Curhaus*. Restaurants, a theatre, conversation rooms and covered walk-ways and promenades began to change the Davos landscape.[10]

The way of life at the *Curhaus* and the other guest-houses and villas that took in consumptives was not the strict regime of the later sanatoria. Spengler recommended that all his patients spent time resting each day, consumed nourishing food and took regular exercise in the open air. However, the routines of his system were not enforced, guests were free to come and go as they pleased. In the 'open' sanatorium of the *Curhaus*, most cases were treated as guests not as patients, which called for will-power on behalf of the cure-guest to sustain the regime necessary to effect a cure.

> Davos demands qualities the very opposite of the resigned sentimentalism in which too frequently the phthisical youth or maiden was encouraged. Here is no place for weak and despairing resignation; here you are not pusillanimously helped to die, but are required to enter into a hard struggle for life. The combat is frequently a tough one. Days, weeks, months, sometimes years of obstinate self-denial and self-sacrifice are required ere the desired result is attained. But attained it will be, if body and spirit work hand in hand and cheerfully assist the grand, simple remedies offered by nature to her ailing sons and daughters.[11]

The Davos climate was the key to healing success: as well as the altitude and rarefied atmosphere, the valley faced south for maximum daily sunshine in every season and was sheltered from the worst of cold winds by the enclosing mountains. The dry atmosphere, high in oxygen, was believed to have healing properties. These qualities made any regime followed by the patients more effective than the same treatment carried out in the lowlands. Spengler decreed no actual *Liegekur*, where patients spent several periods each day lying in the open air on covered balconies. Very ill patients could stay in bed in their room or lie for a short time on the terrace. In less severe cases Spengler recommended an afternoon rest in a half sitting position. There were no *Liegestuhle* in Davos anyway, only tables, armchairs and stools on the terrace.[12] The *Liegekur* that Unger had already encountered at Görbersdorf in 1865 would not be followed consistently in Davos until 1889 when Dr Karl Turban came and opened the village's first 'closed' sanatorium. At Dr Turban's sanatorium, patients followed a strictly timetabled regime with fixed periods of rest several times a day and so were not as free to follow their own interests as those in the open establishments.

Although they had time for outdoor exercise, it was usually spent in taking walks. A report in the *Davos Courier* in 1903 said, 'Always invigorating and bracing, its sanatoria are filled the year through with consumptive patients, who obtain the greatest benefit from its open air treatment. We spent one evening with about half-a-dozen bronzed, healthy-looking men, listening to the band at the *Kursaal* and were surprised to find that each without exception was at Davos undergoing treatment for the dread disease.'[13]

By 1903 there were eight closed sanatoria separate from hotels. These were the *Alexanderhaus* with sixty beds; *Sanatorium Davos-Dorf* with seventy beds; *Internationales Sanatorium* which had forty-eight beds; *Neues Sanatorium Davos-Dorf* which had fifty-five beds; *Sanatorium du Midi* which had sixty beds; *Turban'sches Sanatorium*, the biggest with ninety beds; *St Joseph's Haus* which had forty-five beds; and *Sanatorium Dr Danegger* with an unspecified capacity. As well as these there were twenty-two hotels, including *Kurhause*, nineteen *Pensions*, thirty-one houses offering rooms to rent, two apothecaries and two bacteriologists.[14] That same year, 1903, the *Schatzalp Sanatorium Davos* opened on a plateau 300 metres above the village at 1,864 metres above sea level. It was described as a 'mountain health resort for diseases of the lungs'. This establishment was a luxurious *art nouveau* designed building reached by its own funicular railway. For upwards of 14 francs 50 rappen, patients received seven meals a day, medical treatment, baths, massage, electric light, heating and service.[15]

Few English people, even those who were sick, chose to stay in closed sanatoria, preferring the open system where they could stay in hotels and choose their own doctors. Nevertheless, even sanatoria patients could have an influence on the development of the resort's sporting reputation. A party of fifteen people came out in the Christmas holiday of 1903 to visit their friend Dr Aked of Pembroke Chapel in Liverpool who was a patient at the new *Schatzalp* luxury sanatorium. Spengler's son Luzius was chief physician there. Aked had written home to say 'the doctors declare I shall recover for certain, without doubt; that I shall return to work next May and that I must never ride a bicycle again. I expected sentence of death but I am let off with twelve months imprisonment, not with hard labour.' At the time of his writing, Dr Aked was allowed to walk about for half an hour twice a day at the sanatorium and he claimed that he felt brighter and stronger.[16] Although Dr Aked himself may not have taken part in winter sports, his friends and colleagues from Pembroke Chapel would probably have done so. The *Schatzalp Sanatorium* contributed to the development of winter sports in another important way.

It was built on a plateau, high above Davos and was reached by a funicular railway. This railway was also the first mechanical lift up a Davos mountain that could also be used by tobogganers and skiers who elsewhere had to climb the slopes on foot before they could glide down again.

During stays of many months or even years, cure seekers and their families and friends who visited or accompanied them sought amusement and entertainment, hence the winter-gardens, promenades, meeting rooms and the like built around the *Curhaus*. Indoor amusements included musical evenings, balls, chess, cards, billiards and skittles. In summer outdoor pastimes were excursions into the mountains and side valleys of Davos, collecting wild flowers, walking near the *Curhaus*, tennis, croquet and clay-pigeon shooting. In the winter there were tailing parties in which guests rode on sledges tied together and towed in single file behind a horse-drawn sleigh. There was also sledging and soon ice-skating and later skiing.

One of the first winter sports activities was ice-skating which began on the Davos Lake in the second half of the 1860s. This was not particularly easy as the lake was quite a long way from Davos Platz where the *Curhaus* and a lot of other accommodation were situated. It was also hard work to clear the surface of snow to reveal the ice surface underneath before it could be used for skating. The first ice-rink was built in 1869 in the garden of the *Curhaus*, on the south front which would have been the most sunny side and in a position where those resting could sit and watch. A larger skating rink was constructed in 1873 by creating an outlet from the nearby Landwasser River which would freeze in winter. The land on which it was constructed was owned by Holsboer and nearby, a couple of years later, he had the gas works built. Skating on the well tended rinks was recommended as a suitable pastime for the invalids, the robustness of whom would be a startling revelation to those accustomed to seeing patients undergoing the care and precaution of usual treatments.[17] The number of guests and accommodation of different classes to house them continued to grow and in 1877 a new ice rink was built near the *Hotel Belvedere* in a section of Davos that was to become known as the English Quarter. This rink was soon replaced by an ice-stadium with a pavilion and orchestra.[18]

The British started to arrive in Davos from around 1875, although Holsboer's English wife had gone there with her husband in the 1860s. Davos was first recommended to English health seekers in 1878 by a Mrs MacMorland, wife and mother of the first British family to stay in Davos. 'Several years ago, she wrote, when in a critical state of health, we were led by accident to the

Tailing party, horse-drawn sleigh towing small toboggans,   **2**
Davos Platz

Alpine valley of which the following pages treat, and we felt that the great
good derived by ourselves and witnessed in the case of others from a residence
there, imposed upon us the duty of making the district and its healthy influences as widely known as we could in England.'[19] Mrs MacMorland described
Davos as lying 4,000 feet above sea level, this being fixed as marking the line
of immunity from the disease in this portion of Europe. This is above the line
of beech woods which are found around Klosters, 'which lying over 1,300
feet lower than Davos stands on the debatable ground where the beautiful
foliage of the green thickets cannot make one forget the possible presence of
the enemy', that is the tuberculosis bacillus. Even so, not every where above
4,000 feet presented the same favourable features as Davos. The Engadine was
thought by Davos aficionadoes to be less beneficial as its great length meant it
was cold and inhospitable. In Davos the soil is dry and gravelly and the great
variety of level walks, so important to the patient, must not be forgotten when
summing up in favour of the valley.[20]

As more British visitors appeared in Davos, in typical English manner they
formed clubs and began to organise the sports they took up. The *Hotel Buol* was
the venue for a meeting in February 1889, chaired by Revd. Harford Battersby.
This meeting discussed the formation of a skating club. They resolved to form
a skating club affiliated to the national association of Great Britain, which

would offer training and assessment for the association's proficiency tests and badges.[21] About eighteen ladies and gentlemen enrolled in the new club. The committee members included Revd. Battersby, J. Crewdson Junior and Miss MacMorland.[22] As further evidence of the connection of the development of winter sports with the resort's status as a health resort, Miss MacMorland was the daughter of the first English family to stay in Davos which came for the sake of the mother's health. Crewdson was with his invalid brother and his father, Theodore Crewdson of Northcliffe Hall, Manchester. Theodore Crewdson in November 1889 was trying to find a new position for his valet George Hawley. He put an advertisement in the *Davos Courier* recommending Hawley to potential employers because of his considerable experience of nursing during two years in Davos and St Moritz and his understanding of massage treatment. References for Hawley could be obtained from Dr Ruedi in Davos and F. de Beauchamp in St Moritz. This shows that some invalids stayed in luxury hotels and received nursing care from their own servants.[23] Theodore Crewdson did not intend to return to Davos as his son was now terminally ill and so neither would his other son, J. Crewdson Jr, who could no longer be on the skating club committee.[24]

Ice-skating was an attraction that drew new visitors to Davos. In December of that year, 1889, the *Davos Courier* announced that it was 'glad to hear that there is a possibility of the Misses Cheetham coming to Davos this winter'. Both ladies held first-class badges of the National Skating Association. The editors hoped the shortening of the journey from England due to improved rail services would induce other skaters to pay a visit.[25] The English style of skating though was not popular with skaters of other nationalities. Figure skating, following set movements or figures in strict formation, elegantly, neatly and apparently effortlessly executed, with the unused leg held close to the side, was the form practised by British skaters. They had no time for the showy style of the continental skaters with their flamboyant dances and unused legs held out behind in a sort of arabesque, which looked more spectacular but was thought actually less difficult to perform than figures. This difference seems to emphasise the way the British saw themselves in the colonies and part of Davos was becoming an English colony: quiet and self-assured, secure in the assurance of their own superiority with no need to show off about it. The *Davos Courier* reported to its English-speaking readers that 'complaints had been received at the office of the *Curverein* by non-figure skaters of the balls, gloves, oranges and other objects which were placed on the rink as "centres" by those who aimed at something higher in the art of skating than the monotonous and perpetual

Maria Lichtenhahn Jost, skating in Davos Platz, about 1910   **3**

run round.' The writer conceded that it would be ridiculous of the *Curverein* to ban figure skating but it had made a reasonable request that only balls which would roll when touched be used and that the balls should only be on the ice when actually being used for practice. 'We have occasionally seen ladies and gentlemen use gloves, purses or anything else they can find as centres which are dangerous to others.'[26] Later sports on the ice rink were curling imported from Scotland played by the British and a similar Bavarian game played with stones with wooden vertical handles called *Eisstock,* and also the English game of bandy and its successor, ice hockey. Local Swiss people and visitors of other nationalities also took up some of these activities and games.

In 1872 and 1873, sport-loving guests were reported as riding on small sledges. To the delight of the international community of guests, the *Curverein* laid a sledge-run near the *Curhaus* with two routes, one for riding down and another for climbing up. It was hoped that this might curtail the dangerous practice of riding on the main streets.[27] In a chapter entitled 'Davos for Health Seekers' in Weber's guide to the resort, 'another favourite exercise in Davos was the use of small sledges, propelled down hill by the occupant's own weight'.[28] Sledging also became organised by the English in the 1880s. Friendly races took place between the *Belvedere* and *Buol* hotels. In 1883, under the leadership of John Addington Symonds, an English writer in Switzerland seeking a cure for his respiratory illness, the Davos Toboggan Club was formed and the first organised race was held in February of that year on the road to Klosters. Competitors could be towed on the uphill journey back to Davos in a tailing party behind a horse-drawn sleigh. Two years later Symonds donated a trophy, the Symonds Cup, to be competed for annually on Swiss toboggans, the traditional style of sledge used in the area. Joint winners of the first race for this prize were an Englishman and a Swiss, showing that the event was not confined to members of the English colony. An ice-run for very fast descents by sledge was built beside the *Hotel Buol* in 1884. When an old workman, Marianai, who had worked on the course, passed away suddenly in 1889, an obituary appeared in the *Davos Courier*. Apparently he had been working on the run until the day before he died. His loss, readers were told, would 'be greatly felt by the Committee as he had worked on the Run for the last four years and was well up in the art of making corners and curves and could to a great extent, be trusted to work without supervision. He had been a good subject for amateur photographers.'[29]

Controversy followed the race for the Symonds Cup in 1888. The winner was United States' competitor Mr Child riding sideways on an *American*-style toboggan with spring runners.[30] These machines had to be ridden head first, unlike the Swiss toboggans on which the rider sat upright. A letter to the *Davos Courier* protested about the 'unsportingness of healthy tobogganners using heavy American machines they knew invalids could not use'. For the next three years the Cup was won by sleds ridden head-first. In early contests almost all prize-winners were spending winter in Davos solely for their health. The writer complained that they were not up to using an American toboggan: 'Davos is made for invalids and tobogganing is made for invalids.'[31] Another change in the tobogganing world came in the winter of 1889 when the *Davos Courier* offered 'a hearty welcome to a new form of toboggan which has appeared in our midst. The bobsleigh is the property of Mr Whitney in the *Hotel Victoria*; it is a mighty looking machine consisting of two ordinary Americans connected by a long springboard calculated to hold about ten persons.'[32] Whitney's bobsleigh came first in the trials for the Symonds Cup but was not allowed to take part in the big race itself.[33] In 1903 the first international competition for bobsleighs, the Manchester Bowl sponsored by the Duke of Manchester, was won by a machine called 'Trilby' steered by artist Lawrence Linnell with three other riders.

After six years as president of the toboggan club, the work load had become so heavy that John Addington Symonds had to resign because of his fragile health.[34] To end the controversy, a separate event was introduced in 1890, the Symonds Shield, for Swiss toboggans only.[35] Symonds's successor as president of the club, Harold Freeman, came out to Davos with his family owing to the delicate health of his wife. Freeman himself was in rude health. He excelled in many sports; he had been an international rugby player and had scored the first goal for England from a drop kick against Scotland in 1872. Rowing was another passion and he cycled thousands of miles a year. Freeman worked tirelessly for the club for over twenty years: he designed and even took up a shovel and dug courses; he organised a full programme of events including gymkhanas, novelty races and children's events and international toboggan races. During his first year in office, though, he attracted much controversy relating to unfairness to invalids in the Symonds Cup, due to problems with time-keeping in the races he organised. A complaint was received in the *Davos Courier*, criticising Freeman's arrangements for the international race and the time-keeping. Apparently a competitor who was asked to ride again because of a faulty timer was only 'a delicate schoolboy'.[36] Another letter in the paper the following week questioned the boy's fragility: 'the delicate schoolboy later in the evening went skating and tobogganing'.[37]

Further evidence that some invalids joined in winter sports is shown in the letter of Mr August J. Jaeger, a German-born British citizen staying at the *Hotel Buol* seeking a cure for pulmonary tuberculosis. He refers to having had nasal operations in his letter and anticipates that he may have to have another operation to 'cut and chisel some more and virtually cure that part of my anatomy'. His lungs appeared to be almost healed when he ventured to try tobogganing, of which he begged the recipient of his letter not to tell his wife whom he had promised he would not toboggan. He had been on a sledge with an Irish lady, coming down at lightning speed, when it crashed into a bobsleigh, with the result that he sprained his ankle. The disgusting part of the incident to him was that they were on the *Buol Run* behind the hotel, which is well known as a children's run, where a bobsleigh ('beastly, heavy machine') was never seen until that day. It was on the wrong side of the road on a bend where every toboggan must have run into them; and they did nothing to clear out and make room for us, despite having '*Achtung*' shouted at them. The riders of this bobsleigh were the son and daughters of Lord Balfour of Burleigh.[38] From the tone of the letter it seems it was quite normal for invalids to take part in tobogganing.

Skiing was only introduced to the Alps in the last quarter of the nineteenth century and was slow to become anything other than a pastime for an eccentric minority. Dr Spengler was reputedly the owner of the first skis in Davos, which were given to him as a gift from a Scandinavian guest in 1872. Spengler did not have much of an idea how to use the Lappland hunting skis which were of unequal lengths. For several years they were part of a window display in a sports shop, until Spengler's son Karl tried them out in his parents' garden. A forerunner of skis was snowshoes or *Schneereifen* used by locals to improve mobility in the snow. Some visitors tried snowshoes of various types as an aid to winter mountaineering. However, sometimes skis were also referred to as snowshoes. The *Davoser Blätter* reported in 1875 that some plucky cure guests had climbed up to *Schatzalp* and the Strela Pass high above with the help of snowshoes. The same article recommended that anyone walking or climbing on the mountains in the winter should take plenty of wine or Cognac with them as the mountain inns were closed for the season. As yet there were no skiers to cater for on snow-covered mountains.[39] Water was useless as it would freeze in the cold. The next mention of skis in Davos was in 1883 when R. Paulke, an apothecary from Leipzig, brought his sick wife, family and servants to Davos for a year. His son, Wilhelm, at that time a frail schoolboy but later a famous ski-mountaineer and professor, also hoped to find health and strength in Davos. As well as his school work at the *Fredericianum*, a German school for boys in poor health, Wilhelm enthusiastically took part in sledging, ice-skating, ice hockey and snowballing. For Christmas 1883, his father gave him a pair of *Telemark* skis. 'My ardent wish, to own such wonderboards, was fulfilled', he recounted later. He and his school friends made some of the very first ski-tours using them. Skiing did not yet catch on and the next account of skis in Davos was not made until the winter of 1889/90, when Colonel Napier's Norwegian servant brought a pair with him to the *Villa am Stein*, the former home of John Addington Symonds. Nielsen's servant used the skis around the village. When they left the skis were given to Katherine Symonds, a daughter of Symonds who had been staying in Davos on a long-term basis because of her father's health. She was one of the best tobogganers of the day and was the first of the English visitors to try skiing.

Davos tradesman, Tobias Branger and his brother Johannes were probably the first local people to be enthusiastic about skiing. Tobias Branger was a saddler and upholsterer with his own workshop, who sold articles of all kinds either from stock or made to order. With an eye to the emerging tourism market, he also sold requisites for travellers.[40] Branger had seen Norwegian skis at the Paris Exposition of 1878 and obtained some from Norway in around 1889 or 1890. Tobias and Johannes practised discreetly, to try to avoid the ridicule of their neighbours. On 23 March 1893, the Branger brothers accompanied by E. Burckhardt crossed the Maienfelder Furgga to Arosa with skis and returned the same way. 'On steep slopes they fastened skis together to sit on like a sledge'.[41] The following year they repeated the journey in the company of Dr Arthur Conan Doyle who was in Davos with his wife who had been pronounced as having galloping consumption by her doctor. The Conan Doyles had abandoned their home, sold their furniture and 'made for Davos in the high Alps where there seemed to be the best chance of killing this accursed microbe'. Although given only a few months to live, the 'fatal issue was put off for three years. The invalid's life was happy for it was spent in glorious scenery.'[42] Mrs Conan Doyle did not stay in a sanatorium but after a spell at the *Curhaus* she took rooms at the *Belvedere* with her children and maid, soon to be joined by her husband.[43] Conan Doyle during his stay tried out skiing with the Branger brothers. In some photographs Doyle is shown on skis accompanied by a woman also wearing skis who, according to some descriptions, is thought to be his wife, the invalid.[44] Conan Doyle was a great self-publicist and wrote of his adventure in the *Strand* magazine. Judging by his account not much skiing was done. They walked up to the pass and much of the journey down was again achieved by lashing the skis together and sitting on them.

In 1894, the beginning of the popularisation of skiing as a sport was still six or seven years ahead. Skiers at Davos could almost be counted on one hand and these few were almost all natives, claimed W.G. Lockett, the resort's British Consul.[45] The Brangers had acquired the skis without ever seeing them used and so had no idea of technique other than what they had worked out themselves. It wasn't until 1897 that they procured the book *Lilienfelder Skilauftechnik,* an instruction manual by an Austrian who developed his own skiing method, Matthias Zdarsky.[46] This was the first work to focus on alpine skiing.[47] Earlier instruction was written about skiing on relatively flat land in Norway where the slopes were not nearly as long or steep but that style was not suited to the Alps. In fact, instructions for going downhill on skis were not even included. Standing and moving on flat land was described in a Norwegian manual of 1893 but the reader was told that downhill the skis went by themselves.[48] As the pioneers had discovered, Norwegian skis were unwieldy and not really designed for use on long alpine slopes: Zdarsky's first skis at 2.94 metres long and weighing 4.75 kilograms were quite impractical for running downhill. For his own purposes Zdarsky shortened the skis to 2 meters and made his own *Lilienfelder* fixed bindings which for a long time were one of the leading designs for downhill skiing.[49]

Very few people before 1900 had any interest in or knowledge of skiing technique. This changed when two men, the brothers E.C. (Edward) and C.W. (Charles) Richardson arrived in Davos armed with their own skis. To the amazement of the residents, they made swings and turns to right and left, just like skaters on the ice. They actually skied down the slopes. They had learnt the art in Norway in the winter of 1895–96 and had returned there to ski the following year. In 1901 they came to Switzerland, in sound health, to find snow for skiing. They had been told that Davos snow was too soft and not suitable for skiing until very late in the season. They found it perfect, however, and skied again and again. In 1902 the Richardson brothers wrote an article for the *Davos Courier* with the title 'Davos a ski-er's paradise', a term used countless times since in tourism literature but then iterated for the first time. In the article they extolled skiing as a sport for the truly independent. Unlike the skater and tobogganer, skiers were not tied to rink or run but are free to choose their own path across the vast tracts of unbroken snow.[50] Beyond the initial cost of the ski there was no further outlay for rink or run use, unlike later when the cost of using lifts added to the expense. They concluded the article by pointing out four important things lacking in Davos that would be needed for the village to develop into a skiing centre: a ski club with a resident secretary and, if possible, a professional Norwegian skier attached; really first-class ski and fastenings at a reasonable price and rate of hire; native interest in skiing in general and in jumping in particular; cheap fir-wood skis for the impecunious.[51] Over the next couple of years the enthusiasm of the Richardsons had achieved the things previously lacking for ski sport in Davos. They even taught local boys to ski on barrel staves and helped get the proper equipment put on sale in Davos. With the help of their friends the two Wroughton brothers, who they had met there and who grew to share with them a common love of skiing, they founded the Davos English Ski Club in 1903, a few months before the Ski Club Davos was founded, again with their help. The Richardson brothers suggested the first skiing competitions in Davos. The next year they were among the founders of the Ski Club of Great Britain. The Richardson brothers are acknowledged as the introducers of skiing as a popular sport in Switzerland. The title 'father of British skiing' has been bestowed on E.C.

Richardson, the more outgoing of the brothers.[52] In 1906 Edward Wroughton edited the first issue of *The Winter Sports Annual*, which was soon published yearly by both sets of brothers, the Wroughtons and the Richardsons, who jointly set up their own winter sports publishers whose output continued up until the First World War.[53]

As early as 1876, it was recognised that because of its situation and climate, there were two different aspects to Davos, one which appeals to the tourist, the other to the chronic invalid.[54] According to the first issue of the English language paper, the *Davos Courier* in 1888, rumour had spread far and wide, that in Davos, 'mother nature herself had taken out a medical diploma and was already in possession of an excellent practice, waging deadly warfare against disease'. The rumour had spread not just to the sick but to the healthy too and soon thanks to the excellent facilities for welcoming and amusing invalids, the resorts reputation for amusement and healthy outdoor lifestyle was attracting a majority from those exalting in their fitness.

> Worshippers at the shrine of Mother Nature in her medical capacity and worshippers at the shrine of their own sweet pleasure, compose the present population of Davos, the health-resort.[55]

In the same decade as the first closed sanatoria in Davos opened, Koch, who had one of Spengler's sons, Karl working in his laboratory, discovered that tuberculosis was a contagious disease caused by bacillus infection. This may have caused alarm among healthy visitors who perhaps feared catching the disease from the sick people in their midst. However, Davos was able to combat these fears and at the same time contribute to Switzerland's future reputation as a clean country. Sick people were required to carry a 'Blue Henry' flask to spit into so that no sputum containing the infection could come in contact with other people. All rooms and public places were kept clean and disinfected to kill any traces of the bacillus. Laundry was steamed and soft-furnishing was regularly fumigated. Personal hygiene was also emphasised. Publicity claimed that Davos was actually safer than places that did not have large numbers of tuberculosis sufferers. Elsewhere people had no way of knowing whether they were in contact with contagious people and so no precautions amounting to basic hygiene were taken, thereby allowing disease to spread. The climate was also important, the bacillus found it hard to survive at high altitude. Even so, some guests needed reassurance that they faced no risk of disease from their fellow guests. For this reason hotels opened that did not take invalids. They were styled 'sports hotels' to differentiate themselves from those that took in sick people and their carers and families. The *Fluela Post-hotel* advertised in

1900, that the establishment was not for cure-guests but was reserved exclusively for sporting visitors and tourists. It was recognised as the headquarters of the people who came to Davos 'for sport only, for all the sports and nothing but sport'.[56]

The French-language paper of the community in 1903, referred to 'the two Davoses', one a European centre of sport, the other of the altitude cure.[57] The number of visitors to Davos, both healthy and seeking relief from ailments, continued to grow up until the outbreak of war in 1914. In 1888 there had been a total of 5,381 guests in the resort. The creation of the railway the following year made Davos more accessible and the number of visitors grew phenomenally. Even so, the 1895 edition of *Baedeker's Switzerland* had only this to say of Davos, that it was 'a popular summer and winter resort of consumptive patients'.[58] The 1907 edition of the guide shows the resort remained popular with consumptives in summer and winter but now skating, tobogganing and snowshoeing (with skis) are actively pursued in winter and an international skating competition was held in January on the rink opposite the *Kurhaus*, showing that over a dozen years Davos had changed from being a centre mostly for invalids and health seekers to a place where the healthy could come for pleasure and sport.[59] Just two years later in the next edition of Baedekers' guide, Davos was described as a 'favourite health and sport resort in winter that attracts visitors in summer also', demonstrating its shift in orientation from a mainly summer health resort to a health and winter sports resort.[60] In 1898, Henry Lunn could say that Davos had changed over the last twenty years, and by then there was a perfect network of post-roads and footpaths. The Landwasser had been canalised to avoid flooding of the meadows, peasants had sold land to builders and the result was a town, clustered around the church with excellent shops, a *Gymnasium* (secondary school), *Kurhaus* and English library.[61]

In 1913, the last complete year before hostilities curtailed tourist traffic, most guests had come for pleasure rather than for the cure facilities of the resort. There were 23,531 healthy visitors compared with 10,936 invalids. Davos was not just a health centre but a sports and tourism centre even before the First World War. It was not dependent on one kind of tourist market and this diversification allowed it to survive wars, economic depression and medical changes in the treatment of tuberculosis and other diseases.

Notes

1 *The Sulphur Baths of Alveneu, Grisons, Switzerland (3150 feet above the sea) with the neighbouring mineral springs of Tiefenkasten and Solis. Medicinally and topographically described by Dr Victor Weber*, resident physician, second edition, Zurich, 1883.

2 *Le nouvel ebel manuel du voyageur en Suisse par Richard*, Paris, undated, c. 1835, pp. 389–390.

3 Wyder, pp. 208–222.

4 Ferdmann, p. 37.

5 Ferdmann, p. 50.

6 Ferdmann, p. 54.

7 Ferdmann, pp. 60–61.

8 The contemporary German spelling, with 'C' as the initial letter, is used. In more modern usage the 'C' is replaced by a 'K', e.g. Curhaus/Kurhaus, Carl/Karl.

9 Wyder, p. 83.

10 Ferdmann, pp. 62–63.

11 Weber, J., *Illustrated Europe – Davos*, London, Zurich and Paris, 1876, p. 27.

12 Ferdmann, p. 108.

13 *The Davos Courier*, 17 July 1903.

14 *The Davos Courier*, 2 January 1903.

15 *The Davos Courier*, 2 January 1903.

16 *The Davos Courier*, 17 July 1903.

17 Weber, p. 31.

18 Ferdmann, pp 157–160.

19 MacMorland Mrs, *Davos Platz: A New Alpine Resort for Sick and Sound by One Who Knows It Well*, London, 1878, introduction.

20 Mrs MacMorland, p. 2.

21 *The Davos Courier*, 2 February 1889.

22 *The Davos Courier*, 9 February 1889.

23 *The Davos Courier*, 16 November 1889.

24 *The Davos Courier*, 30 November 1889.

25 *The Davos Courier*, 14 December 1889.

26 *The Davos Courier*, 21 December 1889.

27 Ferdmann, p. 160.

28 Weber, p. 31.

29 *The Davos Courier*, 14 December 1889.

30 *The Davos Courier*, 22 December 1903.

31 *The Davos Courier*, 1 November 1888.

32 *The Davos Courier*, 3 January 1889.

33 *The Davos Courier*, 17 January 1889.

34 *The Davos Courier*, 26 January 1889.

35 *The Davos Courier*, 22 December 1903.

36 *The Davos Courier*, 17 January 1889.

37 *The Davos Courier*, 26 January 1889.

38 Jaeger, A.J., Letter to Sir Herbert Parry, 9 March 1906, Davos Documentazions Bibliotek (DDB)Ref: 01.11.125.

39 Ferdmann, p. 164.

40 *The Davos Courier*, Vol. 1, No. 2, 8 November 1888.

41 Kittle, Fredereick C., 'Down the slopes with Conan Doyle at Davos', *Journal of the Arthur Conan Doyle Society*, Vol. 4, Chester, 1993, pp. 88–103.

42 Conan Doyle, Sir Arthur, *Memoirs and Adventures*. New York, 2002.

43 *The Davos Courier*, Fremden Liste, 24 November 1894.

44 Haldimann, Ueli, *Arosa, Texte und Bilder auszwei Jahrhunderten*, Zurich, 2001, p. 48.

45 Lockett, W.G., *Robert Louis Stevenson at Davos*, London, c. 1930s.

46 Lockett, W.G., 'The Davos English Portrait Gallery, 1.The Brothers Richardson', *Davoser Revue*, Jahrgang IV, Nr. 4, 1929, pp. 99–102, especially p. 99.

47 Zdarsky, Matthias, *Lilienfelder Skilauftechnik*, Vienna, 1896.

48 Uhrdahl, Laurentius, *Lehrbuch*, Christiania, 1893, quoted by Erich Bazalka .

49 Bazalka, Erich, *Skigeschichte Niedrosterreichs*, Verfasst im Auftrag des Landesskiverbandes Niederosterreich Waidhofen/Ybbs, 1977.

50 Richardson C.W. and Richardson, E.C., 'Davos a ski-er's paradise', *The Davos Courier*, Vol. XV, No. 25, 7 March 1902.

51 Richardson, C.W and E.C., *The Davos Courier*, Vol. XV, No. 25, 7 March 1902.

52 Lockett, W.G., 'The Davos Portrait Gallery, I. The Brothers Richardson', *Davoser Revue,* Jahrgang IV, Nr 4, 1929, pp. 100–101.

53 Lockett, W.G., 'The Davos Portrait Gallery, II. The Wroughton Brothers, *Davoser Revue*, Jahrgang IV, Nr. 5, 1929, pp. 126–129, especially p. 128.

54 Weber, p. 2.

55 *The Davos Courier*, Vol. 1 No. 1, 1 November 1888.

56 *The Davos Courier*, Vol. XIII, No. 3, 5 October 1900.

57 *Le Courrier de Davos*, Vol. VII, No. 48, 29 November 1903.

58 Baedeker, Karl, *Switzerland, and the adjacent portions of Italy, Savoy, and the Tyrol, Handbook for travellers*, sixteenth edition, Leipzig and London, 1895, p. 362.

59 Baedeker, Karl, *Switzerland, and the adjacent portions of Italy, Savoy, and Tyrol, Handbook for travellers*, twenty-second edition, 1907, p. 416.

60 Baedeker, Karl, *Switzerland and the adjacent portions of Italy, Savoy, and Tyrol, Handbook for travellers*, twenty-third edition, 1909, p. 442.

61 Lunn, Henry S. and Lunn, W. Holdsworth, *How to visit Switzerland*, London, 1898, p. 311.

3

St Moritz

Parallel with the development of Davos, another Grisons resort, St Moritz, also began a rise to fame as a winter resort from the mid-1860s. St Moritz was already a summer resort for health seekers undergoing hoped-for cures for various ailments at its mineral springs. This makes its origins as a resort similar to those of Davos: travellers from outside the region came seeking health at a nearby spa, although the Davos valley's springs were more distant. Visitors had been documented as coming to St Moritz's springs since the Middle Ages and probably earlier. The first advice on the medicinal effect of the springs was given by Paracelsus who travelled to St Moritz in 1535. The first simple hut by the spring was erected in the late sixteenth century, allegedly by a Polish nobleman as a thanksgiving for his own cure.[1] St Moritz's spa in the area now known as St Moritz Bad was in a valley near a large lake. A village, used as the location for visitors, was sited higher above the lake a couple of kilometres away. Reached by traversing the Albula Pass, St Moritz was relatively more isolated from the rest of northern Europe than was Davos. Most foreign visitors to St Moritz at this time came from Italy. This isolation was to play a significant role in the way St Moritz later developed as a resort when the *Albulabahn* railway eventually reached it in July 1904. In a French guide-book of the 1830s, there were only two lodgings mentioned in St Moritz, the *Ober-Flugi* (*Oberen Flugihaus*) and *Unter-Flugi*.[2] St Moritz's modern development began when a company, the *Heilquellen-Gesellschaft*, was formed by Conradin von Flugi in 1831 to improve and develop the existing spa. In a twenty-year contract with the local council (*Gemeinde*) the company leased the springs for 300 *Gulden* a year. A master builder from Samedan, Johann Badrutt, was commissioned to build a *Kurhaus* that came into operation in 1833.[3] On its ground floor was a hall for drinking the mineral water, a room to warm the bath water, six bathrooms and a room for relaxation (*Liegezimmer*). On the upper floor were two spacious rooms for socialising and exercising (*Spaziersäle*), rooms for administration and for the physician, and men's and women's toilet areas. The *Gemeinde* let the company build using cost-free wood from the locality. Firewood was also supplied free of charge. Another inn was built near the springs on land donated by the *Gemeinde* and with free building materials. More improvements were made after the arrival of Dr Georg Brügger as resident physician in 1847. He drew attention to the lack of comfortable lodgings near the baths, and the terrible state of the roads leading there. In 1852 the contract with the *Heilquellen-Gesellschaft* ran out and the *Gemeinde* erected new baths and improved the street up to the village, St Moritz Dorf.[4] A further contract with another newly founded company was agreed. Six men, led again by Conradin von Flugi with J.B. Bavier (a member of the *Nationalrät*), and Rudolf von Planta of Sameden (a *Landammann*) who were joined by Dr Brügger, Johann Lorsa and Hans Joos. This group founded the *Heilquellen-Gesellschaft von St Moritz*, which later became the *A-G Kurhaus und Grand Hotel des Bains*. The company made a contract with the *Gemeinde* which was drafted mainly by von Flugi. This contract was for a fifty-year lease at 1,700 Swiss francs annually to include all existing installations and stock. It also donated land on which to erect buildings and the right to expropriate private land for this purpose. Even more generously, the company could have wood for building and fuel at no cost, it paid no local tax and was granted pasture rights for a herd of cows to supply the Kurhaus with milk. In return the company supplied all St Moritz residents with half-price spring water and after the lapse of the contract all buildings would be given to the *Gemeinde* unless they were worth over sixty francs, in which case 70 per cent of the additional value would be paid to the company.[5] The company was launched with start-up capital from twenty-four shares of three thousand Swiss francs; further capital was raised from the sale of a hundred further shares at six thousand Swiss francs. The profitability of the company meant it had no difficulty in taking out a loan with interest of 4 per cent. A new *Kurhaus* was erected by the springs and opened in 1854. It had fifty guest rooms, two dining rooms, reading and ladies' rooms, coffee lounges and billiards rooms as well as plenty of offices for administration and stables. In its first year in operation shareholders received 5 per cent interest on their investments and a small dividend. Von Flugi led the company from the start, then he became financial director and treasurer. The agreement with the *Gemeinde* was revised in 1859: the unlimited supply of firewood was only available for ten years and then reduced to a specified amount of wood; the community was no longer obliged to supply building wood; pasture rights were restricted to just five cows; at the end of the contract's life the community would be obliged to pay the full value of the buildings without the 30 per cent discount. The company was therefore improving the resort for the benefit of the community. In 1860 an even more ambitious *Kurhaus* near the lake was built with two hundred rooms for about three hundred guests and a new bath building was erected.[6]

Unlike Davos, Arosa and later Leysin, that had to start their development virtually from scratch, the mineral springs of St Moritz described above had provided a substantial tourism infrastructure to the community, but like the accommodation in the other resorts studied, it was only open to summer visitors as were the other guest-houses and hotels in the village above. One of these was the seventeenth-century house of Johannes von Flugi, *Oberen Flugihaus,* that was bought in 1834 from the Flugi family by Peter Faller from Davos and renamed the *Pension Faller.* This was then acquired in 1854 by Johannes Badrutt of Sameden, the son of the man who had been the building contractor responsible for the first *Kurhaus,* who ran it as the *Engadiner Kulm.* To rebuild the place in 1858, he secured a loan of 28,500 Swiss francs from banker Johannes Töndury, founder of the *Engadiner Bank,* and Sameden man, Andreas Rudolf von Planta. The hotel was further enlarged in 1868, 1875, 1894 and by 1909 it contained 330 beds.[7]

Like Davos, with Alexander Spengler and the legendary two first winter visitors Richter and Unger, St Moritz has its own winter season creation myth. Whilst Unger and Richter and other early Davos visitors like Riggenbach and Holsboer and their contributions to Davos life are well documented, the first people to winter in St Moritz are less well known. The story of Johannes Badrutt's bet with some English guests at his *Hotel Engadiner Kulm* in the autumn of 1864 is often related in stories of St Moritz's history as a resort. Badrutt's wager was that his English visitors would enjoy winter in the Engadine and would not feel the cold. He offered a free stay at the hotel if they came back in winter and enjoyed themselves. If they didn't he would pay their expenses for the trip. Four of the English guests took him up on his offer and returned to St Moritz in November 1864 and stayed there until Easter. This puts the inception of St Moritz as a winter resort a few months before the arrival of Unger and Richter in Davos. The story seems to have been first told by Johannes' grandson Anton Badrutt.[8] Johannes himself made no mention of the challenge which led to the first St Moritz winter season in his introduction to the publication of the *Kulm's* visitor lists in 1880.[9] Again, this story is contradicted by information given in the *St Moritz Post* in 1886.

As a summer resort it has been known for many years. As a place of winter residence
it is only during the last six or seven years it has become renowned. In 1866 one
visitor, and he an Englishman, had stayed at the *Hotel Kulm* during the winter. This
was the commencement of the season that now numbers two hundred visitors or
more. The next winter there were upwards of a dozen strangers enjoying the alpine
climate during the winter months. These figures had increased to twenty-four in
1871. In 1881 there were upwards of fifty or sixty people wintering in St Moritz.
This has grown year by year until there is quite a colony of English.[10]

In most publications there is no clue to the identities of the four, or perhaps
only one, intrepid travellers, probably accompanied by their families. However,
a 1968 publication gives the identity of one of them as Mr Arthur E.W. Strettel
who was quite ill and states that the others were a doctor and a minister
of religion.[11] Unfortunately, the writer does not give the source of his information. In an attempt to discover the identity of these English visitors, the
published records of the *Kulm* were studied to see if they revealed any English
who had been present in 1864 who were also there in 1865. Revd A.B. Strettell, a resident of Genoa, was listed in 1864 and in 1865 an entry was made
for 'Rev und Mme Strettel' from Genoa, revealing inconsistency in either
Badrutt's spelling, handwriting or transcription to a printed form. Strettel who
was an English clergyman resident in Italy became a regular visitor to the
Kulm. Like the first Davos winter visitors, Strettel was to become a benefactor
of and investor in the evolving resort. He initiated and financed the English
church in St Mortiz Bad and the village secondary school in 1867 as well as
opening the *Pension Grunenberg*.[12] Other possible candidates for the role of
first winter visitors are the Watson and Matthews families, Stephen Dowell
and Mrs Christie. The 1864 list includes Dr Watson, Miss Watson and Mr
Arthur Watson. The following year records Mr and Mrs Wattson of London,
possibly a different family but perhaps another example of inconsistency in
spelling. Mr and Mrs W. E. Mathews of Florence were present at the Kulm
in 1864 and in 1865 there was 'Matthews und Familie' of England. Stephen
Dowell appears in the 1864 list but in 1865 there was a Mr Dovell. Again they
could be different people but are also possibly the same individual, a victim of
dodgy handwriting or inaccurate transcription. The last candidate is a woman,
Mrs Christie, who first visited the Kulm with her husband. She had a private
income and came from Scotland. In 1864 Mrs Christie alone is mentioned
but the next year she was there with her little daughters, her *Töchterchen,* not
previously mentioned.[13]

The visitor lists for the *Faller* were also published by Badrutt. Most visitors
at that time were from elsewhere in Switzerland and the few foreigners were

from Italy. The first English guests arrived in the summer of 1845: they were Mr Jupper Curcy, Mr J.E. Cross, Miss Thompson and Miss Otter. They were followed in 1846 by Capt C.P. Rigby and Mr A. Goldsmit, both with private incomes. In 1847 Lt Colonel and Mrs Trollope were guests.[14] No further information about these people has so far been discovered. Faller's guests, like those to other alpine resorts, only visited St Moritz during the summer months. According to Badrutt, this summer season was itself very short, from 10 July to either 20 or 31 August. He wanted to lengthen the season, probably to increase his income in order to repay loans he had borrowed from the *Engadiner Bank*. June, with its long days and glorious meadows, was, he thought, the most beautiful time in the Engadine; autumn months with their clear weather were also favourable. Badrutt fostered the idea that the failure to attract visitors in winter was due to the belief that the climate would cause illness, especially in December, January and February.[15] He praised the pollution-free, calm air, high light levels, sunshine and warmth as having a strengthening effect on a diseased organism; these were things that could only be experienced by spending a part of the winter there. This places his legendary wager with the English guests who were to become St Moritz's first winter visitors in a different context. Far from being merely a bit of fun on the part of a jovial and generous man (although as a person he could nevertheless have been both) the bet was part of a sound business strategy aimed at extending his business and income by lengthening the time his hotel was open during the year. However, the story of the bet could be a myth, or a story told within the Badrutt family and perhaps elaborated over the years before it was made public in the next century.

The rising stream of tourists during the summer months and then in the winter season led to new hotels being opened in St Moritz as well as private houses offering bed and breakfast accommodation. There was the *Villa Flugi*, next to a mill, with fifteen beds; *Pension Bavier* with ten to twelve beds; and the *Pension Thom*. The increase in numbers of guests meant that other large and luxurious hotels were able to open both on the hillside at St Moritz-Dorf and beside the lake near the springs at St Moritz-Bad, without damaging the business of the *Kulm*. By the 1870s the *Engadiner Kulm* was the leading hotel in the village, thanks to Badrutt's effort and improvements. New development was not focussed solely on the spa: in the mid-1870s the luxury hotels *Du Lac* and *Victoria* opened their doors. These were followed by the *Neue Stahlbad* in 1892, the *Palace Hotel* opened by Johannes' son Caspar Badrutt in 1896, the *Hotel Schweizerhof* in 1898 and in 1905 the biggest of all, the *Grand Hotel*, which was to be destroyed by a fire in 1944.[16] Further luxury class hotels completed St Moritz's transformation from mountain village and spa into an internationally renowned high-class resort. These were the *Suvretta House* in 1912 and a year later the *Carlton*. This development was only decelerated by the hiatus of the First World War.

All the capital for these projects came from the same sources. Janet Töndury-Zoya from S-chanf in the Lower Engadine founded the *Bank J. Töndury et Cie* in 1856, which became the *Engadiner Bank* which remained in business until 1932. The bank moved in 1888 to Samaden, at that time the economic centre of the Engadine where most of the region's financiers existed. A list of the founders and boards of directors of the major St Moritz hotels shows that Janet Töndury or his son Gian were involved at a senior level in all of them, for example the *Neues Kurhaus, Hotel du Lac, Hotel Victoria, Hotels Réunis (Bellevue), Neues Stahlbad, Hotel Schweizerhof* and the *Grand Hotel*. In addition to the Töndurys, most management boards of these hotels also contained Henri-Albert Tester, Peter Perini, Andreas Rudolf von Planta, B. Moggi, Henri Alesch of Sameden, Lorenz Gredig of Pontresina and Conradin von Flugi from St Moritz. With the exception of the Flugi family who were shareholders in the *Neuen Kurhaus*, the *Schweizerhof*, the *Grand Hotel* and the *Neuen Posthotel* and the Badrutt clan, the proprietors of the *Engadiner-Kulm, Beaurivage/Hotel Palace, Privathotel* and the *Hotel Caspar Badrutt*, scarcely any local names were on the list of board members of the great hotels, which were or became joint stock companies. Even Badrutt depended on capital from von Planta and the *Engadiner Bank* to buy the *Pension Faller* and for its successive enlargements to create the luxurious *Kulm*.[17] The people of St Moritz let the exploitation of the resort slip from their hands more and more by allowing it to be taken over by outsiders.[18] This experience was repeated at Davos, Leysin and to a lesser extent Arosa where individual financiers with interests in a range of different enterprises invested in the resort infrastructure, for example Holsboer in Davos. Again, similarly, these entrepreneurs were outsiders who recognised the potential of the emerging tourism industry which could cater for the perceived needs of a growing middle class attempting to purchase good health in an environment far away from the pollution of the industrial cities which were often the source of their wealth. These entrepreneurs were often personally committed to the promotion of the resorts because of their own experiences of the health benefits of the climate.

In the discussion of St Moritz above, it has been shown that the infrastructure of a health resort already existed years before its transformation into a winter sports centre. At the time the first winter visitors came to stay, there was already the *Kurhaus* and facilities around St Moritz Bad as well as accommodation up the hill in St Moritz Dorf, an example of which was the *Engadiner Kulm* where Johannes Badrutt was waiting to take them under his roof. This was not the case in Davos where Unger and Richter had to persuade the owner of the *Strela*, the only hotel there, to open up for them in winter. The only possibilities of lodgings in Arosa or Leysin at the time would have been in private houses, unless a landlord could be persuaded to open up and heat his establishment like some visitors to Grindelwald in 1860 (see Chapter 6) seem to have experienced.

The next part of this discussion will look at how and if St Moritz's spa infrastructure helped it develop as a winter resort and why it didn't become a centre for altitude cures like Davos, which was actually lower lying. Davos became a centre for high-altitude tuberculosis cures owing to its position at about 1,500 metres above sea level. St Moritz lying at 1,800 metres would seem to have offered a similar if not even more beneficial atmosphere which could have been exploited by offering facilities for this type of health centre. In the mid-1860s Dr Peter Berry (senior) who as well as Dr Brügger, the spa's doctor, practised in Dorf at that time, induced some English visitors to extend their summer holiday into winter.[19] This information is given by Hans Robertson in his report on the development of the tourism industry in St Moritz written in 1909. In this report there is no mention of Badrutt's wager with his English guests, to persuade them to come to St Moritz in December. Robertson credits Dr Berry with inducing the first English guests to stay in winter. Perhaps Berry's recommendations of an alpine winter on health grounds filled his patients with trepidation and Badrutt's bet was a lighthearted way of persuading them that they would not suffer. It is known that Revd Strettel first came to St Moritz for the benefit of this health. As he stayed at the *Kulm* and Dr Berry was Badrutt's brother-in-law, then he was likely to have been a patient of Berry. From the mid-1860s every year more and more English guests came but for more than fifteen years they remained a discrete group who lived in a single, small community like a big family.

Following the publication in 1877 in England of the book, by Mrs MacMorland, *Davos Platz*, Davos became more and more popular as a centre for English health seekers with respiratory diseases. An English physician, Dr J.F. Holland, had spent many winters with patients in Davos, until the number of English there reached about 1,000 in 1883. This crowd obviously meant that Davos was no longer so quiet or exclusive and so Dr Holland took a small, select company of upper-class English with him to St Moritz. According to Robertson, St Moritz appeared to be less strict than Davos, which seems unlikely as the 'open' style of *Kurhaus* or sanatoria still prevailed in Davos at that time. Patients stayed in hotel-type or private accommodation. They were free both to choose their own physicians and decide how closely they were going to follow medical advice. The following year, 1884, another small exodus began from Davos to Arosa. Dr Holland and his group were encouraged by Badrutt who wrote in the foreword of his published guest book of the *Engadiner Kulm* that he was firmly convinced that a successful winter colony in St Moritz could suit a great number of people. A small winter colony lived in the *Kulm*, which for many years remained the only hotel open in winter. In 1885 there were between a hundred and two hundred guests; by the end of the 1880s three or four hundred. On 28 January 1888 there were 248 guests in St Moritz, 135 English at the *Kulm* and another fifty at the *Hotel Caspar Badrutt*; other nationalities were negligible apart from thirteen Italians at the *Privat-Hotel* where there were also another eight English people. There were only 450 guests over the whole winter of 1888.[20]

It seems the intention at that time was to make St Moritz into a second Davos. Resort publicity resembled that of Davos and negotiations began for the purchase of land on which to build a sanatorium. In the English community an aid fund allowed some sick and convalescent people to stay and be treated by Dr Holland free of charge. Before this could be realised the railway had come to Davos and brought a major upswing to that resort: the number of guests there rose from 6,872 in 1889 to 10,067 in 1890 and 13,220 in 1895. The *Albulabahn* railway which would reach St Moritz in 1903 was planned in 1897. The pass over the Albula had acted as a barrier in winter to the severely ill and frail for whom the journey would have been too arduous. Boring a tunnel through the Albula would allow them to travel to St Moritz by train in warmth and comfort. But did St Moritz now want to attract this kind of person?

The development of a dedicated winter sport resort was still unforeseen. Many people in St Moritz thought there could be two distinct seasons, its usual summer spa season plus a winter altitude cure season like in Davos. In St Moritz-Bad where Töndury was behind most of the hotel businesses, he and his supporters were against this from the start. He saw no benefits, only potential damage, to his existing interests in the spa. The hotels in Bad, a wide flat, open space, were not situated to benefit from winter opening, being in the shade, he claimed. In Dorf too, many were against the creation of a centre for the treatment of lung diseases; among them was Dr Peter R. Berry, the son of the Dr Peter Berry mentioned above as being instrumental in encouraging early winter visitors to the resort. The younger Dr Berry sought to prove that a summer health resort and a winter tuberculosis centre would be incompatible and that tuberculosis should be unconditionally kept out.

In 1898 there was a stormy meeting of the *Kurverein*. Opponents of the health station won and plans for the building of a sanatorium were abandoned.[21] The younger Dr Berry and his followers had a hard struggle but had the intellectual backing of Heidelberg professor Wilhelm Erb. Erb had stayed for fourteen days in St Moritz. He stressed that the development of a lung disease centre would hinder the development of the spa and the summer season. He was adamant that St Moritz was unsuitable for phthisics. In this respect, the existing resorts of Davos, Arosa, Leysin, and the much smaller Montana and Les Avants, were much more suitable.[22] His reason for this opposition was that for much of the winter the village had uninterrupted south-west winds which he claimed often carried dust. St Moritz was all right for those with anaemia, neurasthenia, asthma, malaria or other illnesses whose recovery would not be affected but for those with tuberculosis of the lungs it could have an adverse effect. Erb concluded with the call to halt the development of facilities for tuberculosis sufferers in St Moritz. The development of the spa would not be affected and the winter resort could be advanced simultaneously. His views were circulated widely in medical circles and had the effect he intended.

Although Erb and his supporters' opinion contradicts that published earlier in 1886 by English physician Dr A. Tucker Wise, their opinion was the one that prevailed. Tucker Wise had seen no contra-indications of the summer Alpine climate for those in the early stages of phthisis but not those with hopeless advanced symptoms and who were in a feeble and irritable condition, with high fever and incapacity for gentle exercise.[23] The slow scrofulous forms and fibroid conditions would also receive undoubted benefit. Tucker Wise's recommendations of the Engadine did not specifically relate to St Moritz. All official announcements from the *Kurverein* drew attention to the fact that those infected by tuberculosis of the lungs would find no admission in St Moritz. Hoteliers were obliged to refuse to admit those manifestly ill with the disease. In sales of building land, the construction of sanatoria were forbidden. No provision was made for special hygiene arrangements. This meant that St Moritz and its hotels could focus on a winter season dedicated to sport and leisure and the needs of the apparently healthy.

When the *Grand Hotel* opened in 1905, newspaper reports emphasised that the hotel was for the 'reception of the best grade of travellers', and the directors wished it 'to be clearly understood that the new hotel is in no sense to be regarded as a resort either for tourists on the one hand or consumptive patients on the other'.[24] Guide-books reassured potential guests that lung patients remained excluded (*Lungenkranke bleiben ausgeschlossen*).[25] This was echoed in the visitors' newspaper the *Engadine Express and the Alpine Post*: the article, in German, extols the virtues of St Moritz as a centre for climatic cures in both summer and winter. Health factors in winter were just as effective as summer: the thinness and dryness of the air; the intense rays of the sun; lack of pollution, calmness and above all the opportunities for exercise in the mountains compared favourably with a stay in the South by the Mediterrannean. Having said all this, the article goes on to emphasise to readers that unlike other high altitude health centres, St Moritz was not a place for those with lung disease. The wind is completely wrong for those with tuberculosis: they should go to Davos, Arosa, Leysin or Les Avants.[26] St Moritz was good for people with other illnesses or the healthy who came to enjoy sports.

Despite this denial, there were guests in St Moritz who did suffer from tuberculosis. An Honorary Secretary of the Tobogganing Club, Harry Walker, was a chronic consumptive who was considered uninsurable. Every year he stayed at the *Engadiner Kulm Hotel* where he had subsidised board and lodging. Perhaps his condition was not obvious: a guide published in 1911 said that as the hoteliers were strongly opposed to receiving sufferers, any who went there would be 'sure of a very unfriendly reception'.[27] Walker lived to be eighty years old.[28] Another prominent member of the club was the Hon. Henry 'Harry' D'Olier Grant Gibson, the second son of Lord Ashbourne, Lord Chancellor of Ireland, who had presented the Ashbourne Cup to the toboggan club. Harry Gibson died at Varenna on Lake Como at the young age of only thirty-five. According to his obituary, he was 'perhaps the last of the distinguished all-round sportsmen and pioneers who raised St Moritz into the unique position she now holds'. Another invalid when he made his first visit to St Moritz was John Arden Bott who first came to the resort on account of his ill-health in 1902. He was to dominate tobogganing for the first twenty years of the twentieth century. To help him in his quest for victory he devised a sliding seat for toboggans. He was so committed to the resort that he bought the *Hotel Rosatsch*.[29] Another keen tobogganer was Bertie Dwyer who was asthmatic and also in Switzerland for his health.

Sickness though often hidden was always present. Although a work of fiction, Mrs Aubrey le Blond's *The story of an alpine winter*, captures this undercurrent of sadness. A new arrival to St Moritz, Sybil, is in conversation with a regular St Moritzer: 'Life here seems one constant succession of sports and picnics and merrymakings. Is anyone ever serious? Or is the place an Alpine Monte Carlo with a lot of exercise thrown in?' 'The sadder side of life is not overlooked as you might at first think,' said Lady Livingstone more gravely:

> 'The doctor's wife could tell you many a heartbreaking story, though she would not let you know how many, struggling with poverty, sickness and trouble, she or her husband have set on their feet. Look, too, at the villa on the hillside, with its sunny balconies and homelike appearance. That house belongs to the St Moritz Aid Fund, which helps those who can't help themselves to spend a winter or a summer in the Engadine.' 'I see, poor souls – consumption!' broke in her brother. 'No, not always, though that was my idea too at first. These people are mostly poor gentlefolk broken down from over work, breadwinners who could get quite well if they could only have a few months total rest here.'[30]

Utilising the long hours of sunshine with its additional intensity due to the altitude, Dr Bernhard opened a clinic in St Moritz for patients suffering from surgical, *chirurgicale*, bone or osteo-tuberculosis. (Dr Bernhard was an earlier exponent of heliotherapy, who later inspired Leysin's Dr Rollier.) They lay in the sun with diseased parts exposed to the sun's supposed healing rays. He called his treatment innovation *heliotherapy*. It was this therapy that impressed Auguste Rollier so much that he began his own clinics on the other side of Switzerland in French-speaking Leysin.

Winter sporting activities had taken place right from the start of St Moritz's opening to winter visitors. An Englishman who passed the winter of 1868–69 at Badrutt's *Engadiner Kulm* reported that on average they were out for four hours daily, walking, skating, sleighing or just sitting on the terrace.[31] This gentleman too appears to have been a health seeker, as he informs his readers that he was far stronger at the end of the winter than at the beginning. As evidence of this he says that during his time there he had neither cough nor cold, despite being out in all weathers. He gave these health details in the hope that they would be useful to other people who, like himself, had delicate lungs.[32] The gentleman spoke gratefully of the benefit they had derived from the attention and skill of the resident Swiss physician, Dr Berry (the elder).[33] From the published guestbook of the *Kulm*, the writer of this recommendation can be recognised as probably being Francis Greatheed of London. According to Yeo, whose paper discussing his own, not entirely convinced, views of the benefits of a stay in the high Alps repeats this quotation, the same author, styling himself President of the St Moritz Skating Club, described in a letter to *The Times* how a beautiful surface had been produced on the lake by using a sluice gate and guiding shoots to divert a stream on to the surface of the ice marked out for skating, which began in late October and continued until the end of March or April. The pleasure of sleighing is also enthused about. Nothing short of an actual trial would enable anyone to realise the pleasure of gliding along rapidly in a sledge, under a brilliantly blue sunny sky, with the crisp white snow underneath.[34] This was riding on a horsedrawn sleigh. He goes on to talk of another favourite of the English, young and old, as well as natives, sliding down steep inclines on small sledges constructed for this purpose. He found the speed attainable almost incredible. To describe the English as a group like this could imply there were quite a few of them but at this time numbers of visitors, including English, were small, although in his letter of thanks to the Badrutts at the *Kulm*, Greatheed does say that he with other English friends formed a small club, first for keeping a small circle clear of snow and secondly for renewing the surface whenever it became impaired. This implies that before at least the 1870s, the *Kulm* took no responsibility for providing outdoor amusements as guests had to make their own skating rink.[35]

The following year, 1870, another person wrote describing the party at the *Kulm* as four English, three Germans, three Italians and a French lady. At Mr Strettel's house there were four more English besides Mr Strettel himself, while at Sameden a few miles away were an English couple with five children. That was the total of visitors in the Upper Engadine at that time.[36] This writer's view was judged by Yeo as more balanced than the earlier author because of his more restrained enthusiasm in his style of writing. He says that, healthwise, one gained from the climate but also lost greatly for want of good food. This writer too describes sleighing and skating amongst the amusements as well as the indoor game of billiards. This person also hints at boredom, as in a place like St Moritz then was you were thrown on your own resources in a country covered with snow. 'If you can manage to sleep twelve hours out of 24 you can manage to get through the time', he says, implying that time could drag. He said it was a great experiment coming to St Moritz but wasn't sure it was adapted to any but moderately strong persons who happened to have delicate lungs. The sceptical Dr Yeo, in whose published paper these testimonies appeared, agreed with this verdict. He would have liked to treat the whole thing as an experiment in order to study the results, to be able to find some empirical evidence of the efficacy of this as a health treatment. He felt patients should be under the constant care of a physician who could make regular reports on their progress.[37] Yeo was critical of what he saw as the unscientific conclusions of Dr Spengler and others who made unreserved claims for the success of climatic cures in the high Alps. He felt that no proper controlled experiments or observations had been made on which to base many of the assertions.

A supporter of Spengler's conviction in the efficacy of a high alpine climate against lung disease was the elder Dr Peter Berry who had practised in St Moritz since 1857. Berry, of French Hugenot descent, had been a surgeon with the British Swiss Legion in the Crimean War. His father, a confectioner from Schiers, had fought in Napoleon's army in the Peninsular War and while there he had married a Spanish girl. Peter Berry's sister, Maria, had married Johannes Badrutt in 1843, and lived with him in his family's guest-house, the Bernina, in Sameden. When Badrutt acquired the *Engadiner Kulm* he realised that his guests would require the services of a physician during their stay. His wife therefore wrote to her brother, suggesting he come and set up practice in St Moritz which he did.[38] Peter Berry's and his sister Maria's dual-heritage and international background may have given them English or other language skills and an acceptance of cultures other than their own. These skills would have helped the growing resort become more attractive to English visitors and invalids.

The numbers continued to grow until in early December 1886 there were sufficient English visitors to warrant the publication of an English-language newspaper, the *St Moritz Post,* produced by Freddie de Beauchamp Strickland. It was just eight pages long and was printed in Chur, so getting copy to the printers and the papers themselves back to St Moritz was quite an onerous task. The following year, printing was moved to Sameden. The paper soon began to cater for the English in other resorts and the title changed to *St Moritz and Davos News*. It spread the fame and popularity of the Alps as it was sent to the friends and relations of those in St Moritz and other resorts to all parts of the world. 'Here then was a by no means poor factor toward the development and popularising of one of the most rising health resorts of the last century', claimed the *Alpine Post and Engadine Express* in 1901. As interest in its news spread further it became the *Alpine Post* in 1892. A German-language paper, the *Engadine Express*, came out for a short time and the two amalgamated in 1901.[39]

From the start the English guests took part in winter sports, chiefly because there was little else to amuse visitors during the alpine winters in the, as yet, still primitive resort. Other hoteliers were more cautious than Johannes Badrutt and only about two of the four hotels remained open for the winter until the mid-1880s. One of the English guests, Franklin Adams (who had learned to toboggan in St Petersburg) with the support of Badrutt, improvised a toboggan run about 200 yards long on the north side of the Kulm in 1876.

This was the arrival of organised tobogganing in St Moritz, but on a much humbler scale than in Davos at that time. As in other alpine resorts, the first winter sports activities were sledging, followed by ice-skating. There were soon sledge runs on the edge of the road from Dorf down to Bad, *Badstrasse*, the Village Run on the *Aronastrasse*, the Chantarella Run from above the village, and the Lake Run from the *Engadiner Kulm Hotel* across the meadows down to the lake. As in Davos, tailing parties were a popular amusement with a dozen or more sledges pulled behind a single horse-drawn sleigh.[40] Skating too was a popular pastime and soon there were approaching twenty ice rinks in St Moritz. Famous skaters came to work as instructors; ice festivals with fantastic costumes and gymkhanas, a particular favourite with the English, were held. Skates were sold by the village ironmonger, an early supplier of sports goods.[41]A forerunner of ice hockey, bandy, was played using a small ball rather than a puck. In about 1880 Badrutt imported equipment for playing curling as a pastime for his guests at the *Kulm*. Also at the *Kulm*, tennis was played as a winter game. A court was kept clear and ready, surrounded by snow walls.[42] 'Invalids', though what their incapacities were is not mentioned, were reputedly involved in all these activities.

The guests at the *Kulm* formed their own Outdoor Amusements Committee in 1884 and together with Peter Badrutt, who was by that time running the hotel for his elderly father, decided to construct a toboggan run to rival those of Davos, in the hope of attracting some of the rival resort's tobogganing enthusiasts to come to St Moritz. Since the previous year, St Moritz sledgers had been welcomed in Davos to take part in tobogganing contests but had lost to them for want of effective practice. The new run would help them finally to beat the Davos tobogganers. For Badrutt, it would help make St Moritz a rival to Davos as a resort and so be good for business. Davos had the Klosters Road Run on which to practice as well as race. Badrutt was therefore eager to provide a longer and better course to the existing one already built by Franklin Adams.[43] Johannes Badrutt, the father, suggested that a recent geometry graduate of the University of Zurich, Peter Bonorand who lived in nearby Celerina, offer his services to the Outdoor Amusements Committee to design a course using his excellent mathematical knowledge.[44] A location was eventually chosen and staked out in autumn of 1884 with wooden pegs to make the line of the track. It followed the twists and turns of a steep gully between St Moritz and the neighbouring village of Cresta. When it snowed it was built up with banked walls. The committee comprising George Robertson, Charles Digby Jones, C. Metcalfe, J. Biddulph and W.H. Bulpett, were sure that a track with banks and curves would enable them to achieve much higher speeds than were possible on the Klosters Road at Davos. However, the toboggan runners cut into the snow walls of the track and ruined it; then someone at the *Kulm Hotel* had the idea of icing the banks. Bulpett and Robertson worked hard to complete this task and created a three-quarter of a mile run.

The course was created by five men whose boots were swathed in bandages, linking arms and trudging the line to be staked out until the snow was trampled down for the frost to harden. Making the banks was more difficult: they took nine weeks to construct.[45] A challenge was sent to Davos for a race to be called the Grand National, in response to the name of Davos' own race, the International. Three runs down the new track would make it a distance similar to that of the Klosters Road. A team of ten led by John Addington Symonds crossed the Julier Pass in sleighs by night, eager to meet the challenge. The confident St Moritzers were disappointed when their anticipated victory turned into another defeat by the Davosers, who took the first three places. C. Johnnie Austen beat Minsch the Davos postman who had been joint victor of the first International Race at Davos. According to Symonds's wife, the Davos riders 'were cautious and ran for safety, while the Engadiners, confident in their knowledge of their own course, threw themselves out by the most terrific spills'.[46] This was the beginning of the famous Cresta Run.

In the following year's Grand National race St Moritz did a little better: Minsch won again after St Moritz's leading hope G. Baillie Guthrie, victor of that year's International at Davos, had a fall but another St Moritzer took joint second place. The third year of the event, in 1887, after winning the International Minsch was expected to win the Grand National again but instead suffered the ignominy of disqualification because he had a practice run on the course on the morning of the race, which was against the rules. This event though was overshadowed by the huge excitement caused by a competitor who raced lying head-first on his toboggan. Unfortunately for him he took a number of falls during the three runs of the competition to the benefit of Baillie Guthrie riding in the conventional seated manner on a Swiss sledge. Runner-up was fourteen-year-old Bertie Dwyer, at school in the Alps because of his asthma.[47] Even more excitement ensued the following year with the appearance of an American-style sledge, owned by Davos-based Mr Child. This design was eagerly copied by other enthusiasts in Davos who had them made especially by local craftsmen. Mr Child and his 'American' toboggan was eagerly anticipated in St Moritz where the Grand National on the Cresta Run would provide perfect conditions for a record speed. However, there was speculation as to whether this extra-light machine, ridden head first, should be allowed to compete. Wasn't it cheating to ride a sledge that because of its design was faster than others? It was also unfair as this style of sledging was unsuited to invalids who supposedly were so well suited to the Swiss machines that there were a number of them who generally managed to beat those who were in sound health.[48] The 'American' was not disqualified and the Davos contingent eagerly awaited another victory. This was not to be, as the anti-climax of the episode was that Mr Child decided to withdraw his entry since after inspecting the course, he concluded it would be too fast and dangerous to race. Another 'American' machine rider won for St Moritz although he was not a resort regular but a visitor from the United States. Mr Cohen did not ride head first though but sitting up on his sledge. According to Harold Freeman reminiscing in the *Davos Courier* in 1913, a similar machine to Child's was ridden by Major Wilbrahim, lying flat, who was runner-up to Cohen in the same race.[49]

Tobogganing, evolving from the childish fun of sledging, was becoming a serious, competitive sport, involving sophisticated design of equipment and runs, evolving from the childish fun of Swiss sledging. Toboggan riders began to take their sport seriously, practising regularly. It was suggested that the reason for the consecutive victories of Davos riders in the Grand National was that they practised a dozen or more runs every day for one or two months

American-style toboggan on the street in St Moritz

while those in St Moritz were more complacent and practised for just a couple of runs a day for a fortnight. The Cresta Run and the Grand National event were expensive to maintain and organise but the Badrutts, seeing the potential popularity the run might bring to St Moritz, provided the workmen to build the Run and proposed the formation of a Club led by a committee chosen by visitors. The St Moritz Tobogganing Club was founded in 1885, a couple of years later than that of Davos, and among the committee members were Duke Grazioli, Major Dwyer, the uncle of Bertie, and Bulpett.

Bulpett, with his sportsmanship and enthusiasm, was dedicated to the Cresta. Bulpett and the committee soon realised the 'America' style of machine was the most suited to racing and the Swiss *Schlitten* became virtually obsolete in competition. The lightweight, metal-framed, 'skeleton' toboggan was, according to Harold Freeman, the main organiser of sledging in Davos, invented by Major (at that time Captain) Bulpett in St Moritz.[50] Hans Robertson, writing in 1909, also credits Bulpett with its invention. Steel runners for the toboggans were made in the St Moritz workshop of Christian Mathis but the German and Belgian steel used proved unsuitable. To solve this problem, Bulpett ordered best quality English steel to be imported and arranged for Mathis and the other blacksmiths he employed to be taught how to weld and shape the metal to make the first modern toboggans. This design was improved upon by H.W. Topham, whose sledge was made of steel.[51] With it he won the Grand National in 1892. Mathis' blacksmith business diversified to make and supply toboggans and he received more commissions to make machines. Early in the winter season of 1901 the press could report that he had already received a good many orders for new toboggans.[52]

Another design was that of H.E. Forster who grooved the last few inches of the steel runners of his wooden machine to get a firmer grip on the ice. For the St Moritz Toboggan Club the only rule governing construction of sledges was that 'no mechanical appliance acting as movable steering gear or as brake was used'.[53] Modern designs of toboggan could be ridden at greater speeds without the rider being thrown off at bends and bumps than one on which a person was sitting. This allowed the Cresta to be built with more curves, leaps and twists and the surface made more icy to increase speed, which in turn led to more skill being required and developed to complete the course. Toboggans frequently took leaps of over twenty feet, making the run exciting and exhilarating with more than a hint of danger. This itself was an innovation: those American visitors who had first introduced the new style of sledge were only used to riding down straight runs in the United States.

The Cresta was attracting increasing numbers of visitors to St Moritz who were not invalids but saw themselves as sportsmen. No prize money was offered for the races in either Davos or St Moritz, so they were fit and honourable opportunities for testing the skill of amateurs and therefore appropriate for gentlemen, and also for ladies who, in the early years of its existence, were usually allowed to join in races on equal terms or in separate events. The Cresta became so important and closely tied to the fortunes of St Moritz that when the route of the proposed Engadine railway threatened it, the *Kurverein* put forward the funds to alter the course of the line and build a bridge across the Run.[54]

Sledging sport incorporated further innovations over the next few years. A major development which created further diversification was first mentioned in a newspaper report of 1888. American Stephen Whitney, staying in Davos had introduced a new style of toboggan. In the *St Moritz Post* it was described thus:

> The machine consist of two ordinary 'Americas' connected by a board eight to twelve feet long, and three to four inches broader than the combined toboggans. One end is firmly screwed to the rear machine, while the other is fastened by a pivot bolt to the leader: across the centre of the latter projects to a distance of eight inches on both sides a stout wooden bar for steering with. This machine has been tried on the Klosters course with satisfactory results, but it looks a very dangerous machine to ride.[55]

Whitney's innovation, a forerunner of the bobsleigh, was only intended for one person to ride in the head first manner. This elongation of the toboggan was developed further in St Moritz by Bulpett with the aid of blacksmith Christian Mathis. Bulpett's version had two skeleton sleds with steel runners underneath and a support for a flat board joining the two above.[56] Some works on the history of winter sports credit a character called Wilson Smith with the invention of the bobsleigh. One writer claims that in the winter of 1888–89 the first multi-seater sledge was constructed by a Mr Wilson Smith of America who joined two 'American' sledges together.[57] According to Hans Robertson's report of 1909, the bobsleigh was first created by Townsend in 1888–89 and improved upon further in 1889–90 by Saunderson and Mathis.[58] In the history of the Cresta Run commemorating its centenary we are told that Mr Wilson Smith 'attempted to experiment with a new form of toboggan after he had persuaded the blacksmith, Christian Mathis, to link up two "Americas" upon which he and his friends careered down every available slope'.[59] However, according to *A Centenary of Bobsleighing*, another commemorative publication, Wilson Smith never existed. The writer gives an explanation of this error: the first race exclusively for bobsleighs was held on the Cresta Run in March 1892 at the end of the season when any damage to its surface by the machines' brakes would not have been disastrous. The winning bobsleigh was steered by Mr Townsend and in the one that came second were Mr Nugent Smyth who steered, Mr Wilson who sat behind him, followed by Mr Gordon Duff and then brakesman Mr Pryce Jones. The confusion seems to have arisen out of this report in the local English press: 'Smyth, Wilson' seems to have become Wilson Smith in future accounts.[60] The research undertaken for this work verifies this interpretation, that the inventive Bulpett devised the bobsleigh as well as the skeleton. Bobsleighing quickly became recognised as a separate discipline to tobogganing and in 1897 the St Motitz Bobsleigh Club was formed. The enthusiasm of bobsleighers for their new sport was reflected in the names they gave their machines, such as Blitz, San-toy, Royal Flush, Rocket, Boule de Neige, Joker and Bobs.

Because of the high number of accidents they caused to other road users, sledges and bobsleighs became forbidden on the main roads and they had to use special tracks. The making of the Cresta and other runs remained the task of mostly volunteer labour organised by the Tobogganing Club. Thoma Badrutt, who ran his own hotel, took over responsibility for its engineering and management in 1899. In 1901 he decided to run it on new lines: that was to have the run built and kept in order for a fixed sum of money, with not less than fourteen men regularly at work.[61] This would allow the run to be ready earlier in the season and so allow more time for practice before the big competitions. The following year, thanks to the go-ahead style of Herr Thoma, twenty-five men were regularly at work on the Cresta. Because of the time spent in its construction each year, the Cresta opened in stages, an advantage according to the local paper as novices could learn to overcome its difficulties by degrees.[62] The run itself created a multiplier effect and stimulated further tourist development to accommodate the visitors it attracted. At the village of Cresta where the run ended, the proprietor of the popular tea rooms, the *Patisserie Nüss*, enlarged his premises and made a skating rink in front of the restaurant.[63]

The sport of bobsleighing was becoming more sophisticated and rules were evolving to make the sport more competitive. In the beginning there were few rules. The bob team began by pushing the sleigh until it was moving under its own velocity, at a speed faster than they could run. If at a bend it slowed down, the brakesman and other team members could dismount and push again. A physically strong team could push their sleigh down the track if that was the fastest means on a run in poor condition. This gave an obvious advantage to those who were strongest and made the result of competition a foregone conclusion, where victory would always go to the physically heaviest team rather than the most skilful. In 1901 rule changes were being discussed that proposed that riders must be on board the bobsleigh from start to finish of a race. The vehicle would start off by going down a steep ramp and be propelled by gravity only. This would make the sport fairer and competition more sporting as skill not just brute force would be needed to win. The argument for this echoed the traditional one about the involvement of invalids in sport. The *Alpine Post and Engadine Express* argued that this debate was an appropriate occasion to remind readers that many delicate people come out to the Alps for their health's sake and are incapable of violent exertion. 'Surely it would be churlish, if not unkindly to preclude them from all participation in one of the most enjoyable of pastimes and one they may never have the advantage of again.'[64] Eventually rules were introduced that allowed the team to push to start off and then remain on board until the end of the course was reached.

In 1903 a dedicated bobsleigh run from St Moritz down to Celerina beside the Cresta was made and there were another two runs in nearby Pontresina.[65] Again, it was the support of the Badrutts that enabled the long-anticipated bob-run to come into existence. If the club itself raised five thousand of the twelve thousand Swiss francs cost, then the Badrutts offered to undertake the building of the new run and let the Bobsleigh Club pay off the balance when they were able. In addition to this they would allow the Club to build the first portion of the road going over their property without charging any rent. The commune of Celerina asked for an annual rent of 300 Swiss francs for the part of the run passing over its land with an initial lease of ten years.

The Club acknowledged their indebtedness to Herr Thoma Badrutt, himself a keen sportsman and bobsleigher, as well as to the *Kurverein* which had built a new bridge beside the toboggan run without which the new run could not have been built.[66] The paper published a list of twenty individual subscribers, composed of sportsmen and two women, mostly English, whose gifts ranged from ten Swiss francs up to 650 Swiss francs from Count Hans Larisch, the mean donation being fifty francs, the amount that was given personally by Thoma Badrutt and Christian Mathis. The *Kurverein* had donated 500 francs and a masked ball had raised almost 340 francs.[67] The developments in St Moritz and the popularity of the new sport caused other bobsleigh runs to be created: by the season of 1910/11 there were at least 61 runs throughout the Alpine region, and they were spreading to Austria and Germany.

Most people hired a bobsleigh for the season as to buy one was very expensive because the steel had to come from England.[68] This itself caused demand for bobsleighs themselves and factories for their construction were established. The early leader in the field, justifiedly, was Christian Mathis, the blacksmith of St Moritz. His premises were ideally situated near the *Kulm* and he advertised himself as a manufacturer of toboggans, speciality in skeleton, American and Canadian styles and bobsleigh. A proud boast was that the business exported machines to Davos, Switzerland (*sic*), England and America.[69] After 1920 Mathis was overtaken by *Hartkopf* in Davos who became the major exporter of steel bobsleighs and *Bachman Brothers* in Travers who specialised in wooden machines with a steering wheel, the type devised in Leysin. Using a wheel for steering became accepted everywhere, with only a few locals in St Moritz sticking to the original rope steering.[70] Competition between the rival resorts led to representatives from St Moritz travelling to Davos to take part in races but few St Moritzers went as far as Arosa to compete, where Davos riders did well.[71]

It is unclear when skis first made an appearance in St Moritz or the wider Engadine area. Rumour has it that the first skis in Switzerland came from Germany. A carpenter from Berlin, Samuel Hnatek, came and settled in Sils-Maria, close to St Moritz and made the first skis in the area in 1860.[72] Then Anton Pedrun, Paul Zuan and Johann Caviezel of Sils improved on the design. Another view is that skiing may first have appeared in the Engadine in 1881 when Claudio Saratz experimented with them in Pontresina, a few miles from St Moritz. Hans Robertson gives the date of Saratz's experiments with skis as 1895 and claims this was the only sport actually introduced to St Moritz by local people.[73] As late as 1894, a correspondent of the *Alpine Post and Engadine Express,* looking back from 1914, reminisced that at the time of his first visit to St Moritz in that year, 'Norwegian skis were not then known in the Engadine and the pedestrian was obliged to keep himself to the main roads.'[74]

One of the earliest users of skis for touring in St Moritz was Philipp Mark who later became a ski instructor.[75] He advertised his services in the local tourists' newspaper as a teacher of skating and skiing, giving his address in 1902 as the *Villa Alba*, St Moritz.[76] Skis though remained the preserve of an eccentric minority and did not catch on among the winter sportsmen and women for several years. In 1901, the *Alpine Post and Engadine Express* said that skiing had been cultivated for about ten years by a number of pioneers of the sport. 'The repeated attempts to introduce the ski to visitors and natives at St Moritz have made very slow progress. The English, to whom properly speaking the credit is due of having made St Moritz a sporting-resort par excellence, have assumed until now with respect to skiing rather a passive attitude'. The paper went on to say that recently more interest had been shown and that there were (in December 1901) about a hundred people that skied in St Moritz. It went on to say that a big problem was that few people actually knew how to go about skiing and that 'without proper instruction, however, without know

ledge of how the ski ought to be constructed, without having a notion of how to manage these long pieces of wood in order to be able to glide with them like the wind down a steep slope and to overcome every obstacle without danger, many a one drags himself about for some days only to lay aside his implements again with disappointment'.[77] The paper hoped to encourage more to take up skiing by supplying instructions on how to go about doing it. Skiers learnt on the slopes of the *Kulm Park* and the meadows of Salet.[78]

At that time, the sport didn't even have a proper, fixed name. In publicity of 1901 aimed at encouraging summer visitors to St Moritz to return in the winter, the *Engadinder-Kulm* makes no mention of skiing but lists 'snow-shoeing' among the winter pastimes available to its guests.[79] By then the winter season had extended from October to April. Still in 1902, the local paper was hoping that local people might be encouraged to take up skiing. To the *Alpine Post and Engadine Express*, it was not evident why despite being surrounded by many suitable peaks for ascent on ski, all the St Moritz guides, with the exception of a few who had at least made a beginning, are as yet unacquainted with the ski whereas their colleagues in other parts of Switzerland and in Tyrol had accomplished many a tour.[80]

The German section of the newspaper the *Alpine Post*, regretted that many people tried skiing but soon gave up because it was too difficult and no instruction was available. It also encouraged those who could already ski to practice. Two books were recommended as guides to skiing: one, *Skilauf* by Wilhelm Paulke (who was given his first skis whilst a schoolboy in Davos), published in Freiburg in 1899; the second was *Lilienfelder Skilauf-Technik* by the Austrian Mattheus Zdarsky, published in Hamburg the same year.[81] Zdarsky's Lilienfeld style of skiing was popularised by one of his followers, W. Rickmer Rickmers, who was in St Moritz in the winter of 1902/03. With a private income and no need of payment, Rickmers taught the new style of skiing, which incorporated a shorter ski (or *skee*) and fixed heel binding for the first time giving

Skiing on the street in St Moritz   **5**

more control and, with his wife, led mountain excursions to peaks above twelve thousand feet.[82] However, one of the pioneers of skiing in St Moritz, Philipp Mark, supported the more traditional style of skiing, with the heel support being only to prevent the foot from slipping backward. Mark did not consider the *Lilienfelder* ski practical for the mountains because of the metal it contained, which he believed would keep the feet cold and snap in severe frost.[83]

In 1903 the *Skiclub Alpina* was formed in the restaurant of the *Kulm* with twenty founder members, soon increasing to twenty-four. Emil Thoma Badrutt was the first president and Philipp Mark the vice-president and first instructor (*Ubungsleiter*). It soon launched into activity: it was founded on 9 December and its first outing took place on 13 December. A day later its statutes and regulations were adopted. It would seem that the founding of the Club had been delayed for some reason as the local press had reported in 1901 that a ski club was to be founded that year, with a properly kept run on which races would be held, including leaping competitions.[84] A year earlier it had been reported in the German section of the *Engadine Express* that the *Winterkurverein* had agreed to install a ski-jump and provide a challenge cup for the ski club which was to be founded.[85] In January 1904 it organised the first races for the Engadine ski championship; events were held for men, women and children and the military. There were also downhill and jumping contests. The winners of these first events were as follows: the winner in the distance and military races was G. Paravinici from Silvaplana ; jumping was won by F. Iselin from Glarus, where the first ski club in Switzerland had been formed a couple of years earlier; and Miss Hamilton won the ladies' race. By 1914 the club had 306 members, but this fell to 202 with the outbreak of war. It soon rose back up to 388 members in 1918, twenty-nine of whom were women.[86]

The *St Moritz Ski Club* began soon after the *Alpina Club*. Its object was to help beginners who wished to become ski-runners and it began to employ ski instructors. Its first president was Clarence Martin, succeeded by John Dodgshon in 1904. Mr C.R. Wingfield was the secretary. Other committee members were Mr Perrier, Herr Schuster and Herr Karl, showing the international appeal of the sport.[87] Winners in the *St Moritz Ski Club*'s races in February 1904 were Wingfield, L. Coventry, E.J. Herbert, Dodgshon, Lieutenant Mettler and Perrier.

A major contribution to the development of skiing as a pastime was the establishment of four rescue stations to look out for and assist in any accidents to skiers. The four stations were sited above St Moritz at Alp Giop, Alp Laret, Hahnen See and on the protestant church tower. The rescue stations were paid for by Mrs Weinards, the widow of a man from Rheyd in Germany who was killed by an avalanche near St Moritz in February 1904.[88]

Skiing was an energetic activity as without any mechanical lifts exponents had to walk up slopes before they could ski down. Skiing was an aid to mountaineering rather than a sport in its own right. 'It combines the deliberate progress of the climber with the brisk excitement of tobogganing, with the grace of skating or dancing. The rough hill, with its hot and stony mule path, becomes a vision of coolness and smoothness. Once on the top, the work, if any, is done, and unadulterated pleasure begins. There is plenty of time to enjoy the view at leisure.'[89] This vision of coolness and smoothness, though, was reserved for those who were already physically fit. In the same article, Mark warns the new skier not to do too much to start off with and try 'not to get fatigued in trying to reach a height more quickly, in order to be able to enjoy the fine descent as often as possible before having got your muscles used to unaccustomed labour'.[90] This was to change with the coming of lifts and mountain railways. In St Moritz, Emil Thoma Badrutt launched a company to build a funicular railway from St Moritz-Dorf to up to the Chantarella plateau. It was originally intended to serve the proposed *Kuranstalt* in Chantarella and two further intended health establishments, the *Privatklinik* and the *Kinderheim*. The railway was 450 metres long with a maximum incline of 49 per cent. The concession for the railway began on 1 January 1912, took half a year to build and came into use on 2 January 1913.[91] This opened up the Salastrains area above the village for skiing and the site was ideal for instructors to use to give lessons. The far-sighted Emil Thoma Badrutt saw that skiing had a big future. There were still no prepared pistes and ascents were done on skis with hide, known as seal skin, underneath.

A variation of skiing, was *skikjöring*, in this activity a skier was pulled along behind a horse. St Moritz was particularly suitable for this as *skikjoring* races could be held on the frozen lake. It was introduced in around 1900 by Claudio Saratz from Pontresina, of pioneer skiing fame, and it had originated in Lapland where Lapps harnessed reindeer to pull sledges and from that the idea of pulling skis developed. Saratz had acquired some reindeer and began holding demonstrations. In the first race, in 1906, horses replaced reindeer as draught animals and it was run on the road as the lake was not frozen hard enough to be safe. The race was won by Billy Griggs, who was to become the mentor of the British jockey and race-horse trainer Sir Gordon Richards.[92]

As in the other Swiss resorts investigated, St Moritz underwent a boom in visitor numbers from the years around the turn of the twentieth century, a boom which became an explosion with the arrival of the railway that ended the remoteness and relative isolation of the little community. Statistics give an indication of visitor numbers in St Moritz from early in its development as a resort. Lourssa counted fifty to sixty guests all summer in the 1830s: they were Swiss, Italian and a few Germans. At the start of the 1860s there were about a hundred guests: Italians were copious, Swiss numerous, Germans, Lourssa said, 'as predicted' and for the first time, there were three or four English. In the 1860s and 1870s came a change, the total numbers of visitors reached 200, then 300 and soon 400 guests, of these a quarter, then a third and eventually more than a half were English. The rest came from Germany, Italy and America. In 1862 an American guest had appeared.[93] The first of the winter seasons so described, which have since been continuous, was in 1875 to 1876.[94] In 1888 a weekly visitor tax or *Kurtax* of 70 rappen or centimes per guest in summer raised an income of 5,311 francs for 53,116 guest days.[95] At the height of the winter season of 1889 to 1890 there were just 350 guests in the resort, six-sevenths of whom were English. By the same point in the season of 1898 to 1899 this had risen to 1,800, of whom two-thirds were English. In the year the *Albulabahn* railway reached St Moritz, at the season's height there

were four thousand people in the village and this figure grew over the three succeeding years.[96]

A clearer indication is given if annual guest days are compared, although this data includes summer and winter season totals. Summer season visitor numbers were growing quickly as well as winter. From 53,000 summer and winter guest days in 1888, the total rose to 63,500 in 1889 and again to 86,000 in 1890. The rise was less spectacular with 88,500 guest days in 1891. A massive rise came the following year, up to 107,000, with a slight dip in 1893, down to 106,000. The next year, 1894, the figures increased again to 116,000, before dropping to 78,000 in 1895, falling as low as 74,000 for the next two years running and even lower in 1898, to 73,500 guest days. The total started to rise again to 93,000 in 1899, fluctuating over the next four years from 88,000 in 1900, 98,000 in 1901 and 92,000 in 1902. The figures began to climb again after that to 112,500 in 1903, 122,500 in 1904, a very slight increase to 123,000 in 1905 before leaping up to 140,000 in 1906.[97] The decline in 1893 and 1898 is explained through Americans staying away: the first time because of the World Exhibition in Chicago; the second as a war with Spain prevented many people coming to Europe. In the early 1900s, the numbers of English visitors dropped during the Boer War. This indicates both the vulnerability of tourism to competition from rival attractions and the adverse effects of international politics.

In St Moritz Bad the majority of visitors were German; in Dorf it was more international with visitors from a range of countries. The ease of rail transport and shortened journey times led to shorter stays per guest. Guests had previously stayed for between six and ten weeks and few for less than four weeks. Afterwards visits were much shorter, often between eight or fourteen days, concentrated especially around the end of January and the beginning of February.[98] This led to a growth in the accommodation sector: the luxurious *Grand Hotel* opened and many more small hotels and pensions were built to lodge the extra visitors. St Moritz grew as a winter resort by extending the length of time its hotels could remain open and providing an infrastructure to transport guests and maintain them once they were there. Once the conflict of the First World War began the number of people staying in St Moritz, as in Davos, was suddenly curtailed, only to pick up again in the 1920s. The economic depression of the 1930s followed by world war again caused another temporary crisis for the resort.

Notes

1   Margadant, Silvio and Maier, Marcella, *St Moritz – streiflichter auf eine aussergewöhnliche Entwicklung*, St Moritz, 1993, p. 139.

2   *Le nouvel ebel manuel de voyageur en Suisse par Richard*, undated, c. 1835, p. 395.

3   Margadant und Maier, p. 140.

4   Margadant und Maier, p. 143.

5   Robertson, Hans, *St Moritz – seine Fremdenindustrie und sein Gemeinwesen, eine Kulturhistorische und Volkswirtschaftliche Studie*, Samaden, 1909, p. 31.

6   Robertson, p. 33.

7   Margadant und Maier, p. 151.

8   Badrutt, Anton R., *Mein Wegweiser. Errinerungen eines St Moritzer Hoteliers*, Sameden, oJ.

9   Badrutt, Johannes, *Fremden-Liste vom Engadiner-Kulm, St Moritz, 1842–79*, St Moritz, 1880, Introduction.

10   *St Moritz Post*, 21 December 1886.

11   Riess, Curt, *St Moritz – die Geschichte des mondanisten Dorfs der Welt*, Zurich, 1968, p. 25.

12   Margadant und Maier, pp. 51 and 57.

13   Badrutt, J., pp. 18–21.

14   Badrutt, J., pp. 127–129.

15   Badrutt, J., Introduction.

16   Margadant and Maier, p. 152.

17   Margadant and Maier, p. 155.

18   Robertson, p. 35.

19   Robertson, p. 61.

20   Robertson, p. 61.

21   Robertson, p. 63.

22   Robertson, p. 64.

23   Tucker Wise, A. M.D., *Contra-indications for visiting the High Altitudes with a description of the environs of Maloja, Upper Engadine*, London, 1886, p. 7.

24   *Alpine Post and Engadine Express*, 11 November 1905.

25   Tarnuzzer, Dr Chr., *St Moritz. Engadin, Neuer Führer für Kurgäste*, undated, c. 1908, p. 129.

26   *Engadine Express and The Alpine Post*, 9 November 1901.

27   Behrman, H., and Cayley Mann, J. *Summer Days in St Moritz – letters from the pearl of the Engadine with a short guide, published by the Kurverein*, St Moritz, 1911 (German version, 1910).

28   Seth-Smith, Michael, *The Cresta Run – A History of St Moritz Tobogganing Club*, Slough, 1976, p. 79.

29   Seth-Smith, p. 80.

30   le Blond, Mrs Aubrey, *The story of an alpine winter*, London, 1907, pp. 77–78.

31   Burney Yeo, J. *Notes of a Season at St. Moritz in the Upper Engadine and a Visit to the Baths at Tarasp*, London, 1870, p. 56.

32   Badrutt, J., p. 40; Yeo, p. 56.

33 Yeo, p. 57.

34 Yeo, p. 58.

35 Badrutt, J., p. 40.

36 Yeo, p. 59.

37 Yeo, p. 60.

38 Seth-Smith, p. 11.

39 *Alpine Post and Engadine Express*, 1 June 1901.

40 Tarnuzzer, p. 130.

41 Seth-Smith, p. 18.

42 Margadant und Maier, p. 179.

43 Seth-Smith, pp. 18–19.

44 Seth-Smith, p. 19.

45 Gibbs, Roger, *The Cresta Run 1885–1985*, London, 1985, p. 19.

46 Seth-Smith, p. 20.

47 Seth-Smith, p. 25.

48 Seth-Smith, p. 28.

49 *The Davos Courier*, 31 January 1913.

50 *The Davos Courier*, 31 January 1913.

51 Robertson, p. 68.

52 *Alpine Post and Engadine Express*, 2 November 1901.

53 Seth-Smith, p. 32.

54 Seth-Smith, p. 79.

55 *St Moritz Post, Davos and Maloja News*, 29 December 1888.

56 *Sleighbells*, Davos, December 1889.

57 Riess, Curt, *St Moritz – die Geschichte des mondänisten Dorfs der Welt*, Zurich, 1968, p. 27.

58 Robertson, p. 68.

59 Seth-Smith, p. 36.

60 Triet, Max (ed.), *A centenary of bobsleighing*, Swiss Sport Museum, Basel, 1990, p. 40.

61 *Alpine Post and Engadine Express*, 2 November 1901.

62 *Alpine Post and Engadine Express*, 4 January 1902.

63 *Alpine Post and Engadine Express*, 2 November 1901.

64 *Alpine Post and Engadine Express*, 14 December 1901.

65 Margadant und Maier, p. 173.

66 *Alpine Post and Engadine Express*, 7 February 1903.

67 *Alpine Post and Engadine Express*, 7 February 1903.

68 Le Blond, p. 86.

69 *Alpine Post and Engadine Express*, 4 January 1902.

70 Triet, p. 64.

71 *Alpine Post and Engadine Express*, 28 December 1901.

72 *100 Jahre Skiclub Alpina St Moritz (und Kein Bisschen alt)*, St Moritz, 2004, p. 9.

73 Robertson, p. 68.

74 *Alpine Post and Engadine Express*, 22 December 1914.

75 Riess, p. 27.

76 *Alpine Post and Engadine Express*, 4 January 1902.

77 *Alpine Post and Engadine Express*, 28 December 1901.

78 Margadant und Maier, p. 173.

79 *Alpine Post and Engadine Express*, 1 June 1901.

80 *Alpine Post and Engadine Express*, 11 January 1902.

81 *Engadine Post and Alpine Post*, 4 January 1902.

82 *Alpine Post and Engadine Express*, 7 November 1903.

83 *Alpine Post and Engadine Express*, 11 January 1902.

84 *Alpine Post and Engadine Express*, 2 November 1901.

85 *Engadine Express and the Alpine Post*, 4 January 1902.

86 *100 Jahre Skiclub Alpina St Moritz*, p. 9.

87 *Alpine Post and Engadine Express*, 5 February 1904.

88 *Alpine Post and Engadine Express*, 20 February 1904.

89 *Alpine Post and Engadine Express*, 7 November 1903.

90 *Alpine Post and Engadine Express*, 11 January 1902.

91 Margadant und Maier, p. 135.

92 Rayner, Ranulf, *The story of skiing*, Newton Abbot and London, 1989, p. 56.

93 Robertson, p. 45.

94 *The Alpine Post and Engadine Express*, 4 November 1905.

95 Robertson, p. 45.

96 Robertson, p. 65.

97 Robertson, as above.

98 Robertson, p. 70.

4

Arosa

The third of the Swiss winter resorts to be examined is Arosa, situated on the other side of a mountain ridge to Davos, but further away from St Moritz, in the same canton as both in Grisons. As in Davos, tourism began here in the 1860s. Unlike Davos and St Moritz, Arosa had no prior reputation outside the region as a spa, nor had its climate been praised in medical journals, although it was situated at a higher altitude than Davos, at around 1,800 metres compared with Davos's 1,560 metres above sea level. In 1851 Arosa was a scattered farming community of just fifty-one inhabitants. In the 1860s, an elderly widow, Eva Arduser, began to take in guests at her alpine hut at *Hof Maran* on a plateau above the village. To her guests she was known as 'Alte Eva' but running an inn was not her main occupation. Guests had to wait when she was busy on the farm or until she had tended her animals before she would get them anything. In exchange for concentrated alpine air, visitors had to sleep on sacks stuffed with straw.[1] However, they were well fed with fresh milk and had plenty of *Veltliner* wine to drink.[2] On the other side of Arosa, two or three guests could be accommodated at *Egga*, with hosts Christian Mettier-Mathis and Jori Hold.

By the end of the 1860s convalescent young people from the cantonal capital of Chur were staying with local farming families, showing that Arosa was being seen as a health resort early on in its tourism development. It wasn't until 1890 that the road was extended towards Arosa and post was brought to the community on a coach or sleigh depending on the season, which could also carry passengers. The shortened journey time from Chur, lying at 600 metres above sea level, took six and a half hours to travel and climb to Arosa at an altitude of 1,800 metres. Passengers, including tuberculosis sufferers, could now travel in relative comfort, the new road contributing directly to the development of Arosa as a *Kurort* for the lung diseased.[3] The road also made the journey in winter less arduous and the weight of the tourist season was no longer in the summer. The number of summer visitors at twenty thousand still outnumbered the 12,500 there in the winter of 1895/96, but during the following decade the number of summer visitors doubled to 34,800 at the same time as the winter total increased fivefold to 62,600.[4] The number of permanent residents also increased: there were twenty times more people living in Arosa in 1900 than there had been in 1850.[5] The interests of the summer resort and the winter *Kurort* seemed to be opposed: there was a *Kurverein* and a more recent *Verkehrsverein* representing the separate interests of the two seasons. For summer tourists, woodland paths were laid and benches and signposts were erected. Streets and pavements were also created. Over time, though, the two organisations realised they had a common interest. They united in 1903 to form the *Kur-und-Verkehrsverein Arosa*. One of the merged body's statutes emphasised that the needs of summer and winter were of equal importance.[6]

The journey to Arosa, as it was to St Moritz and Davos, was an onerous task for sickly people travelling to the sanatoria. Arosa was handicapped in its development as it could only be reached by packhorse track, even after a road was built most of the way there from Chur in 1874. Langwies' connection to the city of Chur in that year through the building of a road along the Schanfigg Valley to within a few miles of Arosa was a spur to the growth of its tourism.[7] In 1875 a post service was introduced, providing transport to Langwies, where passengers had to change to pack horses or mules; passengers could also be carried by two bearers on carry-chairs. From the mid-1870s, holiday huts were being rented by Chur families around the *Untersee*, the smaller of Arosa's two lakes. These seem to have been self-catering as enough wood for cooking for the whole summer was advertised for sale for five francs.[8] Other people, mainly young convalescents, came from Chur and stayed in private homes or guest houses; there was one at Inner Arosa '*auf der Egga*' and a second at *Hof Maran*, both of which are described above. A family from Zurich came for a long stay in the small guest house erected by Peter Mettier '*am Stafel*' in 1877.[9] The following year, 1879, Luzi Brunold started taking paying guests in his home *Leineggahaus*, which was soon extended and renamed the *Pension Brunold* in 1880.[10]

Reflecting an increase in visitors, more guest houses opened over a short space of time. The first hotel was opened by Peter Wieland in 1878 at '*der Neuen Wiese*' near the larger lake.[11] Wieland renamed his hotel *Seehof*. The *Seehof* offered good food and fine *Veltliner* wine. To keep guests amused it had its own skittle-alley and organised picnics.[12] In 1880, a business directory in Chur listed only three people in Arosa, whose trade was given as *Gastwirt* (innkeeper). These were Luzi Brunold, Georg Hold and Peter Wieland of the *Seehof*, with the note in brackets afterwards 'only in summer'.[13] By the end of the 1880s *Pension Brunold* was advertised as open in summer and winter, and five of its ten rooms were heated, essential if they were to be inhabited in winter. The *Pension* could accommodate twenty-six guests with space for overflow in the village schoolhouse.[14]

The 1880s, as in Davos, was a decade of development of sanatoria, *Kurhäuse* (cure-houses) and hotels. Arosa's first ostensible health establishment opened in 1883: the *Kurhaus* was on the site of a guest house that had belonged to the Hold family. It had thirty-six beds in twenty-two rooms, ten of which were heated in winter, water-closets and two verandas, the largest covered with glass. Also in that year a second hotel was built, the *Rothorn*, soon to be followed by the thirty-roomed *Waldhaus* built for Christian Hold and Peter Mettier, which could take up to fifty guests at a time. Five of the south-facing rooms had balconies, a feature that was also becoming popular in other resorts.[15]

During the long cure that could last for months or even years, patients developed their own cultural life, which included many activities other than sports. At the *Altein* the patients devised and financed a concert programme for the season, which included the *Gewandhausorchester* from Leipzig and the *Duo Busch-Serkin* and song evenings. There was also a *Patientengemeinschaft Altein* which ensured that no poor patient went without flowers if they had an operation or were seriously ill.[16] It also organised language courses and instruction in business subjects to help with patients' rehabilitation into work after recovery as well as to pass the time.

A Dutch chemist suffering from tuberculosis, Dr Willem J. Janssen, in 1883 decided to leave Davos where had gone for his own cure. He bought land and erected a private sanatorium in Arosa. He married a local woman and went to live in nearby Langwies from where he superintended his establishment.[17] His *Villa Janssen* took in only three or four guests in winter and summer. Dr Janssen also offered secondary school teaching.[18] Another cure-guest of Davos, the German Dr Otto Herwig, had stayed there since 1882 seeking relief from tuberculosis. In the spring of 1883, through melting snow, he came over the mountains, crossing the Strela Pass. Herwig lodged at *Leinegga* with Luzi Brunold where he became Arosa's first winter guest, twenty years after the first winter visitors arrived in Davos. A remark in a travel guide-book had given him the idea to get to know Arosa. While he was there he made enquiries about the climatic qualities of the place. He concluded that before invalids could be invited to come there, the suitability of the place must be seriously tested so they could be prepared for the Arosa winter. At such a height and in such deep snow as lay there for half the year, no lowlander could be expected to stay in such primitive conditions; there were not even any streets.[19] Herwig did not let this deter him from his ambition to establish his own cure establishment there and in the summer of 1883 he negotiated with the local authority of Arosa to buy some land for building. After testing the winter conditions for himself by continuing his stay at *Leinegga*, the next year he built a little house that was to become the *Hotel Herwig*.

During this winter Herwig became the first person in Arosa to use skis. Through contact with his friends and relatives in Germany he had heard about Scandinavian skis and arranged for some to be sent to him so that he could try them out for himself. Without any instructions, he found skiing very difficult, gave it up as a bad job and stood them in a corner, continuing his perambulations around Arosa on the more familiar oval snow-shoes.[20] As a physician he performed some emergency treatments on injured local people but soon had problems with the Chur authorities as his medical qualification was from Germany and so he was not authorised to practice in Switzerland. After taking the relevant medical test, Herwig was able to open his sanatorium. He was joined by his sister, Marie, and together they owned and ran the *Sanatorium Berghilf* which had thirty-four beds in twenty-three rooms. Eight of the south facing rooms had balconies. The whole house had piped hot and cold water, heated corridors and toilets. It also had two bathrooms with showers.[21]

Two years after Herwig arrived in Arosa, four more winter visitors arrived during the winter of 1885 to 1886: two were students from Basle, another was from Dresden and the fourth, the ubiquitous clergyman from England.[22] Other accounts show that among the second small batch of winter visitors following Herwig's arrival were brothers Fritz and Carl Egger and Dr Eduard Geigy of Basle.

In the summer of 1884 Dr Schneider-Tissot, accompanied by medical student Fritz Egger, came to Arosa. In the autumn Schneider went to Langwies and Egger to Davos as they could not find any suitable winter accommodation in Arosa. The next year Fritz Egger returned with his brother Carl and they took rooms at the *Leinegga*. He was a correspondent for *Schweizer Ärzte* and through his writing made Arosa known in medical circles. The Egger brothers had some fish-shaped Canadian snowshoes made to a pattern based on the design of a pair Dr Schneider had obtained from Canada. With these snowshoes they climbed the Weisshorn, walked over the Furgga to Davos, riding down the Kummerhübel on a snowboard, the type of sleigh used by farmers for carrying hay and returned over the Strela Pass. At Christmas of 1885, the Eggers climbed the Rothorn with their friend Dr. Eduard Geigy from Basle. They left Arosa at about 2 am wearing their snowshoes and carrying small sledges on their backs for faster progression down hill on hard snow. It took them ten hours to reach the *Kurhaus* in Davos and then they had to make the return journey over the Strela back to Arosa. In 1892, wrote Carl Egger, skis made of resin appeared and a local carpenter, Engi, used them as a pattern to copy. At that time, eighteen-year-old Carl Staubli, later to become a doctor who worked in Zürich and St Moritz, was staying in Arosa to recover from asthma and to study. He soon followed the Eggers on ski and together they used them to climb the Weisshorn, the *Hörnli* and the *Furgga*. Staubli also made some ski tours alone. In March 1893, the Eggers and a fifteen-year-old French boy climbed the *Rothorn* on their skis. It was during this journey that Carl was able to enjoy a feeling he described as close to flight for the first time when he skied downhill.[23] In the same month the Branger Brothers and E. Burkhardt crossed the Maienfelder Furgga on skis in the opposite direction, from Davos to Arosa and back. After qualifying, Fritz Egger became a doctor at the newly built *Sanatorium Berghilf* in 1888. The next year he opened his own practice in the quickly growing village.[24]

Two more doctors from Germany joined the little community: Dr Jakobi as chief physician at the *Sanatorium Innerarosa*, the *Berghilf* and *Tschüggen* and Dr Römisch at the *Waldsanatorium*. Other men in the medical profession also joined them: Dr Schneider-Geiger, the builder of *Hohenfels* and Drs Fischer and Ruedi, who worked at the *Grand Hotel*. Between 1880 and 1888 the number of Arosa residents grew from fifty-four to eighty-eight. A major development occurred in 1887 when a visitor's tax (*Kurtaxe*) of twenty rappen (centimes) a week was introduced to finance communal facilities for guests. That year, too, the first advertisement for Arosa and the *Waldhaus* hotel appeared. 'Arosa, 6,000 feet above the sea'. Over three seasons it claimed more than twenty people had recovered vitality in the house; 'certainly the best proof of the excellent situation, the healthy air and good appetites of the guests'.[25] Two years later the *Kurverein* (tourist office) sent out the first advertising brochure of its own; the brochure praised the quality of Arosa's spring water, its outstanding milk and the *Veltliner* wine, recommended by doctors for cure patients.[26]

During the 1890s, public facilities for sports widened participation in organised winter sports in Arosa. Just before the start of this decade, the *Davos Courier* reported that Arosa was endeavouring to become worthy of the title it had assumed as 'the rival of Davos'. Two new hotels and a villa were to be built. The aspiration was to establish the place on a secure basis as a summer resort and gradually to raise it into repute as an alpine winter station.[27] Therefore, in 1891 the *Kurverein* created the first ice rink on the village's largest lake, the Obersee, but winter sports seem to have truly taken off in the middle of the decade when the sledge run opened and soon after the Arosa bobsleigh and toboggan club, *Schlittelverein Arosa*, was formed. Its first president was Dr Jacobi of the *Sanatorium-Hotel Tschüggen*. The founding committee comprised three Germans, three Englishmen, two Dutch and only one Swiss person. In a short time it had sixty-seven members. The club organised an international toboggan contest in February 1897. There were events for ladies, men and children. They were joined for this event by sledgers from Davos and Klosters. An additional sledge run was created from *Hof Maran* in 1898, improving facilities further for those staying at the other side of the village.

Ice-skating always had a big following amongst the bodily weak,[28] making it particularly popular in the health resorts and in 1899 a consortium created an ice rink in Inner-Arosa. This ice rink consortium was composed of Dr Otto Herwig of the *Villa Herwig*, his sister Marie Herwig who owned the *Sanatorium Berghilf*, Dr Jacobi also of the *Sanatorium Berghilf* and Nico Hold of the *Bellevue*. Just a year later in 1900, a much larger consortium bought land for a skating rink next to the Obersee. Members of the medical profession who were members of this group were Dr Romisch, Dr Ruedi, and Dr Alfred Schaeuble, another German who was a pharmacist and who like many others had moved to Arosa to benefit his own health. Schaeuble worked in the *Villa Anna*, his own home and dispensary named after his wife, and the *Graubunden Cantonal Sanatorium*. All other consortium members represented hotels, guest houses and health establishments. Other developments in the last decade of the nineteenth century were the introduction of the telephone in 1896 and electric lighting in 1897. A newspaper showing who the guests were and where they were staying, *Die Fremdenliste von Arosa*, was also published for the first time in 1896.

All these developments seem to have had an influence in attracting new visitors to the resort. In 1896 there were 125 guests, a number which doubled in a year to 254 in 1897. Visitors were mostly German, with English being the next most represented nationality.[29] Soon the existing post road proved to be inadequate and in 1903 the road between Langwies and Arosa was widened from 3.20 metres to 4.50 metres. But it was now becoming clear that if Arosa was to compete effectively with Davos and St Moritz, a railway was needed to connect it to the wider world. Already in 1901 Dr Rüedi had broached the idea of a concession for a railway company but his death delayed the scheme until December 1905, when such a concession was granted for an electric branch line between Chur and Arosa. The reason for this was that many lung tuber-culosis patients, especially the seriously ill, were frightened by the thought of the long *Post Diligence* journey to Arosa but were drawn by the comfortable train journey to Davos which could be reached in three hours from Chur or two and a half from Landquart. As they had a choice about where they went to, those with lung diseases would usually choose to travel to Davos, leaving only the fit and healthy to come to Arosa, to where the journey by road took double the time. Once the line to Arosa was opened, Davos and St Moritz were no longer easier to get to. British travellers could reach Arosa in just twenty-five hours from London on the *Engadin-Express*. With its woodland, sheltered situation, beautiful lakes, many mountain tours, passes and excur-sions, Arosa was a popular summer resort. In winter, apparently, there was only a small number of non-diseased visitors. None of the winter-opening hotels specifically ruled out tuberculosis sufferers as guests as those in St Moritz did, although there were establishments built especially for the sick. Even so there were some people who believed that when sportsmen and women had to eat and live together with those with lung disease, it was not very pleasant for either party.[30]

The idea of founding a ski club was raised during the summer of 1903, less than a year after that formed in Davos. At the club's first meeting on 4 January 1904 were Dr Schaeuble, Dr Pedolin, Rell the dentist, Herr Herbert, Pfenniger who was proprietor of the *Hotel Collina*, innkeeper Jundt, mountain guides Juon and Rüedi and the teacher Herr Heinrich.[31] The club statutes were drawn up by Dr Schaeuble, Herbert and Juon. The membership list was left at the *Verkehrsburo,* and soon twenty male and female members had signed up.[32] The membership fee of two francs was the same for both sexes. On 26 January 1904 the first ski races were held and in February the first ski-jump contest was organised. Local contestants in this were Dr Schaeuble, Pfenninger, Jundt, Ruedi, Pell, Ueli Abplanalp, Dr Burkhardt and Dr Amrein, all of them in the tourism or medical professions. It was won by Nädig from Davos.[33]

As can be seen, in Arosa, people in the medical profession and those with professional and financial interests in the development of the resort and the attraction of visitors were all keen promoters and participants in winter sports themselves. Dr Otto Amrein had first come to Arosa from school in 1893 as a patient in the *Sanatorium Berghilf.* He went away to study medicine then

The Lichtenhahn family near Schatzalp Sanatorium,   **6**
Davos Platz, about 1910

returned in 1900 to begin his own practice.[34] Between 1916 and 1933 he led the *Sanatorium Altein*.[35]

Another doctor, Fritz Lichtenhahn, who specialised in tuberculosis and lung afflictions, moved to Arosa in 1910. Previously he had worked in Davos with Alexander Spengler's son, Luzius, at the luxury *Schatzalp Sanatorium*. Well versed in the latest treatments, he set up his own practice, created a heliotherapy clinic for children and eventually established a 'preventorium' for frail children, *Prasura*. Dr Lichtenhahn and his first wife were keen skiers, for a long time he was a committee member of the ski club and in 1916 became president of the Arosa section of the Swiss Alpine Club.[36]

The ski club's first badge appeared in 1906 and the following year a Norwegian, Trygve Myklegaard of Christiania, was employed by it to run a skiing course. By 1908 there were some Arosa skiers who were able to give lessons in the club. The club built a ski-jump near the present Arosa station in 1911 and acquired a couple of huts to shelter members on the mountains in 1912 and 1913.

As the number of visitors to Switzerland reached its pre-war peak in 1913, the *Kurverein Sportkommitee* came into being to jointly promote the different sports. Its committee contained some now familiar names: Dr Schaeuble representing the *Eisbahn AG*, Dr Fritz Lichtenhahn for the ski club, Padrutt Mettier Junior of the *Skijöringclub*, Pfenniger of the *Internationaler Schlittelclub*, Luzi Wieland from the *Schlittelclub Plessur*, Richter of *Photographische Gesellschaft*, Trippel of the shooting club, and even the chess club had representation from Herr Masson.[37] An architect, Alfons Rocco, was president of the sports committee. All these people had a professional or financial interest in Arosa's development and expansion as a resort as well as their own personal involvement with the sports.

In the early years of skiing in Arosa, in the late nineteenth and early twentieth centuries, it was mostly a self-taught activity. The writer Hermann Hesse in 1934 described skiing as having changed a lot since he tried it as a young autodidact of the skill many years before. The soft snow of former years had been made into board-hard slopes and skiers needed to have learned *Christianias* and *Stemmturns* before they could safely venture out, a task that usually took a few days.[38] The first public ski teacher in Arosa, Hans Pfosi, discovered his market niche and organised his first course between 15 and 21 December 1915.[39] However, it wasn't until 1919 that a ski school was begun in Arosa.[40] Another innovation in the field of skiing was when Dr Knoll, the chief physician at the *Bündner Heilstätte*, began to practise sports medicine analysis and later became sports doctor in the *Schweitzerischen Skiverband*, involved in investigating the best ways of training ski racers. He was assisted by Dr Pedolin and Dr Gähwyler who also practised medicine in Arosa. In the area of land conservation which kept tracts of land free for pistes that allowed skiers to run down almost into the village, Beat Stoffel, later owner of the *Hotel Kulm* in Arosa, bought a large part of the meadow near Inner Arosa and around the mountain church from Christian Ambühl of Davos, thus preventing its development for building.[41]

Until 1908 Arosa had no bobsleigh run to speak of; the road down to the neighbouring village of Litziruti, which served as the toboggan run, was used. Bobsleighs had to glide over sledge tracks and holes in the road. At 4,600 metres, it was claimed as the longest and most difficult run in Switzerland and it took five minutes for a bobsleigh to run down to Litziruti. The *Kurverein* was responsible for the building of the snow walls of its thirty-one curves, only four of which could really be classed as dangerous.[42] Bobsleighing was not just a sport for participants but an entertainment for spectators, including non-sports people and health-seekers, who lined the course watching with happy cheers.

For the first fifty years of its history as a tourist centre, Arosa was above all a cure-centre. Most guests did not come for hiking or for winter sports, at least not while they were very ill. Doctors recommended to their tuberculosis and other lung-patients the dry, pure air of the high mountains. A prospectus of 1894 for the *Pension Belvedere* informs prospective guests that the beneficial influence of a long stay in the high mountains on different illnesses had been established for a long time. The wind-sheltered situation of Arosa at 1,760 metres above sea level, above the mirror-like lake between mountains up to 3,000 metres high, combined with its favourable climatic qualities, made Arosa a winter station for weak, nervous and convalescent people, especially those with afflictions of the breathing organs.[43] As in Davos, not all cure-guests stayed in the big hotels and sanatoria; many of them stayed as pension guests or lodgers in rooms. Between 1880 and 1930 many Arosa hotels and some houses were enlarged with the addition of wide balconies on which invalids could place their beds every day. This facilitated the *Liegekur,* the core element of the altitude cure. Patients had to lie on the covered balconies for hours, just as they did in Davos and Leysin. This reduced the functions of the body to a minimum, giving time during which the diseased lungs could heal.

Even in its curative aspect, Arosa's rivalry with Davos is shown. To emphasise its purity of atmosphere, in comparison with Davos, marketing publicity described Arosa as having plenty of space around its buildings, making it so much less urban than Davos. Just as in Davos, St Moritz and Leysin, some people were afraid of contagion from the tuberculosis bacillus. However, statistics showed that the death rate from the disease was actually almost half that of Switzerland as a whole: 7.1 deaths per ten thousand inhabitants a year compared with 13.8 per ten thousand elsewhere in the country during the first third of the twentieth century.[44] However, therapeutic and surgical treatments of the disease led to a successive decline in the total number of consumptive patients from 1920. The significance of this for Arosa was a difficult changeover from a cure to a sport resort and this transition was not always conflict free.

For years Arosa had 'done well' out of illness; in future it would achieve the same from healthy people. According to tuberculosis specialist, Dr Amrein, sport had gained the upper hand by 1926. At this time many sanatoria closed and were refurbished and opened again as sport-hotels, for example the Hotels *Valsana, Alexandra, Eden, Excelsior* and *Seehof.* The *Kulm, Tschüggen* and the *Sanatorium* which was renamed the *Grand* became five-star luxury hotels. Dr Amrein was critical of this development which lost Arosa its valued reputation as a health resort. As a place where people with lung-disease could come in the hope of a cure, the village had become world famous and as a consequence had been seen as a place where only invalids lived. However, the science of disinfection allowed healthy people to live beside sick people with no risk of infection. Even so, Arosa felt it still needed the lung-diseased.[45]

An innovative director of tourism, in position from 1915 to 1920, was Felix Moeschlin who later became famous as a writer. He realised early on that Arosa needed to send out a new message and had to move away from its image of a cure-resort for consumptives. Shortly before he took office, the railway opened in 1914, making Arosa only an hour away from the city of Chur all year round. The post coach had taken at least five hours. Moeschlin saw the possibilities this could offer for the development of both summer tourism and winter sports. He furthered the development of sport arrangements of all kinds. During his time the bobsleigh run was built down to Litziruti and German war-time internees built the first ski-jump.[46] Like the Richardsons had done for Davos over a decade earlier, Moeschlin, in a description of the resort, called Arosa 'a skier's paradise', expounding the tourism cliché.[47] Unlike Davos with the *Schatzalpbahn*, St Moritz with the *Chantarella* and the lifts associated with Grindelwald, Arosa had no mechanical lifts that could be used by winter sports men and women until 1937. Arosa became consolidated as a resort in its own right and not an off shoot of Davos. It had its own aficionados and identity, and its logo, in yellow and blue, echoed the colours of the sun and sky, just as Leysin and St Moritz included the sun in theirs.

Notes

1 Danuser, Hans, *Arosa, wie es damals war, Band 1, 1850–1907*, Arosa, 1997.
2 Haldimann, p. 24.
3 Just, Robert, *Alpdorf und Kurort Arosa*, Zurich, 1908, p. 30.
4 Just, p. 31.
5 Just, p. 51.
6 Just, p. 32.
7 Haldimann, p. 19.
8 Haldimann, p. 24.
9 Mettier, P. und Egger, Dr, *Arosa – Ein Führer für die Fremden*, Chur, 1889, p. 12.
10 Mettier und Egger, p. 12.
11 Danuser, *Band 1*, p. 38.
12 Haldimann, pp. 25–27.
13 Danuser, *Band 1*, p. 39.
14 Mettier und Egger, p. 12.
15 Mettier und Egger, p. 12.

16 Gartmann, Johannes Chr., *Altein – Arosa, Erlebnisse und Gedanklen um eine Höhen-klinik und eine Epoche, Arosa*, 1979, pp. 14 and 18.

17 Danuser, *Band 1*, p. 46.

18 Haldimann, p. 29.

19 Danuser, *Band 1*, p. 49.

20 Danuser, Hans, *100 Jahre Ski Club Arosa 1903–2003*, Arosa, 2003, p. 1.

21 Haldimann, p. 29.

22 Just, p. 29.

23 Danuser, *Band 1*, pp. 87–89.

24 Danuser, *Band 1*, p. 53.

25 Danuser, *Band 1*, p. 42.

26 Haldimann, p. 23.

27 *The Davos Courier*, 26 January 1889.

28 Just, p. 51.

29 Danuser, *Band 1*, p. 117.

30 Just, pp. 37 and 38.

31 Danuser, *100 Jahre*, p. 6.

32 Maran, Fritz, *40 Jahre Ski-Club Arosa, 1903–1943*, Arosa 1903, p. 2.

33 Danuser, *Band 1*, p. 98.

34 Danuser, Hans, *Arosa, wie es damals war, Band 2, 1907–1928*, Arosa, 1998, p. 17.

35 Gartmann, p. 13.

36 Lichtenhahn, Ernst, *Aus der Geschichte de 'Prasura'*, Basel, 2003, p. 2.

37 Danuser, *100 Jahre*, p. 10.

38 Hesse, Hermann, *Arosa, Beschreibung einer Landschaft*, Suhrkamp Taschenbuch, 1970, pp. 163–165, especially p. 164.

39 Danuser, *100 Jahre*, p. 11.

40 Danuser, *100 Jahre*, p. 21.

41 Danuser, *100 Jahre*, p. 13.

42 Danuser, *Band 2*, p. 24.

43 Haldimann, p. 56.

44 Haldimann, p. 58.

45 Haldimann, p. 59.

46 Haldimann, p. 101.

47 Haldimann, p. 104.

5

Leysin

On the other side of Switzerland, in the French-speaking canton of Vaud, Leysin began its development as a health and sports resort in the 1870s, a little later than the others in the study. However, a Leysin pastor mentioned in 1764 that sick people were already coming and staying there, making the unrecorded roots of the village as a health resort perhaps as old as those of Davos.[1] Amongst others in the 1870s, students began to take holidays in Leysin: they could rent a chalet or just take rooms with a family. Some parents from the lowlands put their delicate children to board in the homes of local peasants. Tourism remained only a very small sideline to the agricultural village and Swiss guide-books did not mention Leysin until the construction of its sanatoria in the 1890s.[2] The first dedicated guest-house, *le Chalet*, was opened by Mlle Cullaz to take in travellers passing through or staying in Leysin in 1875. Later the chalet was acquired and enlarged by Dr Auguste Rollier for use as a sanatorium. As in Grindelwald, Davos, St Moritz and Arosa, the village only became attractive to outsiders when the construction of a post road made it accessible from towns with railway stations, in the case of Leysin from Aigle near Lake Geneva. In 1875 a diligence (post coach) service carrying passengers from there to Leysin, coincided with the first recorded tourism.[3] By 1898, Leysin was well known and developed enough to be mentioned in a guide written by Henry and Holdsworth Lunn, published in 1898, although the only noteworthy feature for them was a charming walk by the new road leading up to the village from Sepey. There was a hotel in the village and Aigle could be reached by a footpath in an hour and a half.[4]

After a visit to Davos, Dr Louis Secretin of Lausanne felt so inspired he resolved to create something similar in Vaud. He set his sights on Feydey, an area just above the village of Leysin, as the ideal place. Its geographical situation was good: it was on a plateau, about 1,700 metres above sea level, sheltered from the cold winds by mountains, facing south for maximum sunshine and it was incredibly clear of fog which lay below between 1,300 and 1,500 metres. Secretin asked for advice from Dr Bezencenet as the physician had been pleased with the results he observed from sending patients with scrofula and sickly children for long stays at Veyges and Leysin. A generation earlier Bezencenet's father had also sent his patients from Aigle with skin and nerve diseases to the place.[5] As in Spengler's observations in Davos, tuberculosis was apparently unknown up there in the mountains and several phthisics had placed themselves there for summer stays, with general success.

The first sick foreigner to stay there over the winter was a young German, judged to be in a desperate state. He stayed in the village for several months in 1873 and appeared to regain his health.[6] Following this, several other invalids came to stay in the homes of Leysin people, and the beneficial effects of the climate became known in the outside world.

Following a period of meteorological observation begun in 1886 a meeting was held to discuss the findings. A *Comité d'initiative* formed in 1888 made plans to create a *station climatérique* (a climatic resort).[7] (The committee was reluctant to emphasise the medical element too much, hence this term.) Land was sold by the *Commune* of Leysin to the newly formed *Societé Climatérique de Leysin, SA*, a company created in March 1890, to build and run closed sanatoria like those in Davos. Two chalets began to take in tuberculosis patients in 1891.

Construction work had begun on the site and in August two years later the first 'hotel' to welcome tuberculosis patients was inaugurated.[8] The initiators of medical Leysin were reticent to the idea of creating a 'sanatorium' so they called their 120-bed establishment the *Grand Hotel*. The *Societé Climaterique* financed the building of roads up to Feydey, installed water pipes for running water and built promenades and benches to provide rest for visitors who exercised by walking.

A second luxury development was built close to the *Grand Hotel* called the *Hôtel du Mont Blanc*. Here the developers hoped to create a hotel for people who were in good health or who did not want the discipline imposed by sanatorium life. It had twin chalets connected with it for those who did not want to live in a large community and these were named *le Chamossaire*. This lack of strict discipline was not viewed very favourably by Dr Burmer, the manager of the successful *Grand Hotel*. The *Societé Climatérique* soon acquired and took over the *Mont Blanc* and transformed it into another more regulated curative establishment.[9] After a couple of years the *Mont Blanc* was enlarged and *le Chamossaire* reserved for those with more modest budgets.

Dr Burmer's rigorous methods were not supported unanimously by the *Societé Climatérique*. For example, a wealthy Russian, Parouchev, who joined in 1896 did not agree with the methods used but had no authority to change things. Even so, some patients did manage to escape the strict supervision and got out to enjoy themselves. A former patient, Henri de Beauzemont, relates how he was 'invited by some young people to break the rules and lose the medical surveillance and go for an excursion in the marvellous surrounding mountains'.[10] The exertion caused him to have a haemoptisis, a fever and coughing up blood, so he was forced to rest, proving the physician's advice correct. Beauzemont lost a great deal of weight and so had to take large doses of cod liver oil. Beauzemont makes no mention of sports other than this excursion, a presumed hike. However, he said there was no lack of conversation and reading, photography and innocent little games to make the time pass relatively quickly.[11]

The federal diligence ran right up to the *Grand Hotel* and a telephone system and post office were installed and electricity brought power to Leysin.[12] A narrow-gauge rack-railway carried passengers up to the village and Feydey from Aigle in 1896. The *Grand* was enlarged again in 1906 and the train line extended almost right up to its doors.

The needs of invalids who were not wealthy were not forgotten by Dr Fritz Morin who in 1897 set up the *Société de l'Asile de Leysin*. Its aim was to accommodate patients who were in a modest financial condition. The establishment it created was known as the *Sanatorium Populaire* and it received money to help support it from the firm *Nestlé*.[13] Men and women were segregated. In 1903 it became the 125-bedded *Sanatorium des Alpes Vaudoise*.[14] It welcomed patients from the lowlands of the canton, supported financially by the Vaud government. Not only did this offer the chance of altitude treatment for poor tuberculosis sufferers, it also removed them from the more populous areas where they could spread the disease through contagion. Davos and Arosa also had cantonal state-funded sanatoria, such as the *Züricher Heilstatte* and the *Bündner Heilstatte*. Those patients in state-funded sanatoria would probably not have been able to afford to take part in the privileged social and sporting activities of the wealthy guests. Another state organisation funding sanatoria treatment was the Swiss Army who sponsored the *Clinique Militaire Suisse*, run by Dr Rollier.[15] Here Rollier promoted the cure through sunshine and exercise in the form of light work.

A major event in the development of Leysin and also in the treatment of tuberculosis, a disease which can affect any part of the body, including the bones and not just the lungs, was made when Dr Auguste Rollier moved to the village, bought *le Pension de Leysin* and opened in it a clinic for non-pulmonary tuberculosis. The term 'surgical' (or *chirurgicale* in French) tuberculosis was wrongly used to describe forms of the disease that were treated by surgery, the cutting out of lesions as if they were tumours, a time when it was thought to be a purely local infection. This treatment would not cure the illness, the lesions of which were only symptoms, but could lead to secondary infections and mutilation. Professors Bonnet and Poncet, academics of Lyons in France, were the first to oppose surgery alone and to make use of the sun's rays in treatment. This was developed further by Dr Oscar Bernhard of Sameden, near St Moritz, who claimed to have discovered *heliotherapy* in 1899 after being inspired by the method local peasants had of conserving meat in the sun. In 1902 Bernhard was the first to use *heliotherapy* in Switzerland to heal wounds and then directly onto external tuberculosis, when he opened a clinic in St Moritz.[16]

Rollier's method of *heliotherapy* involved exposure of the body or affected part of the body to the rays of the sun. Rollier described his treatment, which had a good rate of success, in several written works. It made use of the antiseptic action of the sun on diseased tissue. Rollier explained his philosophy thus:

> The air and sun bath, judiciously applied, stimulates the appetite and the diges-
> tive functions and renews energy. Under its influence the number of red corpus-
> cles and haemoglobin content are increased, the blood formula is improved and
> the exchanges become more active. The skin, in proportion as it is pigmented
> and strengthened under the action of the air and sun bath, becomes once again
> the natural garment provided by the Creator. It resists the entrance of germs;
> bronze skin is resistant to microbial dermatitis. One hardly ever finds acne or
> boils, which are often doors to more serious infections.[17]

Photos in Rollier's publications show pictures from before and after helio-therapy treatments. Prior to therapy, patients were shown emaciated, with lesions and ankylosis. After a year or even less of the treatment, the same patient is photographed with an athletic physique, free from lesions and with full movement of the body. Many of these patients were said to still be healthy after twenty years.

> The solar rays only reach low-lying lands after passing through the whole thickness
> of the atmosphere, and the air of the plains is frequently saturated with moisture;
> that of the cities is, furthermore, loaded with dust, smoke and micro-organisms.
> This layer of moisture, dust and smoke, which constitutes what a physician has
> picturesquely described as 'atmospheric slime', forms a screen, which prevents
> a great part of the useful solar rays from reaching the ground. That is why in
> winter, the climate of high altitudes is usually much more agreeable than that

of the plains. At Leysin, more particularly, owing to the fact that the village is situated above the humid atmosphere of the plains, the sun shines frequently in December, January and February with a matchless splendour; since the clear air of high altitudes is freely penetrated by the sun's rays, which thus lose nothing of their beneficient influence.[18]

Rollier's method is seen in photographic images of smiling patients, often children, wearing simple loin cloths, happily engaged in various activities, sporting and non-sporting, in the sunshine. Often almost naked children were shown playing on sledges in the snow or sitting at their desks having lessons in the sun. These images were not always factual representations. This inspired and striking publicity sometimes used models posing for these pictures. An inhabitant of Leysin remembers that his brother one day went to pose for these photos even though he was not at all ill.[19] Spreading awareness of the role of the sun and the near-nakedness of his patients in the cure system he presided over was important to Rollier. For him the skin was much more than a mere

7   Taking a break in Leysin

organ of elimination, in the first place it was an organ of absorption; 'it not only assimilates oxygen from the air, thus contributing to the alimentation of the body, but it is through it that the body absorbs that atmospheric energy (the origin of which is uncertain) which must be considered responsible for the often quite surprising muscular development observed in patients who have been bedridden for many months'.[20]

The sun was to become the symbol of Leysin in later publicity. Rollier expanded his activities in Leysin and in 1909 opened a large clinic, *les Frènes*, followed by the *Miremont* in 1914. To help patients of more modest means finance their own cures, by paying part of their fees through work, Rollier devised *l'Abeille* which opened in 1909 as a work colony for convalescents recovering from tuberculosis. At *l'Abeille* the patients made items such as toys and baskets in order to contribute towards the cost of their treatment. Each year a sale was held and the proceeds shared between the workers, who received the whole amount minus the cost of materials. This income could be used to help pay for their maintenance. This kind of cure method was not confined to adults; there was an agricultural colony for children at nearby Cergnat where young people were instructed in outdoor farming activities which contributed to the costs of their treatment and also provided them with training in skills which would allow them to earn their livings in a healthy environment in adult life.[21] At the home for children thought to be predisposed to tuberculosis and other diseases, *Home les Esserts*, sports and walking played a large part in the life of the children. In winter, under strict supervision, they enjoyed skiing and sledging. This home did not admit children with contagious diseases or those who had to stay in bed. Medical certificates were needed to confirm this. For those children in delicate health. *Les Esserts* offered the opportunity to gain strength in a warm, family atmosphere.[22] Children also did their school lessons outdoors and were photographed at their desks wearing only loin cloths and sunhats.

The much larger *Clinique Manufacture* opened in 1930. Here too, the prescribed periods of activity and exercise were put to use for paid work. Patients became out-workers in light trades, such as watch-spring making, toy making, assembling telephone equipment and sewing, some of them working from their modified beds.[23] According to Rollier and his followers, the work cure helped the spirit. It was also helpful with the psychological problems of loss of occupation, separation from home and dependants and the loss of esteem associated with becoming a burden and an expense.[24] Work also eliminated boredom. Most patients in Rollier's clinics did not leave their beds and as a result, there were few suitably sized areas to be used as dining rooms when the buildings were later converted into hotels.[25] In Rollier's clinics patients confined to their beds lay on their fronts; this position was said to strengthen the abdominal muscles and, combined with the sun's rays, was an additional aid to healing.[26] Workers at the *Clinique Manufacture* worked lying in this ventral position as did children at *l'Ecole du Soleil.* This apparently allowed them: to work long hours without fatigue, assisted digestion, caused the shoulders to be held back, repositioned the back and therefore enlarged the thorax. Rollier insisted this was the natural way to lie as it was the position of choice for babies and young children and peasants who had not been taught to lie otherwise. This seems to echo an almost Rousseauian philosophy of the superiority of human beings left to remain in a state of nature.

Many clinics, sanatoria and smaller private chalets that took in invalids seeking a cure opened in Leysin. As in Davos and Arosa, facilities to amuse them, their healthy visitors and those who came to care for them were needed. Recovering patients and their companions and carers took part in winter sports. A publication of 1894 describes sledging as '*le grand sport de Leysin*'. The writer was not inclined to join in, even though he could hear the sledging parties from his sanatorium. He felt he was wise not to join in that particular activity as that would mean climbing a steep slope for several minutes at least before sliding down. '*Longue la peine, court la plaisir*'.[27] The writer, Henri Hen, preferred Norwegian skiing or ice-skating. He also liked to go walking wearing snow-shoes, '*le bonnes racquettes*', which made hikes easier and more agreeable in snowy weather.

A club for sports of different disciplines was initiated in 1903. The *Journal de Leysin*, initiated in 1901 became the official organ of the Sporting Club. The *Climatérique* in 1907 encouraged the club to develop some light sporting activities to benefit those patients already well on the way to recovery or who were not too sick.[28] Care was taken that none of the events organised, which included ice-fetes, firework displays, cinema shows, toboggan races, skating contests and orchestral concerts, interfered with the ordinary course of treatment.[29] *Heliotherapy* had created a cult of the sun. Sunshine and sun tans became symbols of health and taking part in sport was a healthy activity. The *Climatérique* announced in the *Journal de Leysin* of 1914 that healthy visitors found in Leysin varied walks and sports of all kinds. Many sanitoria boasted lawn tennis, croquet and several skating rinks and there were some excellent sledge runs. Toboggan races were organised in January and February each year by the Leysin Sporting Club against clubs at Avants and de Caux. The use of the word 'healthy' is remarkable here and it refers to visitors, as well as recovering and convalescent patients.[30]

The Sporting Club over time offered bobsleighing, hockey, skating, skijoring and clay-pigeon shooting.[31] However, in terms of sport, Leysin lagged behind Davos, St Moritz and Arosa: *ski de fond* (cross-country skiing), as opposed to downhill skiing, was encouraged for exercise and a ski club was not formed until 1924 when the *Ski Club Chamois* was created. Presumably earlier skiing was not organised or was done under the aegis of the Sporting Club. Bobsleighing was preferred by the men of Leysin and a young engineer there who had worked in the automobile industry developed his own model of bobsleigh in the early years of the twentieth century. This Leysin type had a steering wheel and this style soon became predominant everywhere except in St Moritz where tradition held out for the kind steered by a cord. The firm of *Bachmann Frères* at Travers, in the canton of Neuchatel, acquired the licence to produce the Leysin style of bobsleigh.[32]

Cross-country skiers, Leysin   **8**

A team from Leysin won the gold medal at the first Winter Olympics in Chamonix in 1924. The team's composition is demonstrative of the change in social composition in the village as workers moved in to the community to take advantage of the new opportunities for employment: there was Scherrer (the captain), a communist postal worker; Neveu; brothers H. and A. Schleppi; and Rigazzio, an Italian immigrant. A sport where Leysin also took the lead was ice hockey; the first team in Switzerland was formed there in 1903. The following year a team from Leysin and neighbouring Les Avants went to Lyon to play against the ice hockey club there. Later teams from Lyon, Paris and London went to play in Leysin and Les Avants. In Lyon where matches were played indoors in the *Palais de Glace*, the rink's dimensions restricted team size to seven players but at Leysin the ice hockey team consisted of eight members. In 1908 Leysin was a founder member of the *Ligue Suisse de hockey sur glace.*[33]

La societé d'initiative de Leysin-village was created in 1912 and began to manage footpaths, benches and an information bureau. It devised and ran activities for guests and visitors.[34] It published posters advertising the merits of Leysin to potential patients abroad and elsewhere in Switzerland and produced a guide to the resort. Under its influence the trains to Leysin from Aigle were timetabled to correspond with those of the national network. From 1923 a *societé de développement* extended the network of footpaths, public squares and organised floral balcony contests to enhance the resort's appearance. Yellow signposts were erected to help walkers, still the main sporting activity. To finance its activities, a cure or tourist tax, like Davos, St Moritz, Arosa, Grindelwald and other resorts already had, was introduced in 1926.

The *Societé des Hôteliers de Leysin* was founded in 1934. Its first president was Frederic Tissot who had been active in promoting sporting activities. The Leysin 'hoteliers' were of course, the proprietors of small clinics or directors or administrators of the big sanatoria. Leysin began to be promoted nationally and internationally through the Federation of Swiss Tourism. It was not until 1947 that the *Société de Dévelopement* noticed a decline in the number of nights spent by visitors in the village. However, it did not really perceive a long-term problem as they explained it away as being a temporary phenomenon at the end of World War Two when money was devalued and there were currency restrictions in many countries and a general decline of visitor nights in Switzerland as a whole. The society had failed to realise that there were any problems intrinsic to medical tourism.[35]

Unlike in the health resorts of Davos, St Moritz and Arosa, the medics of Leysin had always successfully opposed the development of tourism there.

Publicity sent out, even in the early 1930s, in several languages to other countries was confined to the medical aspects of the resort and its natural attributes, nature and pure, fresh air, presented to readers with a therapeutic goal. The only statement vaguely touristic was '*la vue splendide sur la vallée du Rhone et les cimes de Mont-Blanc*'.[36] Right from the start, a tentative attempt to attract healthy sports tourists was checked by the *Societé Climatérique* with its taking over the *Hotel du Mont-Blanc*. In 1903 a group from Geneva had the *Chamois* built, hoping to attract a winter sport clientele. It was not successful and a few years later it became another *heliotherapy* clinic. The *Climatérique* had been opposed to the propagation of sport in the resort that would disturb other patients. One of the principles of the cure was strict rest, usually in bed on the cure galleries or balconies, in silence. During the hours of the cure the inhabitants of the village had to cease all activities and noise made by their work. Sport presumably had to follow these rules. A guide-book of the 1920s to Switzerland for English visitors warned that Leysin was different from other Swiss resorts. It was dedicated exclusively to the warfare against disease. Although skiing, skating and tobogganing could be seen there, it was not strictly speaking a winter sport centre. 'Leysin is private property and the only kind of sports enthusiast who is encouraged is he or she who has won health and strength on the slopes around.'[37] Unlike Davos, St Moritz and Arosa where diversification of the tourism product had occurred soon after the resorts became famous as health centres, in Leysin no sustained attempt at diversification or promotion of the leisure opportunities on offer to a healthy public was made. After 1947, despite a recovery of the tourist trade elsewhere in Switzerland, Leysin fell into a long period of decline. The number of patients fell between 1946/47 and 1956/57 from more than 1,200,000 to less than 600,000. The duration of a typical stay in a sanatorium, which was about a year before 1945, reduced to about two hundred days in 1956/57 and down further to one hundred in 1963/64.[38] This was the impetus behind Leysin's conversion to a winter sports and tourist resort in the 1950s.

Notes

1 Desponds, Liliane, Leysin, histoire et renconversion d'une ville a la montagne, Yens-sur-Morges, 1993, p. 17.
2 Desponds, p. 17.
3 André, Maurice, *Leysin, station medicale*, Pully, 2002, p. 22.
4 Lunnand Lunn, p. 156.
5 Domville-Fife, C.W., *Things seen in Switzerland in winter*, London, c. 1925, p. 118.

6   Desponds, p. 20.

7   André, p. 22.

8   Desponds, p. 22.

9   Desponds, p. 23.

10   de Beauzemont, Henri, *Comment j'ai gueri une tuberculose pulmonaire au 3e degré sans médicaments, sans drogues et sans operation*. Leysin, 1902, p. 13.

11   de Beauzemont, p. 12.

12   André, p. 198.

13   Hobday, Richard, *The healing sun, sunlight and health in the twenty-first century*, Scotland, 1999.

14   André, p. 22.

15   Rollier, Auguste, *La cure de soleil et de travail á la Clinique Militaire Suisse de Leysin*, Lausanne, 1916.

16   Desponds, p. 29.

17   Rollier, Auguste, *The International Factory Clinic for the treatment by sun and work of indigent cases of 'surgical' tuberculosis*, Lausanne, p. 5.

18   Rollier, quoted by Domville-Fife, p. 112 .

19   Desponds, p. 30.

20   Rollier, in Domville-Fife, p. 115.

21   Rollier, *The International Factory Clinic…*, p. 5.

22   Prospectus, *Home les Esserts sur Leysin Suisse*, by M. et Mme E. Zitting, undated, about 1925.

23   Reminiscence of Maurice André, former patient, interviewed in Leysin, 2003.

24   Rollier, *The International Factory Clinic*, p. 5.

25   André, p. 31.

26   Rollier, Auguste, *Quarante ans d'héliotherapie*, Leysin, 1944, p. 147.

27   Hen, Henri, 'Souvenirs d'hivernage', *A l'ouvre! Quelques pages vendues au profit de l'Asile de Leysin*, Neuchatel, 1894, p. 77.

28   Desponds, p. 56.

29   Domville-Fife, p. 113.

30   Desponds, p. 56.

31   Desponds, p. 57.

32   Busset, Thomas et Marcacci, Marco, 'Comment les sports d'hiver conquirent les alpes' in *Pour une histoire des sports hiver / Zur Geschichte des Wintersports, Actes du Colloque de Lugano*, 20 and 21 February 2004, pp. 5–33, especially p. 14.

33   Busset et Marcacci, p. 15.

34   Desponds, p. 38.

35   Desponds, p. 61.

36   Desponds, p. 39.

37   Domville-Fife, p. 113.

38   Donzé, Pierre Yves, *Bâtir gérer soigner, histoire des établissements hospitaliers de Suisse romande*, Geneva, 2003, p. 264.

6

Grindelwald

Unlike the other resorts discussed, Grindelwald, in the Bernese Oberland, has a different developmental history unrelated to medical practice. Grindelwald began its life as a tourist destination much earlier than the other resorts under discussion. The first documented visitors to the glaciers, a German Count Albrecht von Brandenburg and an Englishman Thomas Coxe, who worked for the British government in Berne, were there in 1690.[1] In the eighteenth century, the enlightenment and then romanticism created more interest in the natural history of the mountains; superstitious abhorrence was replaced by scientific inquiry and admiration of the sublime landscape. Grindelwald benefited from being accessible from northern and western Europe as it was close to the northern edge of the Alps and it also contained some of Switzerland's most spectacular scenery– two glaciers that flowed down almost to the village, and a beautiful, wide green valley overlooked by the magnificent and seemingly impregnable north wall of the Eiger and the fortress-like cliff of the Wetterhorn. The volume of visitors, however, remained small until the nineteenth century: there was no hotel in the village until 1820, visitors lodged with the minister in the *Pfarrhaus* in preference to the inn or *Wirtshaus*. The minister (*Pfarrer*) kept a visitors' book which shows that a high proportion of his guests were English; for example, on one page from September 1816 there are the names, signatures and messages from fourteen people, all of them English. There were 'Mr William Fisher and Mr Bowes Wright, Anglais, September 18th; Mr H. Smith and Mr I. Southead, English; Madame and Mademoiselle Johnson, Anglais; Joseph Woods who "thanks *le cure* (sic) for his warm welcome", 19 September 1816; Mr Banks, Mr Polbill, Mr Bennett, Mr Buckley, Mr Welch, Capt Greene, Mr Pares, 24 September'.[2] The guest-book also contains the names of members of the German aristocracy and royalty. The sale by the monastery at Interlaken of its economic rights and the relinquishment by the Grindelwald commune in 1820 of these *Wirtschaft-srechte* in the valley by sale to private individuals made inn- or hotel-keeping a viable occupation there for the first time. The creation of hotels meant that the *Pfarrhaus* soon lost its function as a hostel.[3]

The first hotel, the *Schwarzen Adler* (Black Eagle), was founded by Christian Bohren who in his day was already quite a well-known character. In 1787 while walking on a glacier, the ice gave way beneath him and he was suspended over a sixty-four-feet-deep gap. Despite a broken arm from his fall he held on and amazingly found a 130-feet-long passage leading to an opening under the glacier and was able to reach safety. His story made him famous. Bohren thought people would want to come and see him and so in 1798, hoping to trade on his fame, he took over the lease of the *Steinbock*, an inn at Grindelwald. He began building a second hotel on adjacent land, the *Schwarzen Adler*.[4] However, Bohren died in 1817 and the incomplete *Schwarzen Adler* was sold to Samuel Blatter of Unterseen (Interlaken) who developed the accommodation when it was finished in 1820 into what was to be the beginning of the Grindelwald hotel business. The *Steinbock* itself was taken over by Elizabeth Grossman, a well-known boat operator on Lake Brienz, and her husband Peter Rutter. The inn was renamed *Zum Gemsbock*. It later reverted back to the ownership of the *Schwarzen Adler*, retaking its original name of *Steinbock* and becoming an annexe of the hotel. Blatter also built the *Berghotel Faulhorn* where mountaineering visitors could rest, eat and stay overnight after the long walk up the mountain.

The *Schwarzen Adler* was taken over again in 1832 by Peter Bohren and his son Rudolf Bohren-Ritschard, who became known as '*Adlerbohren*'. Like many other Swiss entrepreneurs, Peter Bohren had made his fortune abroad before returning to acquire property at home. He became known as 'Lyoner' as he had been in business in Lyon before returning home, supposedly with a chest of gold pieces. He extended and improved the *Schwarzen Adler*. His son Peter worked hard and became an influential man in the valley, eventually becoming *Grossen Rat*. For a decade the hotel enjoyed the unrivalled reputation as the best house in Grindelwald.[5] In 1843 the *Adler* opened another annexe, the *Gräfihaus*, built for the *Gräfin* (countess) von Schwarzburg-Sonderhausen, when she came to stay. Another royal guest was Dom Pedro II, the emperor of Brazil. The *Adler* remained in the capable hands of Peter Bohren until disaster struck in 1884. Bohren deposited the whole of his summer takings in the *Diskontobank* in Interlaken which subsequently went bankrupt. The bank's director, a brother-in-law of Bohren, tragically committed suicide. Many individuals and companies came to financial grief, among them the *Adler.* Following Bohren's insolvency, the *Schwarzen Adler* was bought by Rudolf Stähli-Forrer from Thun in 1885 and then sold again two years later to the Boss family. The youngest son of the Boss family, Eduard, took over as manager.

Almost immediately following the completion of the *Schwarzen Adler* in 1820 the *Grand Hotel Bär,* an eighteenth-century tavern was rebuilt as a hotel that same year by Christian Burgener.[6] Like the *Schwarzen Adler,* the *Hotel Bär* developed from village inn to luxury hotel. The *Grand Hotel Bär* was sold in 1824 to Johann Jacob Wettach, an innkeeper from Wilderswil near Interlaken. He shared his property among his five children when he married for a second time and kept the hotel in Grindelwald for himself. He renamed it *Bären.* In 1840 it was enlarged and rebuilt in the style of a wide-gabled Emmental house.

When Wettach died in 1841 his wife and children took over the running of the hotel. In 1856 it had forty rooms with sixty beds and was called the *Gasthof zum Bären* when taken over by a company of five Grindelwald men, Christian Bohren (*Herrenführer*), Ulrich Bohren (a miller), Peter Bohren, Christian Burgener (a smith) and Peter Roth (*Gemeindepräsident* – president of the local community). All these were local people. In 1867 the last remaining member of the partnership, Ulrich Bohren sold out to Johann Boss, a coach transport operator from Interlaken. Boss's coaching business had carried visitors all over the Oberland so he already had some knowledge of the tourism industry. Boss had a very large family of fourteen children, of whom nine sons and three daughters worked in the hotel business. Under Boss's leadership the *Bär* soon became the top hotel in Grindelwald and made its mark especially on the English. The English called Fritz Boss, the hotel manager, 'Our Fritz'. He had a reputation for being impetuous but always kind and helpful.[7] It was the first hotel in Grindelwald to have oil lamps and wood stoves in every guest room but it lacked warm water. Eventually the hotel was to have between seventy and eighty coach and riding horses and so a huge number of jobs were created, both inside the hotel and out.[8] Two years after Bohren's bankruptcy, the Boss family bought all the property of the *Schwarzen Adler*, its bakery, smithy and its annexes the *Gräfihaus, Steinbock* and *Schlössli.* Johann's sons Eduard and Adolf took over the *Adler's* management.

Grindelwald celebrates its birth as a winter resort from January 1888, the date of the *Bär* opening an annexe next to the main hotel called the Winterhaus. About twelve visitors, including Mrs Jackson who made the first winter ascent of the Gross Lauteraarhorn and Gross Fiescherhorn, made use of the new accommodation. Other mountaineers there were Gardener and Coolidge.[9] By the second year of opening the *Winterhaus* (winter house) had a small skating rink between the hotel and the street made by flooding the tennis court. Bandy was played there by the English guests, to the delight of the villagers to whom the game was a novelty.[10] By January 1880 the number of guests in the *Winterhaus* had increased to a record thirty-five. When the railway opened a decade later in 1890 the *Bär* and other hotels benefited from the new influx of visitors. In the 1891–92 winter season there were nearly one hundred guests.[11] However in 1892 a great fire broke out in the hotel's roof, caused by sparks, and soon spread by the *Föhn* wind, burning down not just the *Bär* but 116 buildings that were all reduced to a pile of ashes. Arnold Lunn, who as a four- year-old boy was staying with his parents in a chalet nearby at the time, describes picking cooked apples from trees in the garden, baked in the intense heat.[12]

Most of central Grindelwald had to be rebuilt and so contains very few buildings dating from before the fire. The *Bär* was resurrected with three hundred bedrooms, reduced later to 250 when bathrooms were added. Because of their heavy investment the Boss family had worked for decades with no real profit. This was to change in 1907 when a company was formed called *Boss Grand Hotel Bär und Adler AG* which took over ownership and financial responsibility. The sale of shares gave the Boss family a large sum of cash and many shares. Management of the hotels still remained with the family. The hotel was to burn down again in 1941 while it was being used as a military sanatorium during the war. This time it was not rebuilt.

A guide-book of the 1830s told visitors about the two hotels, *l'Ours* and *l'Aigle* (Bear and Eagle), and gives instructions for reaching the village on foot or by horse from Interlaken. In the early nineteenth century a traveller arrived in Grindelwald by *Char* with two horses to Grindelwald but planned to continue with just horses over the Scheidegg to Meiringen as there was no road for a carriage beyond the village. The invalid traveller decided not to bother with the second part of his journey. In fact he was not very impressed by Grindelwald at all. 'To avoid the unprofitable toil of climbing up one side of the hill, merely to descend the other, we determined to return to Interlaken, and proceed by water to Brienz. All that is worth seeing, may thus be seen, almost without quitting your carriage, or the high road.'[13]

Lacking a viable road, most tourists came to Grindelwald on foot, perhaps accompanied by riding or pack horses or mules. For example, in a description of a journey from Lauterbrunnen in 1823 the writer resolved to cross the Wengernalp which would bring us down upon the village of Grindelwald, and therefore set off the following morning at break of day, having engaged two saddle horses which, though we were five in company, would enable us to rest by turns. The horses' owners were to act as guides and to carry the luggage… After five hours toil we reached a chalet upon the top of the mountain, when our guides soon made a fire, brought a pail of cream and a kettle from some neighbouring shepherds, and in less than an hour, prepared for us coffee and the other materials of a comfortable, though late breakfast. Three hours descent brought us to Grindelwald…. The inn where we rested was homely but very moderate accommodation would have satisfied us after a day of such fatigue'.[14]

The most popular route for travellers in Switzerland at this time went from Berne via Thun to Interlaken then to Zweilütschinen to Lauterbrunnen, back to Zweilütschinen or over Wengernalp and the Kleine Scheidegg to Grindel-wald. The path was retraced for the return to Berne. This tour was known as the *Grindelwaldkehr*.[15] The village inns had barely enough facilities for guests and so before the mid-1820s many had sought accommodation at the rectory. As late as the middle of the nineteenth century, some travellers were still arriving in Grindelwald on foot. In 1853 twenty-year-old Joseph Hoyland Fox went with his cousin and future brother-in-law, Frank Tuckett, to Switzerland. They explored for a month on foot, by *diligence*, *voiture*, steamer and rowing boat. In the middle of their holiday they went to Grindelwald. The pair left Meiringen at about 6 am and walked over the Grosse Scheidegg, arriving at Grindelwald at around 4 pm in the afternoon. Their stay was very short and next day they continued over the Kleine Scheidegg to the *Wengen Alp Hotel*. After just one night they got up early again and walked on to Interlaken where they arrived at 10.20 pm.[16] After his marriage Frank Tuckett and his family returned regularly to Grindelwald and he became a pioneer of mountain climbing in the Alps. Joseph's son Gerald was also to come to Grindelwald where he would have a major influence on the development of skiing.

By the 1850s there were enough visitors coming to Grindelwald, even on foot, for its inhabitants to begin supplementing their subsistence agriculture with income from tourism. This is evident from the 1856 edition of *Murray's Handbook*: Its inhabitants were chiefly employed in rearing cattle, of which there were six thousand head on the pastures. Some of the peasants acted as guides. Christian Bleuer, Peter Baumann and Hildebrand Burgener were highly recommended by *Murray's* for difficult mountain excursions. Whole families were engaged in the business: 'The younger females picked up a few halfpence by singing *Ranz de Vaches* at the inns and most of the children were beggars – occupations arising from the influx of strangers into the valley which had exercised an injurious influence on its morals and ancient simplicity of manners.'[17] This attests to its readers' disappointment in the discrepancy between the romantic ideal of the innocent, morally superior mountain dweller as eulogised by Rousseau, Byron and Senancour. Other guide-books of the period make the same disappointed observation: the Swiss were eager to benefit financially from tourists. As the mountain dwellers became aware of what the visitors expected and hoped to see, they did their best to provide it. The Grindelwald valley dwellers became conscious that they themselves had become the object of the tourist gaze. Tourists wanted to see the romanticised lifestyle of the Swiss peasant and as these could provide rewards the peasants were often happy to oblige, damaging their image of non-materialistic innocence in the process which, ironically, was partly what the visitors wished to see.

A publication of 1854 telling the story of an American boy's tour of Switzerland shows several examples of this new materialism when describing the visit to Grindelwald. While walking to the village a man came out of a hut and waited for the boy and his adult companion. The man blew his Alpine horn to let the boy hear the echoes. His guardian paid the man a small amount of money and they went on. Another hut was situated opposite a part of the mountain range where there was a great accumulation of ice and snow that seemed to hang suspended as if ready to fall. Another man stood at the door of this hut holding in his hand a small iron cannon mounted on a block of wood. The man fired his cannon indicating to the travellers that it would start an avalanche. Nothing happened but they gave the man money anyway. 'It is customary in Switzerland to amuse travellers with the story that the concussion produced by the discharge of the cannon will sometimes detach these masses [of snow] and thus hasten the fall of an avalanche; and though the experiment is always tried when travellers pass these places I never heard of a case in which the effect was really produced,' said the narrator.[18]

As the travellers drew near the village of Grindelwald the people of scattered cottages came out as they saw them coming with various plans to get money from them. At one place two little peasant girls, wearing traditional Grindelwald-type costume (or what was thought to be), came out with milk for them. At another house a boy came out with filbert nuts to sell and at another the merchandise consisted of crystals and other shining minerals collected in the mountains nearby. Other children stood beside the road holding little Swiss cottages carved in wood, each item with a small box for its safe transportation. In some cases children had nothing to sell and just held out their hands to beg as visitors went by. There were also 'several lame persons, idiots and blind persons and other objects of misery' (*sic*) that occasionally appeared imploring charity. As these unfortunates were generally satisfied with an exceedingly small donation, it did not cost much to make them all happy.[19]

Although the above account shows that some visitors enjoyed the amusement provided by local people or at least did not mind giving money, recognising how well off they were in comparison, others saw it as a nuisance that was damaging the Swiss reputation. The Grindelwald authorities, through the medium of *Baedeker's guide to Switzerland*, recommended that visitors not yield to any of the attempts made to obtain money from them by songs, performances of the Alpine horn, exhibitions of Alpine animals etc., all of which were forms of begging in disguise.[20] However class distinction and property ownership seems to have defined what constituted begging. It was perfectly legitimate to charge tolls and pontage to travellers, fees to visit an ice grotto, use the ladder-way to climb to see the glacier or to see the camera obscura next to the *Hotel Wetterhorn* at the end of the valley near the Upper Glacier. All these attractions involved payment to the person on whose land they were built. For the propertyless, selling a skill or talent directly to visitors was not acceptable but a form of begging. By the beginning of the twentieth century though, it was boasted that in Grindelwald there were no beggars; everyone was willing to work.[21]

Until after the mid-nineteenth century there was still only a narrow path to the village passable on foot or by horses and riders in single file.[22] Road improvements were decided upon in 1851 but it wasn't until 1862 that traffic began to use the road. Then a six-seater postal-coach service travelled to Grindelwald four times a week along the new road, making it easier for tourists to reach. Proposals by the canton's engineer to extend and straighten the road, making it end near the *Hotel Bär* and cutting out the section of the old lane that led to the *Hotel Glacier* at *Endweg* met with protests from commune members Johann Egger and Ulrich Bohren, at that time a share holder in the *Bär*.[23] A new road was desirable but should follow a route decided by the commune not one that would benefit only a few people. Another proposal put to the *Regierungs-Rath* in Bern followed almost the same route as the modern road, cutting through forty pieces of land, sometimes halving its value. It was said no-one would be served by this new route except the owner of the *Schwarzen Adler*, Rudolf Bohren, who was the brother-in-law of the engineer, Aebi. This route would cut off three inns and the shortest footpath to the glacier. The fact that Aebi had his brother-in-law as an adviser was disturbing for the valley residents and so some time elapsed to allow things to calm down before work finally began in 1875. Fritz Boss, now running the *Bär*, opposed Aebi's and Rudolf Bohren's plan. The voters chose to keep the old route to Endweg.[24] In 1882 an employment creation scheme made further improvements to the road and eventually it was to lead to the *Bär* and the future site of the railway station. Pfarrer Strasser counted 18,000 vehicles travelling to and from Grindelwald between May and October with a total observed of 39,330 travellers using the road between 25 July and 1 October 1887.[25]

Road improvements reduced the journey time from Interlaken by coach or sleigh in winter to only two hours. Interlaken could be reached by rail, making Grindelwald accessible from all over Europe. There were so many visitors from England that the *Bär* provided a room for them to use for religious worship in English.[26] In 1879 a dedicated Anglican church was erected. By 1883 there were ten hotels and pensions in the village, providing about six hundred places for guests.[27] Following the arrival of the *Bernese Oberland Bahn* in Grindelwald and rebuilding after the great fire, in the last decade of the nineteenth century and the first decade of the twentieth century the number of hotels and guests rose again. In 1900 the total of hotels had reached nineteen hotels, with 1,253 beds for guests.[28]

Other hotels came to rival the *Bär* and the *Adler* but in an expanding market here as elsewhere there was plenty of room for competition. For example, the *Hotel Schönegg* began as a private house for Dr Beck of Biel, the *Chalet Schönegg*, in 1868. In the 1880s it became the *Pension Schönegg* and this was bought by Gottlieb Stettler in 1892. It had been extended three times by 1900 when it became the *Hotel Schönegg*, with between eighty and a hundred bedrooms. It was taken over by Gottlieb's son Adolf Stettler in 1910.[29]

As in other resorts before the 1860s, tourism in Grindelwald was confined to the summer months. It was a popular summer destination for tourists and mountaineers. As a centre for mountaineering, Grindelwald, with its imposing peaks attracted many climbers, especially from England, to the challenge of the Eiger, Jungfrau, Wetterhorn and many other unclimbed summits in the 1860s. Famous climbers such as W.A.B. Coolidge, his aunt Miss Meta Brevoort and Lesley Stephen came frequently to the area. It was a principle of English climbers at this time never to climb without guides and porters.[30] This created employment opportunities for local men, taking them away from home for long periods, leaving their farms in the care of their wives. This golden age of mountaineering lasted for the rest of the nineteenth century, an enthusiasm that continues in Grindelwald today.

On Boxing Day 1860, according to Arnold Lunn, a group of young

Englishmen led by the secretary at the Berne Legation went to Grindelwald. If these visitors who stayed at the *Hotel Bär* are to be accepted as the first winter guests, Grindelwald, of the resorts studied, was the earliest to have some form of winter sports tourism.[31] The proprietor was persuaded to open and warm his hotel especially for this group of winter sportsmen.[32] This incident is not mentioned in Rubi's otherwise detailed four-volume history of Grindelwald, *Im Tal von Grindelwald*. However, Lunn in several of his books on the Alps said the party was led by one of the secretaries at the Berne Legation, who coaxed the proprietor of the famous 'Bear Hotel' (*Bär*) to open and warm his hotel for this pioneer party of winter sportsmen.[33] Who the individuals in this party were is not told but in January 1867 Sir Horace Rumbold went to Grindelwald with his fiancée and other English companions, a visit documented by Sir Horace in his own account. Rumbold was minister at the British Legation in Berne who records show was based there in 1860. He therefore could have been one of the visitors of 1860 who wanted to share with his future wife the winter landscape he had previously enjoyed. It is also possible that Lunn confused the date or it is a misprint in the source that has been repeated. On the sleigh ride to Grindelwald from Interlaken, in January 1867, 'thick white clouds completely covered the steep mountain sides of the narrower part of the Lütschine valley, while a chilly mist concealed everything thirty yards distant. The upper valley bathed in sunshine as though some great curtain had raised. A cloudless sky above added to the enchantment of the scene,' enthused Rumbold. He went on to add 'that the blueness of the sky was quite Italian'.[34]

Winter climbing first began around Grindelwald when A.W. Moore and Horace Walker toured the Strahlegghörner over the new year of 1867.[35] Otto Schlaefli relates that Moore and Walker were there between 16 and 27 December 1866 to hunt chamois but then went climbing with Christian Almer, Peter Bohren and Melchior Anderegg.[36] If so, they were the first winter climbers if not visitors in that season to Grindelwald. Details of their visit and mountain tour did not appear in the *Alpine Journal* until August of 1869.

The Gentleman's Magazine published an article by Charles Williams describing his own winter visit in its January 1872 edition. Before setting off, Williams claims he had begged his friends to insure his life. In his account he asserted 'in the most emphatic manner that he who has only seen Grindelwald in summer has not seen it at its best'.[37] W.A.B. Coolidge and his aunt Meta Brevoort came in winter for two weeks in early 1874 to what Coolidge described as 'a wholly different Grindelwald to nowadays. Neither ice rinks nor railways, no hotels open and no tourists but lots and lots of snow. The inhabitants were astounded to see us.' According to Coolidge, a few scarce guests found accommodation at the *Hotel Eiger*. Apparently, it was the influence of Williams' article that induced the pair came to Grindelwald for climbing in the winter.[38] In January 1874 Coolidge climbed the Faulhorn with the hotel porter. A few days later, with his aunt, the guides Christian and Ulrich Almer and three porters he went up the Wetterhorn. The following week they climbed the Jungfrau for the first time in winter.[39] The next day F. Bischoff and the *Adler* landlord, Bohren-Ritschard ascended the Mönch. Schaefli, in his booklet on winter in Grindelwald, told readers he believed it was probably these ascents that induced Bohren to commission the local medical man, Dr Bandlin, to write a pamphlet setting out the advantages of Grindelwald as a winter resort.[40]

During the winters of 1877 and 1879, Leslie Stephen was also came to the village for winter climbing, staying at the *Bär*. While he was there, Stephen met up with Coolidge who was staying at the *Adler*. This seems quite an unremarkable event except for the fact that it was probably the first time two distinct parties of foreign travellers had met up during the winter in Grindelwald.[41]

There were certainly a few winter visitors in Grindelwald from the 1860s but there was no actual winter season of activities for tourists. Those who came were isolated adventurers. There is no evidence that any of these people were motivated by the search for health when they came to Grindelwald. They appear to have been healthy sportsmen and women drawn to the village by the glorious scenery and the opportunity to climb the snow-covered mountains. As most peaks had already been conquered, winter offered new opportunities to become the first to climb a peak in winter. In the autumn of 1887 there were about forty thousand travellers on the road along the valley into Grindelwald.[42] The same source says that in the winter there had only been thirty visitors arriving but the source gives no information about where they were staying. 'Grindelwald was making efforts to become a winter resort,' claimed a local Swiss journal in October 1887. New building was taking place so that a greater number of guests could be taken in the next winter.'[43] This was alluding to the construction of the *Hotel Bär*'s new winter house which came into use the following year, in 1888. Grindelwald in its official celebrations commemorates this event as the birth of winter sports in the village and in the Oberland as a whole. One of the first guests at the winter house was Coolidge who continued to came regularly to Grindelwald for winter climbing with the guide Christian Almer.[44] In that first winter season of 1888/89 there were, according to the *Berner Taschenbuch,* only a few *Kuranden* (guests). In 1891/92 there were nearly a hundred and by 1895–96, about 400 guests.[45]

More hotels began to open in winter and by 1905 there were more than a thousand, mostly English guests, over Christmas and the New Year.[46] Those who came to the *Bär* for winter sports enjoyed sleigh rides, sledging, ice-skating and curling on the hotel's specially constructed ice rink. The first winter sport, as in the other alpine resorts, was sledging. On walks the English visitors saw local people using sledges to transport themselves and larger ones called *Hori* for moving wood and hay and other goods in winter. There were different types of sledge but it was the smallest type, known as a *Beinz*, propelled and steered by the legs and feet that was adopted for pleasure use by sportsmen and women. Grindelwald sledges were lighter and more comfortable than those made in Davos. This meant that it took more work to make one and therefore they were more expensive than the *Davoser*.[47] An alternative means of sliding down icy slopes was on a device called a *Gemel*, exclusive to Grindelwald. It was ridden like a bike with sleigh runners instead of wheels.

As elsewhere in the Alps, bobsleighing soon became a popular addition to the sliding sports available. By the end of the nineteenth century there were toboggan runs, both artificial and natural on every side of the valley. Sledgers could go anywhere without fear of being 'hauled up'.[48] The English guests at the *Bär* formed the Bear Toboggan Club which organised races. There were events for gentlemen, ladies, children, singles, doubles and mixed doubles. Mostly the English kept to themselves but soon local people joined in and rode with them.[49] The main public sledge run was the Village Run but the streets too were permitted to be used. Sleigh rides on horse-drawn vehicles were popular for outings and excursions and for pulling along tailing parties as well as for transport to and from the station.

On the ice, English figure skating and especially curling were favourite pastimes. Skating was in the English style which appeared deceptively simple but was actually extremely difficult to learn and perfect. 'Now the English concept of skating, like the English conception of many other difficult under-takings, may be embodied in two words – nothing easier. Long sweeping curves, smooth complacent turns pianissimo, body erect in a statuesque repose, rebellious arms stoically repressed to the minimum of insurrection, these are the requirements of the English school' was the description of the figures performed by small teams skating in unison given by Daniel P. Rhodes. As an American he could mock the English style and refer without any sacri-lege to the 'bewildering gibberish that you hear now and then from the man in grey as the signal for the intricate evolutions that follow. See them gather in a knot around the orange in the centre, then shoot out on all sides like sparks from a firework pin-wheel, then circle about on the outside forwards and backwards, turning together, all in the same line, till suddenly back to the centre they come, only to sail forth again on fresh combinations.'[50]

The Grindelwald Skating Club was formed in 1891 and the Curling Club in 1898, predictably by English guests staying at the *Bär*. For those new to skating, mountain guides could help them learn. As amusements there were ice gymkhanas and at night fancy dress balls on the rinks, decorated gaily with lanterns, torches, lamps, fireworks and bonfires.[51] The Grindelwald Curling Club was the third organised for lovers of that sport in Switzerland after those of St Moritz and Davos. It soon established itself as the leading curling club when it travelled to Davos and beat the home curling team in its own Jackson Cup tournament for the first of five victories in 1903. The team members were Revd. H.C. Gaye (skip), Mr Muir, Dr Marsh and Mr Barclay.[52] There were also teams representing some of the hotels open in winter: three teams from the *Bär*, one from the *Eiger* and another from the *Grand Hotel Adelboden*. Curling was a sport played and organised exclusively by British guests. There was no mention of the sport in any *Kurverein* literature. Another sport played on ice by the British was bandy, a forerunner of ice hockey, which was played with curved headed sticks and a small ball. A club for that sport, the Bandy Committee was formed in 1902, chaired by Col. Hill. The Bandy Cup was competed for in 1909 for the first time. Ice hockey proper wasn't played in Grindelwald until 1913.

By this time the English style of figure skating had almost vanished from the rinks of Grindelwald, driven out, according to Arnold Lunn, by economic pressures; 'four Englishmen skating a "combined" needed more space than fifty foreigners waltzing in the degenerate Continental style' and hotel proprietors began to think in square metres per skater, with the result that English skaters found they were no longer wanted. Skaters in the English style almost disappeared from the rinks of the Alps.[53] The English style of figure skating emphasised the elitism of the British abroad during the heyday of the Empire.

The English school of skating is severe, hostile to display and imbued with the team spirit. The Continental school is free, individualistic and spectacular. The English skater tries to perform a difficult turn with as little fuss as possible. To the uninitiated the most difficult of English figures looks easier than the simplest of Continental 'threes'. The English skater claims that he is modest, and the Continental skater retorts that of all forms of conceit the English type is the most trying, for it is, in essence, based on the assumption that an Englishman need not do his own trumpeting, since his superiority is too obvious to require vulgar advertisement. 'Combined figure skating' said the patriarch of the English school, 'appeals to me because it is English. No individual display, you know. The team spirit on ice. I like watching good Continental skating just as I like watching ballet dancing, but I pay other people to do my ballet dancing for me'.[54]

Lunn went on to explain that unfortunately team spirit was too 'exacting in its demands for space, since fifty immodest ballet dancers on skates occupy less room than four modest gentlemen registering chaste team spirit round an orange'.[55] A great change from the early years of winter sports in Grindelwald when, according to Rhodes, even the Oberlander skated in the English style, for no other was recognised there.[56]

During the first winter seasons before the turn of the century there was no skiing in Grindelwald; the first skiers did not come there until 1891 and they were just two isolated individuals. In 1889, Gerald Fox, the son of Joseph Hoyland Fox whose visit on foot in 1853 is described earlier, went to Scandinavia with his cousin Tom where there was an international ice-skating contest which they followed with eight days' sledging. Their host at a hotel on Oslo Fjord took them to a local carpenter, had them fitted with skis and then took them on a three hour run across country. They had already been to the *Hotel Bär* in Grindelwald for climbing holidays and in 1891 Gerald and Tom went to the *Bär* again, where there were about fifty people, mostly climbers and guides, although there was little climbing that year because of the weather. Gerald persuaded three members of the Boss family, who owned the hotel and two

Curling on the rink of the Hotel Bear, Grindelwald   **9**

boys, the Kaufmann brothers, to venture onto ski. Most of the other visitors seemed to think them an unsafe means of transport. At that time ski sticks and seal skins for climbing upwards had not yet been invented and mechanical lifts were still undreamt of, the skiers only had a single four-foot-six-inch pole with a steel chisel end. For skiing it was much easier and quicker to carry or pull up the skis to the top of the run on the beginners' slopes, the Church Run and the lower part of the Wengen Alp. Gerald wrote, 'There were no trains and we had to work very hard for our sport. Another day, my cousin and I, with Christian Jossi, went up the Lauberhorn (carrying *luges*), nine and a half hours up and five down, waist deep in snow for hours and very cold.'[57]

Another contender for the accolade of first skier in Grindelwald is described as a Russian but he was actually a British citizen with an English mother and a Russian father. Alfred Belaieff, was born and lived in London. When he first ventured onto skis is not documented but in January 1897 wearing long uncomfortable Nordic skis, Belaieff crossed the Strahlegg Pass with the guide Samuel Brawand and Brawand's brothers Peter and Fritz who shared a single pair of skis. This was the first winter crossing of this pass. To undertake this feat Belaieff could not have been a beginner. His guide, Samuel Brawand, began his guiding career in 1892 and is reported to be the first guide to use skis.[58] He probably gained his confidence on skis practising with Belaieff in the years before 1897. In Grindelwald the mountain guides were quick to recognise the possibilities of skis for high mountain tours and most of the younger guides learnt to ski as an aid to winter mountaineering at a time when those of St Moritz were criticised for their reluctance to do so.[59] Another of the early skiing guides was Hans Kaufmann, one of the boys who had first tried skiing with Gerald Fox. Kaufmann began his career as a guide then became a ski instructor. When Fox's own children came to Grindelwald thirty years later, Kaufmann gave them their first skiing lesson.[60] He later went to America where he began teaching skiing in the Rocky Mountains.

Samuel Brawand went on to make other high tours of the Oberland peaks on ski with the American Daniel P. Rhodes in 1899–1900. Rhodes wrote a book which was published in 1903 which was a humorous attempt to inform the reader about the various winter sports to be experienced in Grindelwald. Rhodes had made his high mountain tour with Brawand as his guide. Brawand had presumably shared his experience of skiing with Rhodes and helped him in his skiing endeavours. Therefore Rhodes was probably ironically mocking the snobbery of some of the English guests when he made the remark that 'skiing is more like golf: in learning it you must submit to instructions and not mind being talked down to by your inferiors'.[61] The relationship was similar to that of the existing relationships between mountaineers and their guides. The guide seems to have been a cross between a servant and a companion. As skiing became more popular, getting skis from Norway was not practical. Grindelwald carpenter Samuel Jossi began to make them himself from ash wood to sell to prospective skiers.[62]

Ski races began to be organised from about 1900 by English guests who were regular winter visitors.[63] Skiers raced down a slope known as the Spion Kop as it was at the time of the Boer War. Later events went downhill from the Männlichen. However, when the Grindelwald Ski Club was formed in December 1902, there was only one English name among the founder members, G.A. Newsom. The club's founding meeting took place at the *Hotel Oberland*, chaired by Emil Gsteiger of the *Hotel Bahnhof*. The honorary president was Fritz Boss of the *Bär*, the treasurer was Christian Burgener and the secretary was J. Jakober-Peter, publisher of the *Grindelwald Echo* newspaper.

Straight away the club began organising races; the first events included only jumping and cross-country. Winners of the visitors' races in January 1903 were Miss Hill who won the ladies jumping with a leap of twenty-one feet three inches and Newsom who was victorious in the speed race, cross-country and jumping, clearing a distance of nineteen feet eight inches. All other events were won by Swiss competitors.[64]

Early skiers lacked what today's skiers would class as basic skills. A correspondent of the *Echo von Grindelwald* wrote to the newspaper reminiscing on skiing in her youth. She recalled that if the run down was too fast skiers clamped the ski stick between their legs to use as a brake. They looked just like witches on broomsticks only they were on the ground and not in the air.[65] Daniel P. Rhodes facetiously described this too in *A Pleasure Book of Grindelwald*. 'As speed over heavily-crusted snow is always high even on moderate slopes, and the guiding difficult, it is dangerous and indeed impossible for any great space to let yourself go without check. You must use your brake with all your might, leaning backward on the pole till you are almost sitting on the ski: hardly enjoyable this, and as laborious as any uphill work you did in the summer.'[66] Other methods of braking were not completely unheard of, at least by Rhodes: 'Men pretend to have seen Dr Nansen come skiing poleless and at full speed over a glacier and stop short on the brink of a crevasse by pressing his knees inward so as to press outward against the snow with the soles of his ski. For my part, I am willing to wait, and to begin cultivating this accomplishment when I have something more than hearsay for a guide'.[67] As an experienced skier who had done high-mountain tours on skis, if anyone was aware of other ways of skiing, it was Rhodes. Dr Nansen was the Norwegian explorer whose book about his crossing of Greenland on ski had been inspirational for many pioneer skiers in the Alps.

When ski clubs were formed, one of their primary aspirations was to bring instructors from Norway to Switzerland. Although there was no ski school until the 1930s, there were two Norwegian instructors working in Grindelwald in 1905. Novice skiers could learn how to make *telemark, christiania* and *stemm* turns with them.[68] In Davos too, at its inauguration the ski club resolved to acquire the services of a Norwegian instructor for the club. Rhodes exclamation of pretend disbelief of Nansen's feats was not so far-fetched in the context of skiing in the early 1900s. The English pioneer of ski mountaineering, downhill and slalom racing, Sir Arnold Lunn, had skied for four or five seasons before he saw anybody link turns on a slope. He remembered walking for two miles to see a native who he was told could do the turn the Norwegians call a *telemark*.[69]

As in other ski centres, early skiers in Grindelwald had to walk up hill carrying their skis before they could glide down. 'It is hardly amusing, this skiing upward in monotonous zig-zags, but you will often have a great deal of it to do if you wish to find the best runs down. But you have already learned from the summer what the winter will be teaching you over again – that with fine weather in the High Alps much of the uphill work which was at first so laborious gradually loses all its terrors. Habit and ever-hardening muscles soon combine to set for you a regular pace, calling for so little thought and effort as to leave you quite free for the enjoyment of every point of view', advised Rhodes.[70] The *Wengernalpbahn* didn't operate a service to Kleine Scheidegg from Grindelwald in winter until the season of 1933–34, although there had been a service from Wengen on the other side of the ridge since 1913. Whilst blasting for the railway up to Kleine Scheidegg from Grindelwald was taking place, Fritz Boss, the owner of the *Bär*, was certain it would not pay.[71] The first lift just for skiers was planned in 1926 but the plans did not come to fruition. It was another ten years before a *Schlittenseilbahn*, a kind of giant sleigh for up to twenty-five passengers with skis and sledges which was pulled up the slope at Bodmi on rollers, came into use. It carried people up to the ski school there.[72]

Unlike in Davos, Leysin, Arosa and to a lesser extent St Moritz, there is no evidence to suggest that any of these winter sportsmen and women or their companions were ill and seeking a cure from the Grindelwald climate or waters.

Although there was no winter season at that time, the first winter visitors probably came to the village in late 1860, giving Grindelwald the earliest documented winter visitors of all the resorts studied. These first winter visitors were in good health and came for leisure or sport. They were not invalids seeking an environment that could restore health, and thus was Grindelwald set apart from the pioneers in the other resorts. This is not to say that there were no entrepreneurs with ambitions for Grindelwald to become a health resort. Rudolf Bohren-Ritschard had plans to make Grindelwald a *Winterkurort* in the real sense of the word. He roped in the local physician Dr August Bandlin to assist in this scheme. In 1875 a booklet by Bandlin entitled *Grindelwald als Winterkurort* was published.[73] The booklet contained a foreword by Prof. Dr. H. Lebert from Vevey who endorsed his colleague's recommendations of Grindelwald as a health resort by approvingly acknowledging the endeavour 'to make a *Kurort* of such a beautiful, sheltered, mild Alpine valley'. Dr Meyer-Ahrens, the advocate of Davos as a health centre, was quoted as writing that 'Grindelwald has so healthy a climate that it was qualified to be allowed to enter the ranks of the climatic resorts'.[74] There would be Alpine milk cures in spring and summer and climatic cures in winter and autumn that would benefit those unfortunates suffering from chest disease. Bandlin and Lebert led the efforts to make Grindelwald into a health resort by recommending it for sufferers of chronic catarrh, asthma, enlargement of the bronchi, tuberculosis of the lungs, with or without fever, recovery for chronic pleuritis patients, those with nervous illnesses and weakness or digestive disorders. An advertisement produced for this campaign headed *Kuranstalt Grindelwald, Gasthof zum Schwarzen Adler*, shows an image with little realism in the mountains drawn in the background. The house for the reception of the sick was provided with the highest comfort. There were balconies sheltered by glass, gardens with evergreen plants, high airy rooms and heated corridors.[75] As usual the treatments would include movement in the open air, baths and showers. However, Bohren-Ritschard and his supporters' plans failed to come to fruition.

The idea was resurrected in 1892 by the new valley physician Dr Hückstaedt in his book *Der Alpenkurort Grindelwald zur Winterzeit* which also raised concerns about the suitability of the village for patients in the advanced stages of tuberculosis, heart disease and a tendency to strokes. Hückstaedt described the valley as a natural 'inhalatorium'; there was a wind-free, moderate winter climate in the valley where it seldom rained in winter.[76] He emphasised the low death rate of Grindelwald of only 57 in 1890 and 58 in 1891. The principal illnesses were: heart disease, pneumonia and pleurisy. Tuberculosis affected only 0.8 per cent of the population but accounted for 3.5 per cent of total deaths, but the disease was listed among the contraindications of a stay in Grindelwald, together with feverish conditions, heart failure and weakness. The resort was recommended for those suffering from asthma, emphysema, chronic catarrh, and predisposition to tuberculosis in the young or for convalescence following treatment.[77]

Joint advertisements for the *Bär* and the *Adler*, when both hotels were owned by the Boss family, referred to Grindelwald as an *Alpen-Kurort* or 'Alpine Health Resort'. The village is described as 'a first-rate winter health resort and rendez-vous for sportsmen'.[78] Attempts to create a health centre in Grindelwald met with no real interest and in 1902, in a letter published in the journal *Winter in Bernerland*, Captain Kettle could write 'it is usual for Grindelwald to be as good as fully occupied and all hotels have a great number of guests, of guests we say not of patients as is so often the case in the Swiss high resorts in winter. Thank God Grindelwald is not suitable for invalids and we don't have those incessant coughs here which so stubbornly persist in other so-called favourable health resorts.'[79] Being at a much lower altitude than Davos, Arosa, St Moritz or Leysin, Grindelwald could not claim the beneficial effects of high mountain air and so could never develop as a centre for tuberculosis sanatoria with the same criteria. Grindelwald winter guests almost exclusively had 'healthy faces and strong bodies; candidates for life not death, happy sports people of all ages'.[80] This was regularly mooted as a positive feature of Grindelwald: 'winter visitors may count on not finding invalids at Grindelwald only those in perfect health or recovering their strength'. There were no poor, emaciated and coughing consumptives, only persons temporarily pale after illnesses or prolonged mental exertion, who would soon be bronzed and strong in the health-giving climate and even these were very rare.[81]

Life in Grindelwald in winter was merry and cheerful – suited to those who need to be stimulated and braced up. Melancholy and black cares soon fly away, visitors would be kept occupied and there was no stiff etiquette, constraint or reserve. For those who needed it, medical advice was available from Dr Huber and Dr Scherz. Other publicity, published by travel agents Henry and his brother Holdsworth Lunn claimed that in Grindelwald in winter the temperature was higher than in lower lying places. 'The temperature may be very low but the absence of damp in the atmosphere modifies the cold so much that when the thermometer is below zero the cold is not felt nearly so much as in England in November when the thermometer stands at forty to forty-five degrees Fahrenheit.'[82]

The number of winter visitors to Grindelwald was enhanced in 1892 when on 7 January Dr Henry Lunn brought twenty-six churchmen to a conference to discuss the reunification of the different confessional groups within the Christian church. There were Anglicans, Methodists, Dissenters and continental Protestants. By day they enjoyed the sports and in the evening they held their discussions. From that conference, for which Henry Lunn had made the travel arrangements, evolved the travel agency of Sir Henry Lunn Limited. Henry Lunn was the first travel agent to appreciate the possibilities of winter sports. The party stayed at the *Bär* which charged him three francs fifty rappen (centimes), when there were about twenty-five Swiss francs to the pound sterling, for three meals a day, use of ice rink and toboggans. Lunn offered his clients a fortnight in the best hotel in Grindelwald and a second-class return rail fare from London for an aggregate of 7 pounds 10 shillings.[83] The second 'conference' in 1893 was held in Lucerne because of the destruction caused in Grindelwald by the fire, but the next year it was back.

From the prospectus detailing the Grindelwald Conference of 1894, it is apparent that it was more of a holiday than a religious meeting. It was described to potential travellers as 'a holiday in the Bernese Oberland with extensions to Mont Blanc, the Matterhorn and the St Goddard [*sic*], Italian Lakes, the Engadine and the Falls of the Rhine with a New Guide to Paris'. The prospectus was emphatic that 'as the first object of these conferences has always been to secure a really refreshing holiday in every sense of the word, no meetings (except in the "Devotional Fortnight" and on the two "Reunion Days") are held till 8.30 pm. The days are devoted to mountaineering and other healthy recreations.' Speakers included clergy, Edward Whymper and social reformer W.T. Stead lecturing about the social problems in Chicago and their lessons for Englishmen.[84] This holiday tour was advertised at a cost of ten guineas unless the traveller made his or her own hotel arrangements, in which case it would be three guineas less. Lunn's guests were warned that if they were not already in training, they should be content with short journeys at first. Only after a fortnight's practice would they know their own powers. On a day's walk chocolate was recommended as a useful substitute for meat and cold tea or coffee made with milk or sugar, for wine.[85] Lunn's conferences were organised to take place in both winter and summer months but the expertise he gained enabled him to extend his business to winter sports holidays without the religious element. The fact that his holidays were inclusive tours and seen by existing guests as 'personally conducted' like a Cook's tour, led to accusations by the elitists that he was making Grindelwald more downmarket.

Even though Henry Lunn never skied he had an immense influence on the development of skiing. Although he was not successful in meeting the aim of his conferences for church reunification, the arrangements for the travel and accommodation were so successful Lunn went on to develop his own travel agency specialising in winter sports for the upper classes, named the *Public Schools Alpine Sports Club*, a contrast to the claim that his tours were lowering the tone of a Swiss winter holiday. Not far from Grindelwald, Lunn bought hotels in Wengen and Mürren, places which became the centre of downhill and slalom skiing through the influence of his son, Arnold.

Attentive hoteliers who opened their businesses in winter recognised that winter visitors needed more care than summer ones because of the long hours of darkness which made them more dependent on what the hotel supplied. Therefore every detail had to be carefully scrutinised, as it would be praised or blamed by the guests.[86] Every larger hotel had its own entertainments committee, formed and run by its guests and backed up by the hotel keeper.

By the eve of war in 1913, Grindelwald could boast that it was both a sports place and a resort of the first range. Water was piped to the whole village, there was electricity for lighting and several hotels with central heating. For safety, the streets in and around the village were cleared with a snow plough and snow roller after every fall of snow, so people could walk on them. Ten private ice-skating rinks with a total area of ten thousand square metres provided plenty of space for skating and curling. The new bobsleigh run from Brandegg to Grund, at 4.2 kilometres, was the longest in central Europe. The *Wengernalpbahn* carried riders to the start in minutes. Toboganners were catered for by a kilometre-long artificial run in the village, while some roads continued to be used for the sport. By this time there were eighty mountain guides, many of whom were good skiers who could lead skiing excursions. Two thousand beds could provide accommodation for guests in twenty-seven hotels in both summer and winter.[87] Its lack of sanatoria for altitude cures meant it was not affected by changes in medicine and tuberculosis therapies following the discovery of antibiotics.

Notes

1 Rubi, *Band II*, p. 19.
2 Pfarrhaus-Gastebuch, 1805–1817, Grindelwald Museum.
3 Hagel, Jürgen (Schriftleitung), 'Die Entwicklung eines Bergbauerndorfes zu einem internationalen Tourisenzentrum, Ein Beitrag zum Problem des Kulturgesgraphischen Wandels alpiner Siedlungen', *Stuttgarter Geographische Studien, Band*

74, Herausgegeben von Wolfgang Meckelein und Christoph Borcherdt, Stuttgart, 1968, p. 48.

4 Rubi, *Band II*, p. 39.

5 Rubi, *Band II*, p. 42.

6 Rubi, *Band II*, p. 42.

7 Rubi, *Band II*, p. 48.

8 Rubi, *Band II*, pp. 46–47.

9 Schlaefli, Otto, *Winter life in Grindelwald*, Interlaken, 1903, p. 8.

10 Schlaefli, p. 9.

11 Schlaefli, p. 10.

12 Lunn, Arnold, *The Bernese Oberland*, London, 1958, p. 160.

13 Matthews, Henry, Esq, *The Diary of an Invalid being the Journal of a Tour in Pursuit of Health in Portugal, Italy, Switzerland and France in the Years 1817, 1818 and 1819*, London, 1820, p. 337.

14 *Travels in Switzerland, Compiled from the Most Recent Authorities*, London, 1831, p. 145.

15 Michel, Hans, *Berner Heimatbücher Grindelwald*, Berne, 1953, p. 21.

16 Fox, Hubert, *An English family and the mountains of Grindelwald and how in 1891 the first ski came to Grindelwald*, Grindelwald, 1991, second edition, 2001, p. 3.

17 *Murray's Handbook, Switzerland, Savoy and Piedmont*, 1856, p. 81.

18 Abbott, Jacob, *Rollo in Switzerland*, Boston, USA, 1854, p. 177.

19 Abbott, pp. 178–179.

20 *Baedeker's Guide to Switzerland*, 1895.

21 Schlaefli, p. 42.

22 Rubi, *Band II*, p. 13.

23 Rubi, Rudolf, *Im Tal von Grindelwald, Der Sommer und Winterkurort, Band III*, Grindelwald, 1986, p. 14.

24 Rubi, *Band III*, p. 15.

25 Rubi, *Band III*, p. 18.

26 Hagel, p. 47.

27 *Echo von Grindelwald*, 8 February 1963.

28 Rubi, *Band II*, p. 63.

29 Rubi, *Band II*, p. 63.

30 Hagel, p. 47.

31 Michel, Hans, *Berner Heimatbücher, Grindelwald*, Berne, 1953, p. 22: Michel, Hans, *Tresors de mon pays, Grindelwald*, Neuchatel, 1953, p. 13.

32 Lunn, Arnold, *Switzerland and the English*, London, 1944, p. 78.

33 Lunn, Arnold, *The Bernese Oberland*, London, 1958, p. 163: Lunn, Arnold, *Switzerland and the English*, London, 1944, p. 178.

34 Schlaefli, pp. 4–5.

35 Rubi, *Band III*, p. 93.

36 Schlaefli, p. 4.

37 Schlaefli, p. 6.

38 Schlaefli, p. 6.

39 Rubi, *Band III*, p. 93.

40 Schlaefli, pp. 6–7.

41 Schlaefli, p. 7.

42 *Freien Oberlander*, Thun, 11 November 1887.

43 *Freien Oberlander*, Thun, 12 October 1887.

44 Rubi, *Band III*, p. 94.

45 *Berner Taschenbuch*, 1898.

46 Schlaefli, p. 10.

47 Rubi, *Band III*, p. 107.

48 Schaefli, pp. 25–27.

49 Rubi, *Band III*, p. 108.

50 Rhodes, Daniel P., *A pleasure book of Grindelwald*, New York, 1903, pp. 168–169.

51 Schlaefli, pp. 24–25.

52 Rubi, *Band III*, p. 135.

53 Lunn, *The Bernese Oberland*, p. 166.

54 Lunn, *The Bernese Oberland*, p. 167.

55 Ibid.

56 Rhodes, pp. 174–175.

57 Fox, p. 8.

58 Rubi, *Band III*, p. 143.

59 *Alpine Post and Engadine Express,* Vol. XXX, No. 11, 11 January 1902.

60 Fox, p. 9.

61 Rhodes, p. 188.

62 *Neue Zürcher Zeitung*, 14 February 1991.

63 *Neue Zürcher Zeitung*, 14 February 1991.

64 Rubi, *Band III*, p. 157.

65 *Echo von Grindelwald,* No. 1, 28 Jahrgang, Reader's letter from Margrit Trachsel-Rubi of Interlaken, 5 February 1988.

66 Rhodes, p. 184.

67 Rhodes, p. 192.

68 Michel, *Berner Heimatbücher Grindelwald*, p. 23.

69 Lunn, *The Bernese Oberland*, p. 165.

70 Rhodes, p. 187.

71 Fox, p. 10.

72 Rubi, *Band III*, p. 233.

73 Bandlin, Dr A., *Grindelwald als Winterkurort*, Bern, 1875.

74 Bandlin, p. 6.

75 Bandlin, p. 19.

76 Hückstaedt, Hans, *Der Winterkurort Grindelwald zur Winterzeit*, Zurich, 1892, p. 12.

77 Hückstaedt, p. 23.

78 Poster advertisement for Hotels Bear and Adler, c. 1890s. Grindelwald Museum.

79 Rubi, *Band II*, p. 54.

80 Gottfried Strasser, quoted in Rubi, *Band II*, p. 55.

81 Schlaefli, p. 21.

82 Lunn and Lunn, p. 271.

83 Lunn, *The Bernese Oberland*, pp. 160–161.

84 *The Grindelwald Conference 1894*, Swiss National Library, p. 7.

85 Ibid.

86 Schlaefli, p. 30.

87 Jakober-Peter, J., *Grindelwald im Winter*, Kur und verkehrsverein Grindelwald, 1913, no page numbers.

7

Transfer of technology

Switzerland, with its wild mountains and natural beauty, became an antidote to the blight of industrialisation and all that went with it, in Britain and later in other countries. The perceived simplicity and purity of the Alps became an alternative to modernism. However, this wild natural environment, or at least the part occupied by tourists, had to be tamed before large numbers of people would be able to get to and stay comfortably in these remote places. The changes that the five Swiss communities in the study underwent between the middle of the nineteenth and beginning of the twentieth centuries were reflections of the changes taking place in the countries from which their tourists came. From remote backwaters, villages were transformed into cosmopolitan communities with facilities and amenities to rival or even exceed those in big cities. For some visitors the amenities themselves became as much of an attraction as the mountain environment. In Switzerland tourism would act as a generator of innovation and a motivator for the adaptation of technology to enable travel, hospitality and leisure to take place and then these developments would act as a multiplier to increase the numbers of visitors.

The main fields of technological advance affecting and affected by Swiss tourism were transport, building, agriculture and its associated food industries and healthcare. These are the same factors that influenced the industrial revolution in other states, illustrating that tourism development is an aspect of industrialisation even though it may appear to occupy a liminal space, both spatially and economically. It was this spatial liminality that was both an attraction to visitors and a stimulus for innovations in transport encouraged by changing tuberculosis therapies, which in turn led to developments in building and agriculture. These developments demanded capital investment in tourism infrastructure and moved tourism into a central economic position in Switzerland.

Through the rise in tourism came the dilemma between modernisation and the backwardness of the alpine natural environment and population based on urban criteria and judgements. It was the urban that defined the imagery of nature and the rural ideal. In the nineteenth century the optical medium of photography created pictures of an idyllic landscape in the minds of the urban population. Round panoramas with changing pictures of alpine scenes displayed in many European cities, created in the mind of the middle class an aesthetic view of the landscape, and these images led to a desire to see the original. The horrible mountains became sublime when seen through a telescope or when confronting the first Alpinists.[1] Modern tourism had led people to the borderline between nature and culture, where the former horrors of nature's wildness could be an aesthetic experience. In England where industrialisation was most advanced, the people, or rather an elite group of them, were the first to enjoy the Alps aesthetically. According to Stefan Bachmann, this developed from an individualistically regarded subjective perception and knowledge to a glorification of the Alps. This interaction between nature and culture, both urban and rural alpine, led to a transmission between science and enjoyment, between a scholarly and a touristic view.[2]

Initially, mountain villages were difficult to reach. The mountains were seen as a barrier to travellers, an obstacle to overcome on the journey between northern and southern Europe. It took a huge cultural shift for the Alps to become valued for themselves. This perceptive shift owed much to the philosophy of the Romantic movement. Before people could begin to find the Alps aesthetically pleasing, others had to take an interest in them. With the development of science the high mountains became an object of scholarly curiosity and thirst for knowledge. The simultaneous rise in interest in the mountain population changed the perception of the *Alpler* from the hitherto 'simple fool who was laughed at', to one of a fortunate free people whose prevailing poverty was glossed over as a sign of easily satisfied morality. In the later eighteenth century the mountain dweller was raised in status to a 'romantic motif' of the experience of nature among painters and poets.[3] The perception was that the mountain dweller remained in a virtuous state of nature. In the Alps 'there lives a simple people, doing good, brave, enemies of ostentation and display, friends of work, not seeking to enslave and not wanting masters,' wrote W. Coxe in one of his letters. Coxe developed this idea, claiming that the Swiss had all the qualities of innocence, above all the '*vertueux Valaisons*'.[4] Tourism itself created a mythical Switzerland modelled in the imagery of the romantic era, a stereotype of lofty mountains and wooden Swiss chalets.

After a hiatus of several years during the French Revolutionary and Napoleonic Wars, when pleasure travel from Britain to much of Europe which involved crossing France ceased, transport to Switzerland for an intrepid elite began on a regular basis. Carriers from London to Switzerland were Delavaud and Emery at Mr Recordon's, watchmaker of Charing Cross, and M. Dejean of Haymarket. These could take travellers to Geneva or Lausanne for twenty guineas in sixteen days (two of them spent in Paris). Distance travelled was about fifty miles a day starting out at 5 am. Six passengers and one hundred-weight of luggage could be carried. Food was provided and passengers travelled in an English carriage drawn by three horses.[5] Tolls and customs delayed cross-Swiss travel. The European communications network was joining up but ignored Switzerland. The confederation state created in the 1815 treaty could not take initiatives and private entrepreneurs did not have the necessary weight of investment.[6]

For travel within Switzerland, conveyances for invalids and timid persons who did not wish to ride a mule or donkey or to walk were *char-a-bancs*, a bench on each side of a cart, said to be like a caravan. A *petit char* was like a sofa on four wheels positioned longitudinally or there was a *Berner Wageli* which was lighter and more convenient but easily overturned, causing some serious accidents, not much used even by 1816. Females, timid persons and invalids could also use *chaises-a-porteurs*, chairs carried by men. Eight porters were needed to be hired to relieve each other. Passengers were advised to sit with their backs to the precipice to escape the horrors of the view while the cheerful songs of the porters would inspire confidence.[7] Grindelwald could be reached via boat on Lake Thun and Lake Brienz to Meiringen. From there it was a nine-and-a-half-hour walk crossing the Grosse Scheidegg.[8]

By 1850 Switzerland was the second most heavily industrialised country after Britain.[9] From 1852 Swiss railway development began, bringing British consultants and contractors to the country. Since 1848 the Swiss had developed a unified monetary system and the railways contributed to the growth of banking.[10] Switzerland also united in a single time zone which made timetabling easier. At this time Britain was undergoing a new phase of industrialisation. Finance capital was being used for railway investment, some of it in Switzerland. Companies were beginning to co-operate across national borders. Service industries were starting to develop and at the same time a second generation of middle class was ready and eager to spend their wealth, often acquired by their parents, on leisure and pleasure, although still needing the justification of health to do so. British tourists began to flock to the mountains in summer. This was possible due to the opening in the 1860s of new rail routes in the south of England. From Paris, connections were available to Switzerland where its own railway system was becoming integrated into a network.[11] The *Compagnie Suisse-Occidentale* connected Paris with Geneva and from there Lausanne and Neuchatel. Travellers from Germany were also provided with rail links to Switzerland from the north. Towns like Interlaken, Lucerne and Montreux became towns of passage, centres where tourists pass through.[12] From there they could connect with post vehicles, *diligences* or *voitures* to take them further into the mountains.

Compared to other European nations, Switzerland was quite backward when it came to the development of transport infrastructure. Three things held back the development of railway construction in Switzerland: the absence of a general political interest in transport of the level normally expected in a modern nation; insufficient financial resources coupled with the poor will-power of capitalists; and an extreme distrust by the public of railways that took longer to overcome than elsewhere.[13] A great number of peasants tried to oppose by force the proposals for the first railway lines over their villages' territory. The first track in Switzerland was laid in 1844 by *la Société des chemins de fer d'Alsace*, which lengthened its line from Strasbourg in France right across the frontier to Basle, 1,800 metres of which crossed Swiss territory. At this time Britain had 3,600 kilometres of track. By 1850 Switzerland had 25 kilometres of line while at the same time Britain had 10,500 kilometres, preunification Germany had 5,850 kilometres, France 3,000 kilometres Austria-Hungary 1,580 kilometres and ununified Italy had 620 kilometres.[14]

In 1851 in a triumph of liberalism, a law reserved the building of Swiss railways to the private sector. The quality of projects was the responsibility of the cantons. In 1856 a line opened between Berne and Geneva. Some lines used foreign capital, for example from the French bank *Crédit Mobilier*. Only the *Compagnie du Nord-Est,* managed by Escher, used Swiss capital. Escher's bank *Crédit Suisse* founded in 1855 was modelled on the *Crédit Mobilier*.[15] New routes in the 1860s connected England with the Continent. The London–Chatham–Dover Railway broke the monopoly of the South East Railway in 1861 and developed routes across the English Channel, such as London to Paris through Dover and Folkestone. Two years later, in 1863, the port of Harwich opened, linking the Great Eastern Railway to mainland Europe. Once they reached Paris connections were available to Switzerland. *La Compagnie Suisse–Occidentale* linked Paris with Geneva, Lausanne and Neuchatel. Through tickets could be bought in England, although *Cook's Circular Tickets* did not go as far as Grisons where Davos, Arosa and St Moritz were situated.[16] Grindelwald was therefore much more accessible from Britain than these other places in the earlier days of Swiss tourism before the last quarter of the nineteenth century.

By 1860 railways had reached Lucerne, Chur and Thun. From Chur travellers could go on by other means to Davos and St Moritz or even Arosa. From Thun a steamboat on the lake took passengers on to Interlaken from where they could reach Grindelwald. Aigle was linked by rail to Montreux and Lausanne giving potential access to Leysin.[17] A cog railway reached Leysin from Aigle in 1897.[18] After a slow start compared to other more industrialised countries, Switzerland had 1,263 kilometres of rail in 1865; 2,439 kilometres in 1880; and more than 3,091 kilometres in 1900. There were also many small local railways, for example in 1883 figures show there were 3,600 kilometres in the network augmented by 1,390 kilometres of local tracks.[19] This was an intrinsically irrational system and as early as 1865 fourteen out of the sixteen Swiss rail companies were losing money, leading to an inevitable rail crisis. In 1897, 95 per cent of shares in the *Gothard* company and 60 per cent of those in *Central Suisses* were in the hands of foreigners. The Swiss Confederation nationalised the railways between 1901 and 1909, except for some narrow gauge routes such as the *Rhaetischebahn* and the *Berner Oberland Bahn*, which remained in the hands of local companies. The nationalised federal railway began a programme of electrification in 1916 during the coal shortage caused by the First World War.

By the latter part of the nineteenth century Swiss railways were linked to the wider European network. Trains made Switzerland accessible in a day from Paris or two days from London.[20] By 1898 railway companies were advertising tickets for trains from Paris to Berne and Interlaken in fifteen hours. Passengers could also go via Calais to Basle and then onwards.[21] Advertisements for the *Hotel Engadiner-Kulm* told prospective travellers that St Moritz could be reached twice a week by 'special through train deluxe, the *Engadine Express*, from Calais to Thusis'.[22] When passengers could ride right into St Moritz the local newspaper advertised that the Albula line's trains were heated and, unlike on a sleigh-ride, there was no need to wear special clothes on the journey.[23] The increase in rail passengers travelling to the alpine centres led to an increase rather than a decline in the number of horses in use for local transport in the resorts. For example, in Arosa there were only three in use in 1886 whereas in 1896 there were thirty-seven and by 1906 there were eighty-two horses in use to draw vehicles to carry goods and supplies as well as take visitors to the station and to and around the village.[24] In St Moritz in 1920 there were two hundred horses at work in St Moritz, owned by thirty-seven different people.[25]

An idea first put into action in 1866 by the American Sylvester Marsh when he built the first cog railway to the summit of Mount Washington near Boston was soon transferred across the Atlantic for use in the Alps. This technology was adapted for the construction of mountain railways in Switzerland by engineers such as Nicolas Riggenbach, Romain Abt, Eduard Locher and later on, Emil Strub, who in a relatively short period of time had constructed many cog-railways around the country.[26]

The age of a transport infrastructure that could carry tourists right up into the mountains themselves, making the high Alps no longer the preserve of the mountaineer, began in 1871 with the opening of Riggenbach's *Zahnradbahn Vitznau-Rigi*. Its engineer, Friedrich Wrubel, described the new *Rigibahn* as an 'epoch making triumph of railway technology'. Wrubel was private secretary to the Zurich industrialist Adolf Guyer-Zeller and was involved in the building of the highest railway station in Europe, on the Jungfraujoch at the culmination of the *Jungfraubahn*, 3,500 metres above sea level. In 1898 the stretch of the *Jungfraubahn* to the Eigergletscher opened. In 1912 the entire line to the Jungfraujoch was completed. The *Jungfraubahn* was a continuation of the *Wengenalpbahn*. It opened to winter passengers for the first time in 1913, thus taking skiers, tobogganers and other sports men and women up to the Kleine Scheidegg from Lauterbrunnen and Wengen with ease. By 1910 there were more than forty mountain railways, with a capital investment of a hundred million francs, in operation. A return on capital dividend reaching 9 per cent between 1873 and 1913 stimulated a mountain-railway-building fever, with accompanying speculation and euphoria.[27] The *Rigibahn* and its successors were built with urban capital.

New forms of energy such as electricity also characterised these developments. Hydroelectricity supplied a non-polluting form of energy, not just to the railways themselves but to workshops and lodgings.[28] This capital transformed the Alps into a space of intervention by investors. A negative aspect of this, identified by Bachmann, was a profound cultural change. Formerly the mountain peaks had taught young people the art of climbing, an understanding of nature, a love of the country and a dream of higher accomplishment. They were places of education and simple solidarity. When the peaks could be reached without effort or will power they lost this educational aspect as they could be reached by anyone on a train and seen by all on picture post cards.[29] There were even hotels on some mountain peaks. The centres on which this study focuses were no exception to this development. The world's first cable car, the *Wetterhornaufzug*, opened in 1905 at Grindelwald. In 1907, around St Moritz, a drag lift up Muottas Moragl opened, followed in 1913 by a drag lift up to Chanatarella. Emil Thoma Badrutt launched a company to build a funicular railway from St Moritz Dorf to Chantarella plateau. It was to serve the planned *Kuranstalt* at Chantarella (later the *Hotel-Chantarella-House*). It was also intended to serve two further health establishments: the *Privatklinik* and *Kinderheim*. The track was 450 metres long with a maximum incline of 49 per cent. The concession began on 1 January 1912 and it took a half year to build. It eventually came into use on 2 January 1913.

The building of the *Chantarellabahn*, a small cable-drawn railway, opened up the Salastrains area for skiing. More and more ski instructors now gave lessons on this sun terrace above the village. Emil Thoma, a keen sportsman, had the foresight to realise that skiing had a big future. There were no prepared pistes and it was still troublesome to climb up to the areas preferred for skiing, even with 'seal skin' hide on the lower surface of the skis. Plans were put into action to continue the track higher up to Corviglia. With this purpose, the share company *Aktiengesellschaft Drahtseilbahn Chantarella-Corviglia* was formed in 1928. The new cable-drawn railway line was built over the summer, ready for opening on 19 December. Its success exceeded all expectations, and Corviglia became the ideal of the whole skiing-world.[30] In 1935 another, more simple type of drag lift was constructed up to the Silvretta area above St Moritz, making it the world's premier resort for skiing facilities.

St Moritz's rival for this claim, Davos, had its first mechanical lift from 1907, before the lift up Muottas Moragl was built; the *Schleppseilbahn* (tow-rope lift) on the area known as Bolgen was thought for a long time to be the first of its kind in the world. However, it turned out that one at Schollach in Hochschwarzwald that opened in 1906 and was patented in 1908 was the first. Where Davos did take the lead lift-wise was with the installation of the first hoop lift or *Bügel-Skilift* which opened in 1934. The lift ran continuously, travelling 270 metres and climbing 70 metres, powered by a 24-horse-power motor. It was used by the Davos Ski School free of charge. Guests at hotels associated with the ski school could use it for 50 rappen and all others were charged one franc for a half day. Skiers were happy not to have to struggle up the slope any more.[31]

There was no winter opening of the cog-railway line all the way up to Kleine Scheidegg, from Grindelwald until 1933 but a short stretch was in use up to the top of the bobsleigh run to carry riders and their machines to its start. The *Bobbahn* was constructed beginning beside a small station of the *Wengernalpbahn* at Brandegg. It was ready for use in 1913 but never got fully established because of the War a year later. It reopened in the season of 1921 to 1922 and ran three trains daily between Grund and the *Station Bobstart* at Brandegg. It was used mostly by English bobsleighers but later local residents got a taste for the sport. In 1931 the *Bob-Club Grindelwald* came into being, created by Swiss sportsmen.[32]

Later sports people could enjoy a ride up the slope on the other side of the valley using a *Schlittenseilbahn,* a giant sledge that could carry twenty to twenty-five people with skis, sledges and bobsleighs pulled up on rollers underneath by a tow-rope, before sliding down. Although it was first proposed in 1926, nothing came of the scheme for another ten years when such a lift up to the ski school at Bodmi was installed, the *Funi-Bodmi.*[33]

In St Moritz protests kept railway building from the side of the lake, 'thanks to engineer Dr von Schumacker and Prof Dr Gerlich who put the case for St Moritz to the *Bundesrat* which threw out the bill brought forward by the *Rhaetischebahn,* the Rhaetian Railway Company. If the railway was to go on to Maloja it would have to tunnel under St Moritz, which it never did. The station had to be near the Innfall bridge and new roads took travellers on to *Post Platz* and by lake to Bad. The tunnel into the village was 1,460 metres long and cost an estimated 1.087 million Swiss francs to build.'[34] In Davos, similar protests by existing sojourners were made with less success against the proposal to bring a railway into the village because of the perceived pollution and also the threat to the resort's exclusivity and prized pure atmosphere. In Davos the railway construction scheme itself was initiated by people with powerful interests in the resort, led by Jan Holsboer.

The railways not only brought more and more tourists into the Alps but also created new working-class communities of migrant workers to build them as well as skilled, unskilled and clerical workers to operate them. Huge numbers of construction workers came from Italy and railway workers migrated from elsewhere in Switzerland. Navvies and their families lived in small towns of tents. The village of Preda on the other side of the tunnel leading into St Moritz was formed by workers on the railway. This new working class brought with it class consciousness and protests against the dangerous and sometimes fatal conditions in which they worked. Newspaper reports aimed at an upper-class English-speaking readership did not usually discuss the hard lifestyles of the workers on whom their lives of luxury depended and showed little sympathy for the plight of these people. One reported that Sameden authorities soon smothered an attempted strike amongst the men employed in the Albula Tunnel a few days ago. Apparently two Swiss and an Italian came out on strike there and threatened all kinds of things against other workmen unless they joined them. Four hundred and fifty men threw down tools unless their terms were agreed to although the paper claimed that the greater number had probably no idea what they were really demanding. Three leaders had suggested blowing up the dynamite magazine, it reported. Police arrested the leaders. One of the strikers was banished for a year; the other two were imprisoned and fined. The rest resumed work as happily as before.[35] It is unlikely that just three men could frighten hundreds more into going on strike against their will and the statement that before the strike they were happy cannot be taken as evidence of contentment about their working conditions by the majority of workers.

As well as jobs on the railways there was a great demand for people to work in the service trade which led to seasonal immigration in those trades too. Formerly Swiss villagers had travelled away from home to find such work. Now they could remain at home and enjoy full employment in occupations serving the tourism industry. Tourism, though, is dependent on the economic conditions in other countries, which is particularly noticeable in crises in the countries from which visitors come.[36] For example, the number of visitors from America declined during its war with Spain at the end of the nineteenth century; the Boer War affected travellers from Britain.[37] The First World War prevented people from many countries reaching Switzerland. The depression of the 1930s was also severely detrimental to tourism.

Post stage coaches first began to venture across the Alps in about 1832. The roads were in a primitive state and the high passes, especially the Grimsel and the Gemmi, had reputations of being regular death traps. The postal service was organised for the transportation of letters and parcels, which was more profitable than carrying passengers.[38] As roads improved, the number of passengers and services increased. The bright yellow post-coach, or federal diligence as it was known, remained popular even after the railway penetrated many of the valleys it served. Leysin benefited from a postal coach from about 1880. When the *Grand Hotel* opened, the post was delivered directly to the occupants of the sanatorium.[39] From 1880 to 1884, the combined thirteen alpine lines of those days transported 698,937 passengers. Nine lines survived and kept running for more than twenty years after that and could still boast 847,238 passengers between the years 1905 and 1908.[40] The post-coach routes in the Grisons survived longest, until 1889, as there was no railway in the canton except for twelve miles of track leading to Chur, the regional capital. Chur was also the centre of the federal post coaches from where eighty to a hundred passengers would leave each morning for the Engadine and Italy.

Davos and St Moritz were important branch postal stations, points of arrival and departure for other routes over mountain passes.

> At dawn, everything is still deserted and silent in the streets of *Coire* (*Chur*). But at the post-office, 'what a contrast,' wrote a traveller in 1865: 'There is life, agitation and a general hustle and bustle; postilions in bluish-grey coats trimmed with red in their shiny water-proof hats, are busy polishing the reins getting their whips ready… Conductors, men of an Italian type, in their coquetish outfit are busy moving hither and thither, chattering like magpies and piling up letters, packages and bags in their boxes; others in wooden shoes put the last touches to the horses' trappings amid lively shouts of "Hue!"and "Dia" resounding loudly in the morning's silence. It is a scene of brisk animation around the four big coaches that are going to start in a moment either for the Splugen and for Tarasp, or else for Disentis and the Bernardino… The postilions, perched high on their lofty seats, the reins of their five horses tightly held together, are merely waiting for the signal to start: "*maitre de poste*", holding the list of travellers in his hands, with an air of importance, shouts passengers' names and points out their seats. Amid a tremendous din and commotion, the heavy vehicle rumbles through the streets of old *Coire* (Chur), followed by a concert of barking, howling dogs.'[41]

The first motor postal bus came in service on the line between Berne and Utzigen in 1906. Its maximum speed on the flat was twelve and a half miles an hour which dropped to only six miles an hour uphill. Smooth tyres made the ride so bumpy that baskets of eggs and other produce were damaged by the journey. The route was neither popular nor profitable and so it was a while before similar vehicles were introduced elsewhere. In 1909, one of the first rural routes was so unprofitable it had to be withdrawn and replaced by the old horse-drawn diligence it had replaced. The end of the First World War saw a number of motor lorries decommissioned which were adapted by the postal authority to serve as coaches. In 1919 the first motor route crossed the Simplon and from that time motor buses replaced the horse-drawn service throughout Switzerland, establishing a national network of motor coaches. In the winter of 1924 some buses replaced their wheeled chassis with caterpillar tracks to keep services running through the snow.[42] The postal motor coach was not simply a machine offering transportation faster than horses. It soon became an attraction in its own right. In 1931 of three hundred thousand passengers carried, three-quarters of them made circular trips back to their destination, riding solely for the pleasure of doing so.[43] The postal bus service was not a rival to the railways but actually extended its reach. Through tickets could be bought for trains connecting at stations with the easily distinguished yellow buses to take passengers further to areas where the railway did not reach and these continue to do so.

The first motor car appeared in Grindelwald in 1904, soon followed by the first road accident in 1905.[44] However, in Grisons where Davos, Arosa and St Moritz were situated, motor cars were banned from the roads by the cantonal government in 1900 and the ban wasn't lifted until 1925.[45] Campaigns for and against automobiles were active in the canton throughout that time and a referendum finally agreed to allow motor cars into the region. While the ban was in force, drivers had to leave their motors at the Grisons border or else hitch horses to the vehicle to draw it to their destination. Arosa did not allow full access to motor traffic on the village's main street until 1927.[46]

Transport technology, in the form of road and then railway and tram building in the latter part of the nineteenth century, followed later by motor vehicles, led to the integration of the formerly remote alpine regions and industrial civilisation. There were electric trams from St Moritz Dorf to Bad, and also to Pontresina, Morteratsch, Sils, Maloja and Samaden.[47] Trams also traversed between Davos Platz and Davos Dorf.

Bachmann refers to the aesthetic depreciation of the landscape caused by railway building but by the late twentieth century, tourists were seeing the railways as an enhancement of their mountain experience that promoted nostalgia among populations that had grown up with the motor car.[48] Around every curve on the alpine lines and by spectacular viaducts groups of people (usually men) gather with cameras and video equipment to take pictures of the trains. The railway is at the centre of an integrated system of transport linking the tourist to resorts and attractions. It is Switzerland's key component of an infrastructural network that includes buses, narrow gauge and mountain cog and cable railways and cable cars, gondolas, chair and drag lifts that penetrate deep into the remotest parts of the mountains.

Changes in the structure of employment brought changes in agriculture, especially the transition from grazing and cattle rearing as exclusive occupations to the tendency to regard agriculture as a supplementary source of income. Since the late 1960s there has been a reversal of this trend and large agricultural enterprises have emerged and small non-viable farms abandoned. In Grindelwald, due to the *Alprecht* (mountain laws), which passed rights from generation to generation all alpine pastures are still the property of local farmers. The Alps are co-operative property; sale to non-residents of the community is prohibited.[49] This helps protect the land surrounding Grindelwald from other commercial development and preserves the pastures as open spaces which can be used by skiers in winter.

From ancient times, Swiss shepherds and herdsmen have moved up to the lush alpine pastures with their herds every summer. For about three months cows, oxen, sheep and goats graze and wander on the Alps, that is, the high mountain grass lands, while below in the valleys farmers harvest the hay for winter feed. Cows are milked morning and evening and the herdsmen traditionally prepared cheese and butter. Compared with this life of freedom for the animals, in the winter they are confined indoors in cowsheds for about sixteen weeks. In modern times this has become inextricably linked with Swiss tourism. Tourists and hikers love the beautiful green, lush Alps (the grassland below the rocky peaks but high above the valleys). The sensory delights of visual of the landscape and auditory pleasures, such as the warm, cheerful clanging of cow bells, possibly enhanced and increased due to the effects on the brain of changes in the composition of the clean, fresh air coupled with increased bodily activity contribute to the physical and psychological experience by visitors of the alpine pastures. Dairy farming, its products and imagery are indeed essential to any holiday in Switzerland. Post cards depict alpine chalets (the summer homes of herdsmen), cows wearing bells, alphorns, grassy alpine scenery, or in winter those same pastures transformed into winter-snow-covered slopes, pistes for skiing, traversed by mechanical lifts, operated by many of the same farmers and herdsmen during the quieter winter months in agriculture. Typical souvenirs are model cowbells, wooden cows, goats and chalets or items containing two-dimensional images of these things. Food served in restaurants usually contains cheese or is garnished with it – no holiday is complete without a fondue or raclette evening. Creamy milk chocolate is also eaten while out and about or taken home as a gift.

Therapies recommended by physicians to lowland patients they sent to the Alps had long incorporated milk as integral to treatment or a primary aspect as in the milk cure. This use of milk brought technological advances as well as changes in the way cattle were bred and managed. From the early twentieth century, *Kur-Milch* was advertised in the Davos tourist press as being prepared using the scientific principles developed by Dr N. Gerber of Zurich. Milk came from cows that were kept under vetinary supervision, with high standards of hygiene in the cowsheds and milking stalls. Laboratory control in its preparation guaranteed the milk's freedom from tuberculosis, diphtheria, scarlet fever and typhus. This was a response to the discovery in the 1880s that tuberculosis was caused by bacillus infection and that its microbes could be present in milk. Also, in cities, milk was a far from healthy product often adulterated and contaminated. Water added to thin it down also introduced bacteria and therefore potential disease. Advertisements appeared in the tourist press for 'Milk for the cure – free of all germs'.[50]

A way of making alpine milk safely available anywhere all year round was developed in 1866 by two American brothers who established the *Anglo-Swiss Company,* Europe's first condensed milk factory at Cham. A year later in 1867 a chemist from Frankfurt called Heinrich Nestlé began baby food production in Vevey. He developed a powder from milk and rusk as a substitute for breast milk, which is credited with contributing to the lowering of infant mortality amongst unweaned and small children. In 1905 *Nestlé* joined with the *Anglo-Swiss Company* and became the brand leader in condensed milk.

Milk chocolate was invented by Daniel Peter. He discovered a way of mixing milk, sugar and cocoa using methods similar to those used to make condensed milk. He produced a bar of chocolate called *Gala Peter* in Vevey from 1875. The marketing of chocolate benefited from the legendary health properties of alpine milk. Milk chocolate was used for nourishment by mountain travellers. As it was made of cocoa, sugar and clean uncontaminated milk from the best Swiss pastures, it was seen as a way of getting safe milk to everyone wherever they were in the country. Chocolate was recommended as a healthy and nourishing food for mountain sportsmen and travellers;, being in a bar, it was easily carried. Importantly, too, it did not cause thirst. It soon became a favourite with children; anyone who had a few rappen (centimes) could give it to their children. As a health food it was claimed that it could be used to stop diahorrea or relieve constipation. In 1929 Peter's firm was taken over by *Nestlé* together with the firms of *Cailler* and *Kohler*. Another more recent Swiss-milk-based product is the soft drink *Rivella*, which was made from 1952 onwards.[51]

The growth of alpine resorts and health centres led to changes in agricultural practice. As demand for milk increased, the time of year for calving was brought forward to give a longer period when cows were producing milk. There was a transition to primacy of grazing and cattle rearing exclusively and a tendency to regard farming as a supplementary form of income. The yield of milk per cow increased so although the output of milk went up, the number of cattle didn't rise over the last half of the twentieth century. Cows' milk is now almost universally used and there remain comparatively few goats and sheep on the Alps. Luckily for the tourism industry and mountain lovers, the importance of pastures preserves the alpine landscape.

As the number of residents rose so did the demand for milk and with that the price also rose, and production became intensive. Milk prices in Arosa rose from 9.4 rappen in 1838, to 11.5 rappen in 1858 and 20 rappen by the 1880s.[52]

In the last decade of the nineteenth century the amount of small livestock, sheep and goats, remained constant. For locals, too, the use of goats' milk declined and cows' milk became usual.[53] In Arosa in 1866 there were seventy-seven sheep, sixty-eight goats and fifty-one cows. In 1896 there were forty-five sheep, seventy goats and seventy-one cows. Rapid developments around the turn of the century meant that in 1906 there were sixty-six sheep, fifty goats but one hundred and ten cows. The same phenomenon was evident elsewhere in the tourist regions of Switzerland. During the third quarter of the nineteenth century, cheese and butter as well as milk became more expensive. All milk that was produced was consumed.

To allow enough milk to be available for the tourists and patients, cows had to be put to the bull earlier in the year. Cows had usually given birth to their calves in December but the winter season began in November when there was already a high demand for milk which lasted through to April. Calves needed to be born during the dead season in September and October so that milk could be available by November. Intensive dairy production lasted through the winter. Cattle were fed on high-energy foods to increase the milk yield. By spring there was a small surplus of milk. Calves were fattened during the summer and then sent to the butcher to provide meat for the winter season. This resulted in the intensive use of meadowlands; the whole farming community worked hard at hay making. More cattle meant more manure which added to the fertility of the land. The use of manure had been unknown before and better food for the cattle was the result and hay became available for winter fodder. The price of milk rose fourfold. This intensification of dairy farming as well as the expansion of hotel, commercial and house building created a competing demand for land for agrarian production or building plots and as a consequence land values shot up.[54]

Tourism also affected pig raising; hotel waste food could be fed to pigs so there became more of them. In 1886 there were only thirteen pigs in Arosa, the number remaining constant for the next decade, but in 1906 there were forty-six. All these extra animals supplied food to the hotels. Sausage machines became popular together with new cuts of meat transforming the way people ate. Trout became a popular dish which had previously only been eaten by people in towns. Bread baking too had to be done daily in industrial proportions when in the past stale bread baked only once a year and stored was eaten.

These changes in food affected the dietary tastes of local populations as well as tourists. In the sanatoria seven meals a day were eaten between six in the morning and nine at night: this represented luxurious feasts compared with the earlier main meals of alpine communities. Other changes were that young Swiss people drank less milk and water and more wine. They also bought clothes and stockings instead of spinning, weaving and making things at home. A guide-book of the early nineteenth century had informed its readers that 'Men in Grindelwald were tall, robust and well made. They live chiefly on a milk diet and work their own wool for clothing, and export cheese and cattle.' In Arosa it was warned that: 'Travellers needed to take their own bread', probably because of the above-mentioned tradition of annual baking.[55] By the end of the nineteenth century neither of these statements was wholly true. Houses had always been made of wood, except in St Moritz and the rest of the Engadine, but prosperity for some meant houses began to be made of stone.

Other social changes were that young alpine people were out of the home more, either at school, working in tourist-related industries or joining in the new sporting activities. Christian Branger advertised his restaurant *Bergadler* in Davos, telling English visitors that it was selling *Löwen* beer from Munich and that pigs' trotters were served on Sundays. In the same paper his brother J. Branger advertised mats, carpets and wallpapers for sale in his shop. Toboggans, skates, ice spikes and shovels, modern heating stoves were available at the store of Schneller und Hemmi in Davos Platz.[56] These were not items of consumption normally bought by alpine people, at least not before the tourists arrived.

Under the influence of the manufactured attire of urban Europe, not just the style of dress of native Swiss was affected by contact with the wider industrialised world; experience of the mountains created new fashions and innovations in functional fabrics and outdoor clothing for visitors. Cecilia Fox, granddaughter of Joseph Fox, went to Grindelwald for the first time in 1910 when she was fourteen. At the age of eighty, she recalled of that visit 'we had long skirts, with buttons down the front and tapes with holes so that we could hitch them up'. Hitching up skirts was imperative for young women wanting to fully enjoy the sports on the slopes, either climbing up or sliding down them. Cecilia Fox had also worn nailed boots and carried an alpenstock. She remembered 'large hats with veils attached for when one got near ice or snow were worn as were *viyella* blouses (you must not wear wool when you are going to sweat) and gloves so that your hands don't get sunburnt'.[57]

Living in places covered in snow for much of the time or where it was sometimes very wet with rain in summer meant that keeping the feet dry was a preoccupation for men and women. This was a difficult task for members of a social elite for whom, at home, appearances were of paramount importance. The local English-language papers in Davos and St Moritz frequently carried articles about the importance of wearing the correct footwear, as did guide-books.

The snow boot is certainly open to criticism in respect to such elegance as depends on moderation in dimensions! The by-name of *gouties*, which was bestowed on these encasements in the early days of our English colony at Davos suggests as much art criticism in one word as might otherwise be conveyed in a hundred. Snow boots were not however the original winter footwear of Davos visitors. When people first came here for the winter season forty or fifty years ago, the great Rubber Age had not set in. Leather still reigned supreme on our snows.[58]

The age of rubber referred to was also a colonialist reference; rubber became available for use in mass production because of the imperialist occupation of countries like Malaya where the trees supplying the raw material grew. It is interesting to read what was written on the subject back in 1878 in the book about Davos by Mrs MacMorland, which appeared in that year bearing the title *Davos-Platz; a New Alpine Resort for Sick and Sound in Summer and Winter by One Who Knows it Well*. She wrote:

> Vanity as regards foot and headgear must be laid aside. The extremities should represent antipodes. Strong nailed boots and thick gaiters, suitable for Siberia ought to be associated with a broad-brimmed straw-hat like that of a West Indian planter. The propriety of keeping the feet warm and dry cannot be too much dwelt upon, as neglect in this respect is speedily visited by punishment in the form of colds and catarrhs that may seriously imperil the good effects of Davos air.

A misplaced regard for fashion could be displayed by many people, especially ladies, who tried to convince themselves and their more sensible friends that it was 'impossible for them to bear the weight of heavy shoes and gaiters'. Women who were really anxious to regain their health had to 'conquer this feminine weakness, and insert their feet into a pair of hobnailed boots, with plenty of room to spare for a double layer of felt soles. If they preferred it, they could conceal their flannel-lined Wellingtons under their skirts.'[59] The newspaper in 1915 admonished:

> The Davos lady of today who trips along the snowy Promenade in the daintiest of boots or shoes, to say nothing of semi-transparent stockings, is either living proof that these early ideas were mistaken or she is a very foolish person, far be it for us to decide which. That she has really no insuperable dread of looking clumsy about the feet is evident when she goes out skiing in thick worsted socks and boots like tubs. There can be no doubt that the snow boot was really an improve-ment in several respects upon hob-nailed boots or even Wellingtons. Rubber makes a decidedly good non-slip sole for walking on snow, and a well-lined snow

Maria Lichtenhahn Jost, skiing near Schatzalp,
Davos Platz, about 1910

boot is certainly about the warmest wear to be had. Still, the inherent slipperiness of the ordinary boot or shoe can be overcome, and one certainly does notice from winter to winter a growing tendency to cast off the bulky snow boot in favour of the more elegant article. Whether this is a sign of wisdom or weakness, we will not take it upon us to say.[60]

For men, too, boots were important, two pairs could be brought from home and hobnails could be hammered in by cobblers in Switzerland. Recommended clothes for men were a tweed suit, knickerbockers and a morning coat and dark trousers to wear in the evening in hotels. It was not essential to wear evening dress. Ladies also needed a strong tweed skirt that could be shortened for long walks and blouses as well as boots for walking. They also required a smarter dress for evening wear but were warned that low dresses were not worn in hotels. A second walking dress was necessary in case of accidents.[61] Sunhats could be bought in the resorts themselves and did not have to be carried in the luggage. These would have veils attached to protect the wearer's face from the sun as no sun protection creams or lotions were then available. It was unnecessary to bring all the clothing needed out in one's luggage as it could be purchased in the resorts themselves.

The tourist press in the resorts carried advertisements for the kind of clothing tourists would need to wear for the various activities during their stay. For example, the *Grindelwald Echo* advertised *Billige Sportschuhe* (cheap sports shoes) for sale. Gentlemen's sports shoes were made of *Chromleder* with strong double soles, and were waterproof. Ladies' sports shoes were made of the same leather in a choice of brown or black. Boys' and girls' shoes were also for sale. Only men's shoes were advertised as strong and waterproof.[62] A method of preserving the natural characteristics of leather whilst making it waterproof was to use chrome salts in the tanning process which produced 'chrome-leather'. This process was discovered around the turn of the century twentieth century, another example of the application of technology to the alpine lifestyle.

For women, movement was restricted by the convention of wearing corsets; if they were removed for sledging and skiing in the day, stays were still practically compulsory under garments at all other times, especially for evening wear. In the Edwardian period the corset reached its most extreme form but at the same time, especially among women involved in sports, the convention was beginning to be challenged. Corsets were manufactured in a range of styles for different activities. A special ski corset appeared in 1911 but some progressive young women were replacing the corset with girdle and brassiere.[63] For skiers wearing long dresses, underwear was of course of primary importance. Not only was warmth required of the garments but in the case of a fall, petticoats and even knickers might be on display. Dark colours were advised as brightly coloured underwear could be quite spectacular when the wearer was rolling about on the floor. Special ski outfits for women came on the market in the years before 1914 that could be purchased in London. Harrods was one supplier of such costumes. Women soon began to dispense not only with corsets but with long dresses as well. Photographs from around 1920 show young women dressed in short knee-length dresses with thick stockings on skis. Some of them even began to wear trousers. Discussions as to the morality of this mode of dress concluded that women in trousers lacked the grace and beauty of one in a flowing dress swirling down a meadow. Not just propriety but even moral codes were breached and trousers were banned in some resorts in Bavaria. Not only were trousers ungraceful, there was also no flow to a lady's skiing. There was also a fear that trousers would de-sex women, wearing them could indicate lesbian liaisons or bisexual affinities.[64] Some women wore trousers but carried a skirt to put on over the top when back in the resort or in a restaurant or perhaps for photographs. Not everyone agreed with this verdict; English women ski racers of the 1920s were described in a letter to Arnold Lunn, as being the first girl skiers in the world to be well dressed. Their long straight legs encased in even longer beautifully tailored flopping dark blue trousers, caused the most open-mouthed wonder and astonishment in *Mittel-Europa*. And when these slim creatures could also ski it was really too much! Up until then, women skiers had been baggily clad, khaki figures with cold cream streaked across their sun-burned noses, and rucksacks on their strong backs. Ski clothes with any chic or style for women were completely unknown.[65]

The technologies used in construction were also transferred to the growing alpine resorts. In 1816 there were three hundred houses made of wood in Grindelwald.[66] The conception, financing and production of the great structures like that of the railway network created at the same time the conditions for the development of a new type of edifice in the resorts, the hotel. This was the result of new types of construction techniques, using new materials like steel. Hotels represented modern palaces and '*chateaux de la haute bourgeoisie*' or just social climbing by middle-class guests who were buying into this lifestyle temporarily.[67] Architectural developments carried the message of tourism into the rural zones and the Alps. The implicit message of hotels was that not only people could be mobile but also furniture and urban architecture could be transferred. The style of decoration, usually *art nouveau* or *Jugenstil* in the case of the grand hotels, showed a style of life which was luxurious, even aristocratic or monarchic.[68] However, simple lodgings, in the ubiquitous chalets or modern buildings, stood beside luxury palaces. In Davos and St Moritz modern buildings outnumbered the traditionally styled ones, giving the resorts an urban feeling. The bronze pillars in the vestibule of St Moritz's *Hotel Engadiner-Kulm* were unique in Switzerland at the time they were erected.[69] In Leysin massive sanatoria in *moderne* or *art nouveau* styles dominated the area overlooking the village. In Arosa, and especially in Grindelwald more of a mixture of building styles, modern and traditional, prevailed.

Other building projects were the laying of promenades and pavements, in Arosa a promenade was constructed in 1906. An advertisement for just one small hotel in Davos, the *Pension Villa Freitag*, illustrates this building boom clearly by listing some of the amenities it had access to. It was a 'small modern pension, well situated in the centre of the English Quarter, near the skating rink, ice-run, English church, English library and British Consul. It had comfortable, well-ventilated rooms with balconies, central heating, bathrooms, modern sanitation and electric lighting throughout. It also had a telephone, served excellent cuisine and had a dark room demonstrating the rise in popularity of photography among the middle class.'[70] Another hotel with its own dark room was the *Hotel Victoria* in Davos Dorf. It also had an English-style open fireplace.[71]

On a grander scale, the *Hotel Engadiner Kulm* in St Moritz advertised that it possessed 'every modern comfort, heated throughout; all the rooms, public and private were lit by electricity, covered terrace, baths in the house. Two full-sized lawn tennis courts, golf links, two hydraulic lifts, English physician in the hotel; omnibus to the mineral baths'. In line with British tastes, all sanitary arrangements were by Lowe and Sons of London.[72] The innovative Badrutt had installed the first new-style water closet and water pipes in Switzerland throughout his hotel.[73] Davos Platz had a supply of clean drinking water from 1873, thanks to the initiative and investment of a consortium led by Dr Wilhelm Beeli. The water system was extended and improved in 1883 and in 1884, to serve the growing town, five-kilometre-long water pipes carried more water from the Fluela Valley. Sanitary improvements to carry away sewerage were also carried out to prevent the spread of disease.[74] The four hundred villagers of Leysin had been provided with drinking water by five local springs. In 1891, the *Société Climatérique de Leysin* incorporated a reservoir fed by a spring in its plans for the *Grand Hotel* and this was extended by a pipe to the *Mont Blanc* when it opened and eventually piped water flowed to the whole village.[75] Arosa had been supplied from a number of private and communal springs but in 1900 an improved supply of piped water became a centralised responsibility of the community.[76] Since the 1860s and 1870s, a report of 1909 claimed, the 'rural toilet' had disappeared in private lodgings.[77]

By the turn of the century, in place of symmetrical barracks with small, defectively furnished rooms, thin plank walls, difficult to close windows and everything of a primitive standard, hotels appeared in St Moritz, in the style of an English club or the castle-like *Palacehotel* or American style hotels combined with the new Berlin style of ostentation and refined use of space and technical achievement.[78] All these modern installations attracted more and more visitors. There were five main types of Swiss hotel: *Passanten-hotels*; *Luftkurhotels* for summer occupation only; *Luftkur und Bade Hotels* for summer use; *Luftkurhotels* with central heating and winter sports facilities for year round occupation; sanatoria with corridors and *Liegehallen*.[79] Sanatoria buildings and many hotels were constructed with balconies on the south side to get maximum sunshine. 'The open air galleries are constructed upon the corbel system so as to avoid the columns and supports which in projecting galleries intercept the solar rays. The sunlight will thus be able to penetrate well into the rooms. To conduce to this end, the bay of each room occupies all the space available for the purpose'.[80] The north-facing sides of the buildings was occupied by hotel services or accommodated servants and hotel or sanatoria staff. Hotels and sanatoria in Davos and in Leysin, mainly had flat roofs, to prevent snow sliding off down the slopes of the traditional pent ones, that could injure people passing by outside.

By 1912 there were twelve thousand hotels with 385,000 beds across Switzerland, most with modern sanitation, central heating and electric lighting. Investment in hotels at that time totalled 1.3 million Swiss francs, representing a thirtieth of all national investments. The massive investment level of 1912 was not reached again until 1960.[81]

Lighting was initially provided by candles or more luxuriously, oil lamps, but soon gas lights supplied from small, local gasworks provided the fuel. The Davos *Kurhaus* and the street in front of it were lit by gas from 1874, thanks to a small gas works initiated and financed by Jan Holsboer. Soon gas lights were illuminating the main streets of Davos from about 1881.[82] This illumination was a cause for consternation to John Addington Symonds who the following year inveigled that Davos was descending into 'an ill-drained, overcrowded, gaslighted centre of cosmopolitanism, disease and second rate gaiety'.[83] St Moritz too had its first gas works in 1874 which supplied gas for lighting to the grand hotels in St Moritz Bad.[84]

Another investment related to energy and infrastructural development was electricity. This technology was pioneered in Switzerland by Johannes Badrutt in his *Hotel Engadiner-Kulm* in St Moritz from 1878. After a visit to the World Exhibition in Paris, Johannes Badrutt saw electric lighting for the first time. He didn't rest until he had his own small power station. Apparently, people came from near and far to see this wonder, light that burnt without being set fire to and without a flame.[85] The other resorts in this study soon followed St Moritz by installing electricity: Leysin installed electric lighting in 1896;[86] Arosa in 1897. Although these modern innovations were an attraction for guests and other visitors, to the conservative part of the population everything new was an abomination and Johannes Badrutt had to struggle against much initial hostility.[87]

The telegraph had put Grindelwald in communication with the outside world in 1866. It was first connected to the telephone network in 1892, when there were only four subscribers, the hotels *Eiger, Glacier, Beausite* and *Adler*. By the turn of the century in 1900 there were still only nineteen users. Arosa got its first telephone in 1896. The *Grand Hotel* in Leysin had advertised a telephone from about 1893. Those without telephones were reliant on the telegraph to receive important news by telegram. All these adaptations of technologies developed in other more industrialised countries affected the local resident communities as well as the tourists. Craftsmen profited from the construction of cable cars, ski lifts and holiday chalets.

The same Paris Exhibition that had so enthused Johannes Badrutt with its display of electric lighting also featured the Norwegian skis that inspired the Branger brothers of Davos to obtain their own. They were among the first Swiss to experiment with them and then to copy and to sell skis to others.[88] Other craftsmen had manufactured sledges, bobsleighs, skates and other sports equipment, importing the materials from which to make them, such as steel.

Sanatoria made use of the natural healing properties of the alpine environment and patients had to follow a strict regime of rest, exercise and nutrition. For the resorts to develop by attracting guests who were in good health they had to overcome the stigma attached to illness and fears of contagion by the infectious disease of tuberculosis. Davos hotels used a steam laundry to ensure the thorough cleaning of linen. The laundry had a separate disinfecting department and most hotel rooms and corridors had linoleum floor covering, which could be disinfected to kill microbes.[89] Outside of their hotels or sanatoria, sufferers from tuberculosis were required to carry a flask, a *Spucknapf* or *Blaue Heinrich*, to cough and spit into to prevent infected sputum landing on the ground or bacilli being carried in the air. Publicity for the resorts emphasised that far from being at risk of infection from tuberculosis, visitors were likely to be safer than in other places where it was not known who or how many people carried the disease or where they were.

In the field of medicine, the clinics and sanatoria in Davos, Arosa and Leysin were leaders in tuberculosis care. Heliotherapy as well as open-air altitude cure treatments were carefully researched in all five of the resorts studied although never implemented on a commercial scale in Grindelwald and were discouraged in St Moritz. In Davos and particularly Leysin these treatments were practised on an industrial scale. Another aspect of health care pioneered in the Alps was the nurturing of the psycho-physiological connection between mind and body as illustrated in the hour a day of respiratory gymnastics performed in some of the clinics of Leysin. This was linked to the daily exercise regime practised in the sanatoria throughout the centres in this study.

Sanatoria had the latest radiography and surgical facilities and offered the most effective treatments then available. Later on, this concentration of medical expertise meant that Swiss resorts could offer excellent casualty treatment for victims of winter sports accidents.

All these adaptations of technological developments in the five resorts studied demonstrate how any initial attraction of a life of simplicity in the mountains was soon subsumed by the desire to live with all the comforts modernity could offer to the wealthy.

> I remember the warnings and admonitions which certain anxious spirits address from time to time to town dwellers, who, they say, take with them all the burden of the town's social demands- obligations in matters of dress, dinners, concerts etc to their health resorts, whither they pretend to go to find relief for over-strung nerves. Utterly unfounded and proceeding from inadequate knowledge of life as it really is. The back to nature doctrine of Rousseau is erroneous, nature is not synonymous with lack of culture. This doctrine ought not to be preached to us during the four or six weeks of our summer vacation when we benefit by a change of environment and the absence of professional and other worries.[90]

Nature and purity of atmosphere were no longer enough to attract visitors to the mountains of Switzerland. Guests became unwilling to sacrifice their luxurious lifestyles for the sake of a Rousseauian ideal of simplicity and demanded the latest in technology so they could live in the comfort to which they had become accustomed, even in the remotest alpine valley.

Notes

1 Boyer, M., 'Les Alpes et le tourisme', *Tourisme et Changements Culturels/Toursimus und Kultureller Wandel; Historie de Alpes/Geschichte der Alpen*, ed. Thomas Busset, Luigi Lorenzetti, Jon Mathieu, Zurich, 2004, pp. 118–130, especially p. 122.

2 Bachmann, Stefan, *Zwischen Patriotismus und Wissenschaft – die Schweitzerischen Naturschutzpioniere*, Zurich, 1999, pp. 94–96.

3 Bachmann, p. 94.

4 Boyer, p. 24.

5 Coxe, Henry, *The Traveller's Guide in Switzerland: Being a Complete Picture of that Interesting Country*, London, 1816, p. xxxi.

6 Berger, Anton, *Histoire Economique de la Suisse*, Lausanne, 1983, p. 287.

7 Coxe, p. 2.

8 Coxe, p. 163.

9 Wraight, John, *The Swiss and the British*, Salisbury, 1987, p. 239.

10 Wraight, pp. 242–244.

11 Tissot, Laurent, *Naissance d'une industrie touristique – les Anglais et la Suisse au XIXe siecle*, Lausanne, 2000, p. 164.

12 Desponds, p. 49.

13 Berger, p. 287.

14 Berger, p. 287.

15 Berger, pp. 284–285.

16 Tissot, p. 164.

17 Berger, p. 286.

18 André, Maurice, *Leysin, station médicale*, Pully, 1993, p. 22.

19 Berger, p. 285.

20 Berger, p. 296.

21 Lunn and Lunn, p. 324.

22 *The Alpine Post and Engadine Express*, 1 June 1900.

23 *The Alpine Post and Engadine Express*, 7 November 1903.

24 Just, p. 40.

25 Margadant, Silvio and Maier, Marcella, *St Moritz – Streiflicher auf eine aussergewöhnliche Entwicklung*, St Moritz, 1993, p. 189.

26 *Jungfrau Railway, Bernese Oberland, Swittzerland*, third edition, Zurich, oJ, c. 1907, p. 4.

27 Bachmann, p. 99.

28 Heiss, Hans, *Les grandes étapes de l'histoire du tourisme, 1830–2002, Tourisme et Changements Culturels*, pp. 45–59, especially p. 51.

29 Bachmann, p. 100.

30 Margadant and Maier, p. 135.

31 Morgenegg, Hans, *Der Skilift auf Bolgen, Davoser Revue*, 78 Jahrgang, No. 1, March 2003, pp. 40–43.

32 Rubi, *Band III*, pp. 112–113.

33 Rubi, *Band II*, pp. 232–233.

34 *Engadine Express and Alpine Post*, 23 November 1901.

35 *Engadine Express and Alpine Post,* 9 November 1901.

36 Kröner, Arlinde, 'Die Entwicklung eines Bergbauerndorfes zu einem internationalen Tourisenzentrum. Ein Beitrag zum Problem des Kulturgeographischen Wandelsalpinen Siedlungen', *Stuttgarter Geographische Studien,* Herausgegeben, von Wolfgang Meckelein und Christoph Borcherdt. Schrifterleitung: Hagel, Jürgen, *Band 74,* p. 115.

37 Robertson, Hans, *St Moritz – seine Fremdenindustrie und sein Gemeinwesen, eine Kulturhistorische und Volkswirtschaftliche Studie,* Samaden, 1909, p. 65.

38 *A century of Swiss alpine postal coaches,* Geneva, 1932, p. 17.

39 André, p. 199.

40 *A century of Swiss alpine postal coaches,* p. 44.

41 Muller, A., 'Suisse et Lombardie', 1865, quoted in *A century of Swiss alpine postal coaches,* pp. 43–44.

42 *A century of Swiss alpine postal coaches,* p. 45.

43 *A century of Swiss alpine postal coaches,* p. 47.

44 Rubi, *Band II,* p. 75.

45 Margadant and Maier, p. 191.

46 Danuser, *Band 2,* p. 185.

47 Lunn and Lunn, p. 324.

48 Bachmann, p. 100.

49 Kröner, p. 116.

50 *The Davos Courier,* 12 December 1903.

51 Wyder, p. 94.

52 Just, p. 40.

53 Just, p. 40.

54 Just, pp. 44–45.

55 Coxe, p. 163.

56 *The Davos Courier,* 12 October 1889.

57 Fox, Hubert, *An English family and the mountains of Grindelwald and how in 1891 the first ski came to Grindelwald,* Grindelwald, 1991, second edition, 2001, p. 10.

58 *The Davos Courier,* 13 November 1915.

59 MacMorland, p. 39.

60 *The Davos Courier,* 13 November 1915.

61 Lunn and Lunn, p. 75.

62 *Echo von Grindelwald,* 7 January 1928.

63 Allen, E. John B., 'With a minimum of fatigue': women's skiing before World War 1', in Ulla Palmgren (ed.) *The 2nd FIS Ski historical conference,* Lahti, 2001, pp. 117–133, especially p. 120.

64 Allen, 'With a minimum of fatigue', p. 121.

65 Mrs Kiare quoted by Arnold Lunn, *The story of ski-ing,* London, 1952, p. 96.

66 Coxe, p. 163.

67 Heiss, p. 49.

68 Ibid.

69 Badrutt, Anton R., *Mein Wegweiser – Erinnerungen eines St Moritzer Hoteliers,*

Samaden, c. 1965, p. 18.

70 *The Davos Courier*, 13 January 1898.

71 *The Davos Courier*, 2 January 1903.

72 *The Alpine Post and Engadine Express*, 1 June 1901.

73 Badrutt, p. 16.

74 Ferdmann, Jules, *Der Aufstieg von Davos*, second edition, 1990, pp. 206–207.

75 André, p. 189.

76 Danuser, *Band 1,* p. 137.

77 Robertson, p. 47.

78 Robertson, p. 47.

79 *Festschrift zur 40 Generalversammlung des Schweizischen Ingenieur und Architekten-vereins*, Chur, 1903.

80 *Le Sanatorium Universitaire International*, Leysin, Switzerland, c. 1930.

81 Berger, p. 298.

82 Ferdmann, p. 190.

83 Pimlott, J.A.R., *The Englishman's holiday: a social history*, Hassocks, Sussex, 1945, p. 209.

84 Margadant und Maier, p. 95.

85 Badrutt, p. 16.

86 André, p. 198.

87 Badrutt, p. 20.

88 Kittle, Fredereick C., 'Down the slopes with Conan Doyle at Davos', *Journal of the Arthur Conan Doyle Society*, Vol. 4, Chester, 1993, pp. 88–103.

89 *The Davos Courier*, 2 November 1900.

90 Behrmann, H., translated by Cayley Mann, J., *Summer Days in St Moritz – letters from the pearl of the Engadine with a short guide, published by the Kurverein*, St Moritz, 1911, p. 21.

8

Who were the first winter sportsmen and women?

To understand the beginnings of winter sports in Switzerland and the special role played by the British in the development of these pastimes into organised competitive activities, an understanding is needed of who the people were that decided to leave their homes and spend up to six months at a time in the winter Alps. These people were able to maintain themselves and sometimes their families without having to be engaged in paid employment during the time they were away. They were evidently of independent means or else their relatives at home were willing to finance them. The family income therefore was high enough to support an adult member who contributed nothing for at least part of the time and who was valued highly enough to make their health or happiness worth the expense and in some cases, perhaps, sacrifice.

Many went to the Alps on medical recommendation, either alone or with relatives and friends as companions. They took lodgings near to each other and formed small communities where they tried to live as if they were in England or, more accurately, in a British colony in the decades of Britain's imperial zenith before the Boer War. The communities actually labelled themselves 'English or British colonies' as an indication of identity. The small villages they adopted as their winter homes were recreated as mountain sports resorts which in many ways were the image of English tastes and fashion, for example hotels where they stayed were provided with open-fireplaces in the English style rather than following the Swiss tradition of tiled stoves. Churches were built for Anglican worship, English libraries created, newspapers written and produced and British Consular services established in some resorts. In Davos, the area around the hotels *Buol* and *d'Angleterre* where many of the British had their lodgings became known as the *English Quarter*.

Winter sportsmen and women were strangely loyal to one particular resort, returning to it year after year. In Davos they even referred to themselves

Skiers outside the Hotel d'Angleterre,
Davos Platz, about 1905

11

Davosers. In the Bernese Oberland were found *Wengenites* and *Mürrenites* who favoured Wengen and Mürren, early centres of downhill skiing. 'Local patriotisms have played a great role in British ski-ing history,' noted Sir Arnold Lunn, himself a pioneer of both ski mountaineering and downhill and slalom racing.[1] The British hotel guests worked together to organise their own entertainment, theatricals, balls and games. They also organised outdoor amusements in the snow which soon evolved into organised winter sports with their own aficionados, specialised equipment, competitions and formalised rules.

For this purpose, they formed special committees; frequent reports of their meetings appeared in the pages of the guests' press, such as the *Davos Courier* and the *Engadine Express.* The subjects for this chapter have been identified using these newspaper reports as sources of names and information about what activities they were involved in while they were in Switzerland. These reports show the prominent role these people had in the development of these mountain villages into resorts open in both summer and winter time. Often these articles and other contemporary literature produced in the resorts give a detailed picture of the character and personalities of the early winter sportsmen and women; sometimes they just give a name on a hotel guest list beside the location of their permanent place of residence. These reports give no indication of what kind of life the visitors had when they weren't in Switzerland. Where the funds came from to pay for their long stays abroad is never mentioned, neither is their occupation, family and educational background and personal circumstances. This chapter will attempt to present short biographies of some of the late nineteenth- and early twentieth-century British winter visitors using information from census, birth, marriage and death records from England and Wales and other documentation of the time.

Scrutiny of hotel guest lists and other reports published in local newspapers often reveals a visitor's full name and home town which provides a key to access United Kingdom census data and other reference sources, such as the *Oxford Dictionary of National Biography*. Where a visitor is described as English, it can also refer to Irish, Welsh or Scottish guests. They were usually all called 'English' by the Swiss. When a title is given with a name then it can be assumed that the individual and his or her family were members of the aristocracy or nobility, just as 'Revd.' or 'Dr' indicates a person's professional status. Another potential clue to status is in which hotel or other accommodation a visitor stayed. This, though, can be misleading as some hotels were more prestigious than others; however, presence on the guest list of a high-class hotel may not be an indicator of either wealth or status. Hotels had different classes of accommodation, ranging from luxury suites to simple rooms for servants and accommodation for their own staff. Some of the names on guest lists may belong to servants such as maids, man-servants, sick and children's nurses, governesses or companions accompanying their employers.

Starting with the very first British winter visitors to Grindelwald, they were already resident in Switzerland working at the British Legation in Berne so they had not travelled such a great distance. The minister in charge there was Sir Horace Rumbold, a title and occupation placing him firmly in the upper class. In St Moritz the first winter visitors were also reputedly English, the possible candidates for this role include Revd. Arthur Strettell and Stephen Dowell. Arthur Edward Strettell was born in 1845 at Taplow in Buckinghamshire, the son of Alfred Baker Strettell and his wife Laura van Sittart. The 1881 Census says that Arthur Strettell's father was vicar of St Paul's Church, Canterbury. The father had graduated from Trinity College, Cambridge in 1836. There was a daughter, Alma, living at home who had been born in Savignon, Italy. The mother was not there at the time of the census. This information is significant as not only can we place Arthur solidly within the middle class as both a clergyman and a clergyman's son but as part of a family that had travelled and spent time abroad. His mother's family name is not English and she was staying in Italy at the time his sister was born. The residence of Arthur himself given in the *Engadiner Kulm*'s guest book of 1865 was Genoa, showing he was quite comfortable living and travelling abroad. Strettell also alludes to being a health seeker in St Moritz in his message written in the hotel guest book.

A second of those probable first winter guests to the *Engadiner Kulm* in 1865 was Stephen Dowell, born in Shorwell on the Isle of Wight where at the time of his birth his father was the rector. The family then moved on when Revd. Dowell became the incumbent of Gosfield in Essex in 1848. Stephen was among the first intake of pupils to Cheltenham College in 1841. Dowell went on to study at Corpus Christi College, Oxford from where he graduated with a Bachelor of Arts degree in 1855. He then took articles with London solicitor R Bray. In 1863 he began studying for the Bar at Lincoln's Inn. Nine years later, he gained a Master of Arts degree. Stephen Dowell was twenty-seven at the time of the 1861 Census, staying as a visitor with the Bray family in Surrey, which would make him thirty-one or thirty-two years old during that first winter at the *Kulm*. Dowell was a keen sportsman who played for the Marylebone Cricket Club and England. His family background also gave him strong links to the clergy although he himself was a member of the legal profession. In his legal career he became Assistant Solicitor to the Board of the Inland Revenue. His historical and legal writing means that Dowell fits into the intellectual type of guest. His book *The Income Tax Laws* was published in 1874; he then diversified into history with *The History of Taxation and Taxes in England from the Earliest Times to the Present Day*, which was published in four volumes and came out in its second edition in 1888. Dowell died of pneumonia in 1898 at the relatively young age of sixty-four.[2]

An early St Moritz ice skater was Francis Greatheed, born in 1850 in Norwood, London. His parents were Revd. Samuel Stephenson Greatheed and Margaret Stephenson. Samuel Stephenson, Francis' father, had studied at Trinity College, Cambridge. A famous organist and composer, Revd. Greatheed was rector of Corringham in Essex. He was an original editor of the *Cambridge Mathematical Journal*, and composer of the *Sequential Book of Early Church Music*, the oratorio *Enoch's Prophecy*, the *English Gradual* and many other religious works. Francis's grandfather was Samuel Greatheed, an army officer who became an independent minister and joint founder of the *London Missionary Society* and was the first editor of the *Eclectic Review*. The well-known English radical Francis Place's daughter Annie was governess to Samuel's daughter. This background puts Francis within a middle-class religious and intellectual milieau. His father died in 1887. Francis never married and in

1891 he was living with his brother John, a Church of England clergyman, in the Rectory at Corringham in Essex, which seems to have been a living held in the family. John had previously been Curate in Boston, USA and in Bombay, India. Brother John had studied at Trinity College, Cambridge, like their father. Their older brother, Stephenson, was also a clergyman. By 1900 Francis was a gentleman living on his own means in Bournemouth. Other brothers were William who was a solicitor and Christopher who was a deputy conservator in the Imperial service in India. Francis himself died relatively young in 1904. In St Moritz Francis was accompanied by his only sister, Dorothea, who was ten years older than he was and who outlived him by five years. His lack of a profession may indicate that Francis had some kind of health problem, as the other men in his family all had occupations.

Already from just four examples it is evident that nineteenth-century British travellers to the Alps were strongly represented by clergymen or those with church connections. In the small sample of almost a hundred people investigated here, there are about twenty of them, around 20 per cent. Clergymen were often keen ice skaters and they were frequently represented among the Victorian skating clubs of Switzerland. In 1875, Revd. Harford Battersby was staying at the *Hotel Buol* in Davos where he was on the committee of the skating club. At home he was vicar of St Johns in Keswick where he was probably already an outdoor enthusiast as he lived in the Lake District. He was a founder there of the annual Keswick Meeting to encourage Christian unity. As president of the Keswick Library Society, he organised the opening of the library on Sunday afternoons to draw young men from the streets and into harmless and intellectual activities.

St Moritz ice skater Revd. Ernest Dudley Lampen was thirty-one years old in 1901. He was married in 1898 but his wife was not at home on census night 1901. He was born in Leeds, the son of Revd. Stephen Lampen, rector of Tempsford, Bedfordshire. In 1891 he graduated with a Bachelor of Arts degree from Balliol, Cambridge and gained a Master of Arts degree in 1899. Ordained a deacon in 1892, he became a priest the following year. His church career began in Ventnor between 1892 and 1895; he then spent a year in the parish of Fisherton in Wiltshire. Between 1896 and 1899 he was chaplain of Holy Trinity, Pai in France whilst also being vicar of Selsey in Sussex. He doesn't seem to have settled as a vicar, and between 1900 and 1901 he was Association Secretary of the South-East District of the *Church Pastoral Aid Society*. During this time he was a regular visitor to the skating rinks of Davos. He was still unsettled and went abroad again, to Chateau d'Oex where he was chaplain between 1902 and 1907.

Such was Lampen's love of his adopted mountain home, he wrote a guide-book to entice or assist new visitors, *Chateau d'Oex: Life and sport in an Alpine Valley*. A rather derisory review of the work in *The New Age* accuses it of being amateurishly written. Lampen was commended, though, as his 'honest, calm, ingenious, banal, clumsily-expressed enthusiasm obtains your sympathy in the end'. He was also praised for his attempts to get to know the local people, who he did not refer to as 'the natives', unlike some other English visitors. Lampen's was not the kind of temperament that regarded Switzerland as 'a cross between a switchback and a frozen pond'.[3] From Chateau d'Oex, Lampen moved on to St John of San Remo where he remained for twelve years, although during the First World War he was back in Chateau d'Oex as chaplain to interned British soldiers. Remembered as an old Davoser, the British Colony had a collection and posted a cheque to him after sending a telegram of welcome to the prisoners.[4] Lampen ended his career in Switzerland at le Ressat, Chateau de Blonay in Vaud.

Though not a member of the clergy himself, Ormond B. Hake was born in 1860 and had close family links with the Church. He was the fourth son of Robert Hake, a canon at Canterbury Cathedral. He was acknowledged as an expert on tobogganing and contributed a chapter on the subject to a book, *Skating and Figure Skating* by J. M. Heathcote and C.G. Tebbutt that was published in 1892. By 1901 Hake was married to Janet and living on his own means. At that time they were staying with Ormond's brother Lewis who was vicar of Wrysbury in Buckinghamshire.[5]

Llewelyn Powys, another writer, was born in 1884 and sent to the *Clavadel Sanatorium* in Davos in December 1909 after suffering a pulmonary haemor-rhage caused by tuberculosis. Llewelyn was the eighth of the eleven children of the vicar of Montacute in Somerset. His mother was also a clergyman's daughter and related to the poet Cowper. As well as clerical and intellectual connections, Llewelyn had some overseas links. One of his brothers lived in East Africa and he travelled there himself as well as to America and later to the West Indies. He had been a school master but life in the sanatorium gave him the time to read and develop his own writing skills. He recovered enough to return home but had to go back to Switzerland in 1912, where he brought on another haemorrhage after foolishly walking over the mountain pass between Davos and Arosa.[6] He was well enough to go home and resume his literary career but his tuberculosis and other complaints recurred so he went back to *Clavadel* in 1936 in a last attempt to save his life. He died there of a burst duodenal ulcer in 1939.

Dr Charles Frederick Aked, born in 1864, was being treated in Davos in 1903. Unusually for a Davoser, he was described as a radical socialist and was Baptist minister of Pembroke Place Chapel, Liverpool. He emigrated to the United States where he became naturalised in 1907 and worked as minister of Fifth Avenue Baptist Church in New York before moving to San Francisco. Aked maintained his radicalism and was an enthusiastic supporter of women's suffrage.

Sidney Parry of Windlesham was one of five boys between twelve and eighteen who were boarding pupils of Ward Travers Burges, vicar of St Michael's, Shrewsbury at Parsonage House at the time of the1881 Census. His father John Parry was a clerk in holy orders lodging at 2 Park Villas, Windlesham with landlady Margaret Franklin who had no husband at home and three young children. Sidney's mother Latatia had been born in Barbados, putting him into another common category of visitor to Switzerland, those who had overseas connections.

Another from a clergy family though not actually a clergyman himself was Freddie de Beauchamp Strickland, editor and founder of the *St Moritz Post*. He was born in 1859, the son of Henry Strickland, a missionary curate to the Lord Bishop of London, according to the census of 1861. The family does not appear in subsequent census data and so was perhaps resident overseas, undertaking missionary work.

An entrant in a clay-pigeon shooting contest in Davos in 1903 was another clergyman, William H. Longsdon. The 1901 Census shows him living in the parish of St George the Martyr in Southwark although he was born in Yorkshire. At the time of the census he had three children, the eldest of whom was five.[7] As the reference used to identify Longsdon was the result of the shooting contest, there is no clue as to whether his whole family were in Davos or just William alone.

Yet another member of the clergy resident in Davos was Charles Mourilyan, born in Sheerness in 1870. In 1891 Charles was a university student of twenty. His father Thomas Langley Mourilyan was a retired staff commander in the Royal Navy. They were living in Canterbury. In 1901 Charles was a Church of England clergyman in Attleborough in Norfolk. In 1913 he married Lucy Barton in Kensington.[8]

Other visitors to Switzerland appearing in the hotel guest books who had close clergy connections were Thomas Minshull of Great Malvern who was nineteen in 1881, living with his curate father Thomas. The daughter of the vicar of Filkins in Oxfordshire, Margaret S. Cunnynghame, who was born in Durham in 1855 was also there.[9]

Christianity also played a defining and important role in the lives of the Lunn family. An important figure in the popularisation of winter sports through his *Public Schools Alpine Sports Club*, founded in 1905, was Henry Simpson Lunn. He was born in Horncastle in Lincolnshire in 1859, the son of a greengrocer and Methodist lay preacher. Henry himself studied both medicine and theology at Headingley College in Leeds and Trinity College in Dublin. He was ordained as a Methodist minister in 1886. The daughter of a canon, Mary Moore, became his wife and in 1887 they travelled to India where Henry worked as a missionary. His son Arnold was born while they were in Madras. After a year though Henry's health broke down and he was forced to return to England. Henry now turned his missionary's zeal to reform within the church. His outspoken comments on the waste of money and overstaffing in the Methodist Missionary Society who he had worked with in India and also political criticism led to his resignation from the ministry. He then became a minister of the American Methodist Episcopalian church resident in Britain.

Church unity was another focus of Henry Lunn's zeal. It was that aim that lay behind the Grindelwald Conferences which he organised between 1892 and 1896 and from which his future career as a travel agent evolved. He resigned as a minister of religion in 1895 and concentrated on his travel business. His opposition to the Boer War did not lose him his friends in politics or in business and in 1902 he organised his first tours to Adelboden and Wengen. He formed the *Public Schools Alpine Sports Club* in 1905 to escape the potential stigma that could have been attached to his clients travelling as part of an organised tour. Organised tours carried middle-class associations and were therefore something members of the upper class, guarding carefully their social status, were anxious to avoid being associated with. Lunn also founded the *Hellenic Travellers' Club* with Lord Bryce in 1906 and *Alpine Sports Club Limited* in 1908. Henry was granted a knighthood in 1910.

In some ways Henry was unlike the usual wealthy visitors to Switzerland of the time although as a clergyman who had travelled and worked overseas, he, and his son Arnold especially, who was born abroad, were typical in others. Where Henry differed was that he was not born into a very rich family and that he gave all the wealth he made from his entrepreneurship to promote church unity, the original aim of the Grindelwald Conference. As a Christian, he felt guilty about profiting so much from his industry. After giving £22,000 to the Assyrian and Iraq Committee in 1925 to help those suffering from persecution, in 1928 he put into action a scheme to divest himself of all his property and to form an incorporated society which would provide the necessary funds for the future continuation of the publication he had founded, *The Review of Churches*. This was issued to clergy of all communions to support movements for church unity and international peace and to further religious and social ends.[10]

The son of Sir Henry Lunn, Arnold, because of his father's interests and schemes, was born into a typical background for an enthusiast of Switzerland and winter sports. He was born abroad in India, was brought up with a strongly religious background with clergymen on both sides of his family, travelled widely and had a Swiss German nurse, making him fluent in the Bernese dialect. He attended a good public school, Harrow, followed by Balliol College, Oxford. Although he studied for a legal profession, he chose not to be called to the Bar. His titled father at one stage in his life was a wealthy man. Sir Henry's enthusiasms created the lifestyle which nurtured Arnold, who was also later knighted. Arnold was skiing from the age of ten and crossed the Bernese Oberland on skis at the age of twenty. He devised the slalom and downhill skiing races and campaigned to get them accepted as events in the Winter Olympics. He also started the *British Ski Year Book* in 1919. His own son, Peter, was a skier and captain of the Great Britain Winter Olympic team in 1936. The Lunn family highlights the difficulties of counting and assessing individual backgrounds as they could have been accompanied by other family members who are not included in the survey. For instance, both Lady Lunns, the wives of Sir Henry and later Sir Arnold, travelled with their husbands, as did children and some servants, employees and friends.

St Moritz colony member, John Arden Bott, was a toboggan enthusiast whose innovative designs contributed enormously to the development of the sport. He was born in 1875, the son of Francis William Arden Bott of Somersal Hall, Derby. He studied at Trinity Hall, Cambridge from 1893, where he was an athletic blue and prominent oarsman before he became a railway contractor and engineer in 1897, skills which he was able to use in his designs for sledges which he adapted to have sliding seats. His wife was also a keen tobogganer. In the winter of 1901 to 1902 the Arden Botts were staying at the *Engadiner Kulm* with their family and servants, an entourage of seven persons, though only John has been described here. Bott enlisted in the Royal Fusiliers in 1914 where he became a captain. He died suddenly in 1917 of heart failure.

At the same time as the Arden Botts were staying at the *Engadiner Kulm*, in the winter of 1901 to 1902, Percy Fox and his wife of Tunbridge Wells were also there, together with the Misses H. B. and E. Fox. Not all of these four people have been individually researched either; only Percy has been included.

The author E.F. Benson was a regular at St Moritz. Edward Frederic, known as Fred, was born in 1867 in Berkshire at Wellington College where his father Edward White Benson was head master. His father became Bishop of Lincoln then Truro and later Archbishop of Canterbury. His mother was Mary Sedge-wick Benson who was described by Gladstone as 'the cleverest woman in Europe'. After her husband's death she set up a lesbian household with Lucy Tait, the daughter of a previous Archbishop of Canterbury. Fred was educated at Marlborough College and then King's College, Cambridge. He worked for the *British School of Archaeology* in Athens and then for the *Society for the Promulgation of Hellenic Studies* in Egypt. E.F. Benson was famous as a novelist, some of his most famous work being the Mapp and Lucia stories. He also wrote an early guide to winter sports. In 1904 he was part of a team from St Moritz that skated in Grindelwald in its skating cup competition. Such was his skill that he represented England at figure skating. Fred, who remained unmarried, and two of his brothers were gay. His unconventional lifestyle and background may have contributed to his feeling happy living away from England in the more relaxed atmosphere of St Moritz, although he fitted in sufficiently well to become Mayor of Rye between 1934 and 1937. He also became a justice of the peace and was awarded the *Order of the British Empire*. Benson died of throat cancer in 1940.[11] Benson's sister was also keen on winter sports and took part in skating contests in St Moritz. Although from an elite clerical background, Benson also had an extremely unconventional lifestyle, another factor uniting some members of the English communities in Switzerland.

Another author with an unconventional lifestyle was John Addington Symonds who made Davos his home, convinced he could maintain his health nowhere else. In common with many other Swiss health seekers, he was the son of a physician. Unlike most others, though, he had been raised in a liberal, Christian Socialist, though puritanical, milieu. His mother died when he was only four years old and he and his sister were raised by a stern aunt. Educated at Harrow before going to Balliol College, Oxford, he then got a fellowship to Magdalen but his health broke down and he went to Switzerland, although he had been planning to go to Egypt. Symonds had romantic relationships with first a chorister at Bristol Cathedral and then with another chorister, feelings he tried hard to suppress. The collapse of his health was blamed by his doctor on sexual repression.

Symonds' first residence in Davos was the *Hotel Buol* where he developed a close friendship with Christian Buol, the proprietor. He met his wife Janet North during his trip to Switzerland. Tuberculosis was diagnosed in a lung in

1865. His maternal grandfather and his sister also died of the disease, as did his eldest daughter, Janet. He seriously began his literary career at this time as his poor health precluded any other sort of profession.

Although on medical advice he was married, he remained a homosexual. Symonds began an affair with a Clifton schoolboy in 1868 that lasted for four years. He even took the boy with him to Switzerland. Symonds and his wife had agreed on a platonic marriage in 1869 which freed him to live openly with his sexuality. He did not hide his homosexuality and wrote the book *Male Love* as well as many other works on more conventional themes. He was nominated for a professorship of poetry at Oxford in 1876 but was forced to withdraw his application because of his defence of pederasty in his *Studies of the Greek Poets*.

In 1881 he moved into his own specially built house *Am Hof*, near the English Quarter of Davos. In his home in Davos, Symonds could live as he chose, a bohemian lifestyle, free of all taboos. He played an active role in popularising the resort through his writing. Though a writer, his earnings from this did not form his main income. His affluent lifestyle was financed by investments in land and railways as his earnings from literature were quite small. He was a promoter of tobogganing and President of the Winter Sports Club and the Davos Toboggan Club. He bought two Swiss farms, helped many young men get started in business and financed the Davos *Gymnasium*, a secondary school for boys.[12] He was committed to Switzerland and the Swiss, not just the English Colony, and he made friends with many local people in Davos.

One of Symonds' daughters, Margaret, who became Madge Vaughn after her marriage, spent many years in Switzerland with her father. She became the lesbian lover of Virginia Woolf, herself the daughter of regular visitor to Switzerland the climber, writer and academic, Lesley Stephen. Another daughter of Symonds, Charlotte, met her banker husband Walter Leaf in 1894 in Davos where he had gone climbing. Leaf was a frail boy but was well enough to go to Harrow and then to Trinity College, Cambridge. He was director of the London and Westminster Bank from 1914 and chairman of the Institute of Bankers from 1919. Leaf was also a classical scholar and member of the Alpine Club.[13] He spent summers in the Alps climbing so was not really a winter visitor until he met his wife.

The youngest of the Symonds girls was Katherine, born in 1868. She married Charles Furse, a well-known artist and son of a clergyman. Furse suffered from tuberculosis and spent the winter in St Moritz in 1880s. From 1900 he was compelled to spend each winter in Davos because of his illness.

It was in Davos that he met and became engaged to Katherine Symonds.[14] As he became more ill in 1903 and 1904, Furse and Katherine toured the Alps, the Riviera and Madrid in the hope of some relief for his condition. This was unsuccessful and Charles Furse died in 1904, leaving a young widow with two sons. Katherine became Dame Katherine Furse after working as nursing director of the *Women's Royal Naval Service* during World War One. After the war she joined Henry Lunn's travel firm and was also the representative of the Ski Club of Great Britain in Switzerland. She was the first British woman to achieve a gold badge for the first class ski-running test of the Ski Club. Dame Katherine was president of the Ladies' Ski Club. She also did much work for the Girl Guide movement. She became head of the Sea Guides and Director of the World Association of Girl Guides and Sea Guides.[15]

Also with an unconventional lifestyle, related to his sexuality, was Hector Munro who was born in Burma in 1870. His father Charles was a colonel in the Indian Staff Corps there. From the age of two, Hector Munro lived in Devon with two strict, unmarried aunts while his father remained abroad. He was educated at Exmouth and then Bedford Grammar School. His father returned from Burma in 1887 and took his family on extensive travels on the Continent. Davos was to become almost a second home to the family, a place where, as his sister Ethel Munro, asserted 'We let ourselves go!'[16] Apparently, between sketching, tennis, riding, amateur theatricals and natural history, practical joke followed practical joke as if he was living out the plots of some of his future ironically humorous stories. While he was in Davos, Hector visited John Addington Symonds. Ethel observed that he and Symonds 'played chess together and found they had a taste for heraldry in common'.[17] In fact they had other things in common too. Both were writers, sportsmen and gay.

At the age of twenty-three Hector went back to Burma where he joined the police but retired after only fifteen months owing to malaria. He then took up journalism and writing as a career. Using the pseudonym *Saki*, he wrote political satires for the *Westminster Gazette*; he also acted as foreign correspondent for the *Morning Post* in the Balkans, Russia and Paris. Hector Munro had only a few intimate friends and never married. As a closet homosexual, he moved on the fringes of polite society, like several others who frequented the Swiss winter season. In his stories he described the colonies as 'a sort of modern substitute for an oubliette, a convenient depository for tiresome people'...used as 'a sort of refuse container'.[18] His unconventional lifestyle may have made Munro feel that his family put him into the 'tiresome' category or the 'social misfits' he referred to elsewhere in his short novel *The Unbearable Bassington*.

Hector went off to Burma so perhaps he was thinking of himself when he wrote of the ostracised person, 'If he had unlimited money at his disposal he might go to the wilds somewhere and shoot big game. I never know what the big game have done to deserve it, but they do help to deflect the destructive energies of some of our social misfits'.[19] His experiences of ex-pat life in Switzerland also appeared in his work. One of the characters in his story gave 'Grindelwald a sinister but rather alluring reputation among a large circle of untravelled friends as a place where the insolence of birth and wealth was held in precarious check from breaking forth into scenes of savage violence'.[20]

In Davos he must have been aware of the many sick people in the resort which triggered the following candid remark that shows his doubt of conventional wisdom: 'Stagnation while one is young he justly regarded as an offence against nature and reason, in keeping with the perverted mockery that sends decrepit invalids touring painfully about the world and shuts panthers up in narrow cages.'[21] In 1908 he moved to London before volunteering for the army on the outbreak of war, even though his age of forty-four meant he was exempt from the call-up. He was killed in the trenches in 1916.[22]

A contemporary fellow writer who stayed at the *Belvedere* in St Moritz was Robert Erskine Childers and his three sisters, the Misses Childers. He, like several other members of the English colonies, had studied at Trinity Hall, Cambridge. The Childers family were no strangers to tuberculosis: their father had died of the disease in 1876 and their mother was in a home for incurables before she died in 1882. Erskine Childers and his sisters went to live with an aunt and uncle in Ireland. In later life he developed a cough similar to his parents' tuberculosis symptoms. He became interested in liberal politics, and between 1895 and 1910, he was a clerk in the House of Commons. He served in the military in the South African War. He was also an author and wrote the novel *The Riddle of the Sands*. A passionate convert to Irish Home Rule, Erskine Childers was shot as a Republican by the Irish Free State government in 1922 for carrying a gun.[23]

Another group of people, some of whom have been discussed above, who made up a disproportionately large section of the English colonies in Switzerland were those who already had connections abroad or who were born into families that travelled or lived overseas. Some of these had been posted to the colonies either as administrators or in military service. Others were members of families where one or more members were immigrants. These people were therefore used to being away from home for long periods of time. Their international lifestyle equipped them with the skills needed to co-exist with people of other cultures, have servants of other nationalities and to communicate in languages other than English. For some of them life in a colony, even an improvised one, perhaps felt more like home than actually living in Britain itself. After years abroad some of them might have found it difficult to fit in back at home.

Norwood Young was a resident of the *Hotel Victoria* in Davos for the seasons between 1888 and 1890 at least.[24] Norwood was active in the Toboggan Club and was one of those from whom tickets could be obtained to use the Buol Toboggan Run.[25] At home he lived at 70 New Finchley Road, Hampstead – in 1881, with his parents, Ralph Young who was a retired major general in the Royal Engineers and his mother Juliet. This was a much-travelled family, used to a cosmopolitan lifestyle as Juliet had been born in Greece and Norwood himself in the East Indies in 1860. His brothers and sister were also born abroad, as the 1871 Census gives Punjab as the birthplace of Sarah and Julius and the youngest child, Dalhousie, was born in Madras. Confusingly it also records Punjab as Norwood's birthplace. At this time the household had a nurse as well as three other servants. Norwood was a solicitor's articled clerk. The household had three servants, a cook, a housemaid and a parlour maid. Norwood married Ada Meakin in 1901 and is listed in the Plantaganet Roll of Blood Royal, showing he had upper-class family connections.

Although he was not British, and not strictly speaking an immigrant to the country, Phillippe Perrier, a St Moritz skier who came sixth in the races of February 1904, lived in England. He was the son of the French Consul in London.[26]

Harold Freeman was born in 1850, the son of a famous historian and Oxford professor, Edward Augustus Freeman. Apparently the only foreigners Edward Augustus Freeman admired were the Swiss Germans, which may have had an influence on his son. No occupation is recorded for Harold; he lived on his own means, probably inherited from his wealthy grandfather, John Freeman, a colliery owner. Harold did have some commitments, however; one year the *Davos Courier* reported that he would be late arriving in the resort because of business. At the age of eleven Harold went to the Madgalen College School before going to Marlborough, a public school well known for outdoor sports, a strange choice as it seems his father Augustus despised all games and sports. At Oxford he studied at Oriel College, where in 1869 he became a member of the first Oxford University Rugby Club Committee.

Harold excelled at all sports: in 1871 he represented England in the very first international rugby fixture in Scotland, the only other rugby-playing nation at the time. He scored a magnificent drop goal to help in the first-ever English international victory against Scotland at the Oval the following year, 1872. The next couple of years he played in the international matches of 1873 in Glasgow and again at the Oval in 1874. In the 1873 game Freeman played in normal dress shoes because a cobbler did not complete wet-weather modifications to his boots in time for the game. In 1874 his drop goal was England's only score which won the match ten minutes from the end. His own team was Marlborough Nomads, a very influential rugby club at the time. Later he played for Wells.[27] Freeman was also a cycling enthusiast who rode over ten thousand miles a year. He was a keen and expert rower.

In 1881 at the time of the census he appeared to be living alone with just servants for company at his home at Abbots Langley in Hertfordshire. His wife, Alice, who was born in Wellington, New Zealand, was head of another household in Hastings where she lived with their children. This seems to confirm that Harold first went to Switzerland for his wife's health. Living by the sea was thought to have therapeutic properties so when not in the Alps Hastings might have been a reasonable alternative. The couple had three children, Edward born in 1876, Mary born in 1878 and Eleanor born in 1879. When in Davos the family made their home in the *Hotel Buol* then later on they made the *Sport Hotel* their base. Harold was secretary of the Davos Tobogganing Club for many years and worked with amazing energy to prepare courses, organise races and gymkhanas as well as competing in them himself. His children were also keen tobogganing competitors. Edward Freeman joined the army and was killed in the First World War in 1916. Harold did not recover from this emotional blow and died soon afterwards.

Fitting the model of English colony members having lived abroad or being part of a travelling family is Mr F. St. Clair Ferran who lived in Cheltenham with his widowed mother. He was a guest at the *Hotel and Pension Bellavista* in Davos in 1903. The 1891 Census reveals that Francis St Claire Ferran was born in Bombay, India in about 1876. He was the eldest of six children, the two eldest being born in India. One sister was born there in 1880 and a second sister was born in Hemel Hempstead in about 1883, showing that Francis probably lived abroad for the first five to seven years of his life. Their mother was a widow by 1891 but had sufficient income to have three servants in their Cheltenham home and so could perhaps afford to send Francis to Switzerland.

Lord Redesdale was skating in Davos in 1903. He was born Algernon Freeman-Mitford in 1837 and grew up to be a diplomat, writer and Liberal politician. He went to Eton and Christ Church, Oxford. In 1858 he joined the diplomatic service and served in St Petersburg, Peking and Japan. He resigned from the diplomatic service in 1873. As an author he wrote *Tales of Old Japan*. He was knighted to the *Order of the Bath* in 1882, and between 1892 and 1895 he served as Member of Parliament for Stratford on Avon. He was created Lord Redesdale in 1902. He died in 1916 in his eightieth year.

Another son of an immigrant was Alfred Belaieff, one of the very first skiers in Grindelwald in the 1880s. He was born in about 1866 in Marylebone, the son of Abraham, a merchant born in Russia. His mother Clara was born in London and had two daughters as well as Alfred. The household had two servants, including Harriet Belaieff, born in Essex, presumably a relative. Grindelwald sources usually describe Alfred as a Russian, resident in London. The census reveals that he was only half Russian, from a family well integrated into English life. Alfred would have been a British citizen and a native speaker of English as his mother tongue.

Another son of a migratory family was James Schloss who was born in London in about 1858. His father Joseph was a merchant, born in Bavaria according to the 1881 Census when they were living in Hampstead. His uncle and cousins in the same household had been born in France, as were the servants. Indicative of a search for good health which led him to Davos, in 1891 James was living on his own means at the age of thirty-two at the *Chine Hotel* in Christchurch on the south coast of England where he died in 1900.

Stizia Bello was three in 1871; he was born in London and his older brother, eleven-year-old Theodore, in Manchester. His father, Doamanchia, was a commission agent born in Turkey but a naturalised British subject and his mother was from Manchester. An uncle was the governor of Spakia in Crete. The Bello family home was in Victoria Terrace, Balham in 1871 and 1881 but had disappeared from the records by 1891, shortly before he spent his winters at Davos.[28]

Davoser Lewis Novelli was born in 1847 in Manchester. In 1881 he was a barrister staying at the Langham Hotel, Portland Place Marylebone with his twenty-one-year-old wife Mary Jessie. His father John was an immigrant born in 1835 in Trieste, at that time part of Austria.[29]

Two of the only three English patients at the *Schatzalp Sanatorium* listed in 1903 also had overseas connections. Constance Allardice was born in 1880. Her father David's occupation was listed in the 1881 Census as a South American merchant. He had apparently resettled in Cheshire after living in Chile for several years. There were eleven children in the family, the older ones all born in Chile. Even one of the four household servants was from Chile, more evidence that they were at ease with people of other nationalities. The number of servants also indicates a prosperous household.[30]

Another of the British guests at the *Schatzalp* was Manchester man, Ben Abrahams. He too was born into a family which had lived abroad. Benjamin was born in Manchester in 1873 but the birthplace of his father Moses was Poland. The 1881 Census shows that immigrant Moses was a photographer and part of Manchester's growing Jewish community.[31]

The third British person staying at the *Schatzalp*, who was accompanied by his own servant, was printed in the *Davos Post* as Mr A.B.M. Midleton lived at Chirk Castle in North Wales. No person called Midleton can be found living at Chirk Castle in any census but a search of the internet and census reveals that Chirk Castle was the North Wales seat of the Myddelton family. Having passed through the female line, the family name at the time of the 1891 Census was Biddulph. There was an Algernon H.M. Biddulph resident with his mother, sisters and twenty-one servants. An older brother Robert was a scholar at Eton. The family name was changed to Myddelton, like that of their ancestors in 1899. Financial problems meant that Chirk Castle had to be leased out for a while from 1911. It is assumed that the name A.B.M. Midleton in the *Schatzalp* register is a transcription error as Chirk Castle contained only one household of family and staff and that the sanatorium visitor was Algernon Myddelton.

Other Davos guests staying at the *Hotel Victoria* in 1903 were Mrs Wyatt Smith, her two daughters and their maid of Guildford. The census of 1901 reveals that Ellen Wyatt Smith was a fifty-six-year-old widow living on her own means. Her unmarried daughters were thirty-three-year-old Lucy and Dorothy who was twenty-four. This was another family that had spent time travelling and living abroad, the census also reveals that Lucy was born in Buenos Aires.

At the *Hotel Buol* in 1906 was A.J. Jaeger who wrote regular letters to the composer Sir Hubert Parry who gave him financial support. Jaeger was forty-one at the time of the 1901 Census and he was living in Fulham with his wife Isabella Donkersley, a talented violinist who had studied at the Royal College of Music.[32] August Jaeger was a British subject born in Dusseldorf, Germany in 1860. He left the authoritarianism of Bismarckian Germany in 1878 when he was eighteen. He and Isabella had two children. August's sister and Isabella's mother lived with them so when August was away being treated for his illness life must have been hard for Isabella left at home. The letter to Sir Hubert reveals that Mrs Jaeger was forced to help maintain the family by playing in concerts and by giving music lessons during his absence. She had difficulty finding work in the form of pupils or engagements 'for there's nae luck about our House, except that we are devoted to each other', Jaeger wrote to Sir Hubert Parry.[33]

August Jaeger himself was a music publisher's clerk, according to the census of 1901. He worked at the London music publisher *Novello* and was a close friend of Edward Elgar. Jaeger offered Elgar advice and helped him publish his work. After a discussion with Jaeger, Elgar rethought many famous musical passages, including the finale to *Variation on an original theme (Enigma Variations)* and the climax of *The Dream of Gerontius*. Jaeger himself was immortalised by Elgar in his *Nimrod Variation*. Nimrod, the great grandson of Noah, was the great and noble biblical hunter, a pun on the German word for hunter *Jaeger*. This ninth *Variation* was an attempt by Elgar to capture Jaeger's noble character and depict a night-time walk the two of them had shared, discussing Beethoven's slower movements. A character representing Jaeger appeared in Sir Frederick Ashton's ballet production of *Enigma Variations*.

Burnt out by his work and suffering from tuberculosis, Jaeger went to Davos in the winter of 1904 to 1905 while still having his salary paid by Novello's. After a few months back at home, he returned to Davos the following winter. He wrote to Elgar describing Davos as 'this Godforsaken, lonely Hole in the d- Alps'. Davos did not cure him and he left the place for good in the summer of 1907 when he was pensioned off by Novello's. On 2 December 1908 Jaeger wrote in a moving letter to Walford Davies 'I'm only waiting from day to day for the time when I get confined to bed, never to rise again. When I think over it all, and realise how beautiful life is and what work I might or could do, and what intellectual beauty there is still to be brought forth by men of genius – and how very soon I shall be dead to it all, dead to family and friends and sunshine and green fields and symphonies and quartets and poetry and pictures and all that makes life the great thing it is, then my heart feels heavy, heavy as lead, and tears flow readily.'[34] This poignantly and movingly demonstrates that life was not all light-hearted fun and games in the cure resorts. August Jaeger died of tuberculosis in the spring of 1909, leaving his wife and two young children under ten. A memorial concert was held in his honour in January 1910.

Another man who entered the clay-pigeon shooting contest in Davos who came from the professional business class who also had a migratory background was George Hoghton who was twenty-seven in 1903. His father was born in the United States and was secretary to three railway companies. In 1891 they were living in Bromley, Kent. In 1901 George's father was a railway co-director who would have been able to maintain an ailing son in Davos. The family may have had two homes as George and his sister Ethel were living in Dorset and were described as son and daughter of the head of household although no actual head is listed there. Interestingly, Annie Shaw, a hospital nurse, is living in the household, indicating that there was possibly illness in the family. There were two female cousins staying with them, including Adele Froes who was born in Brazil, demonstrating further the family's international connections.

Some of the earliest British visitors to go to Davos, Sir Edward Frankland and his German wife Sophie, were there in the early 1870s because of Sophie's tuberculosis. She died there in 1874. Sir Edward was a renowned chemist and analyst for the London Water Supply. He was a professor at the Royal College of Chemistry. He had worked in Germany where he met Sophie before moving back to Britain.[35]

Roland Humphrey though born in Bournemouth was the son of a retired member of the Bengal civil service whose home was in Weston, Somerset. His mother, who accompanied him in Davos, was born in Calcutta, India in 1843.

A fellow bobsleigher in St Moritz was Gordon Duff who was born in about 1878 in Shanghai, China. His mother Ellen and his sister were born in Shanghai too. The family was living in Dulwich, Camberwell, London at the time of the 1891 Census where his father Henry in 1891 was living on his own means. They had just two servants.

The Clowes family, William, Ethel and their teenage son Geoffrey lived in Davos for several years from around 1900 because of William's ill health. Geoffrey joined in with the social and sporting activities of the resort. The 1891 Census shows that the family were living in Kingston, Surrey at that time. Although originally trained as a barrister after leaving Kings College, William worked as a journalist and writer specialising in the navy. One of the books he wrote was the *History of the Royal Navy*. He also travelled frequently to America, studying the racial difficulties in the southern states for *The Times*. In 1902 William received a knighthood. The Davos trip was unsuccessful as a cure and Sir William died at home in 1905.[36]

In 1881 Hans Hamilton Benn, born in Cork, was living in London with his widowed mother who had been born in Sri Lanka. He studied engineering and married in 1894. His brothers were barristers. He is missing from the 1901 Census so could have been away from Britain at this time, possibly in Davos.

John Somervail Clerk was born in Glasgow in 1855, the son of a merchant who employed three clerks in his business. In 1880 he married Dora Carew in Kensington. Dora was born in India in 1860, so the family had overseas connections as well. In 1881 the couple lived in Marylebone and John held no profession or trade. As well as three domestic servants, there was a professional nurse in the household, perhaps indicating illness in either John or Dora. By 1891 they had two small children who were away from home at a small school in Eastbourne although they were only eight and five years old at the time. Daughter Dorothy remained at school in Eastbourne until she was past eighteen years old and son Ronald went to Malvern College before going to Merton, Oxford and then becoming a schoolmaster at Windlesham School. Tragically, Ronald was a captain killed in battle in 1915. John and Dora were still living in Windlesham.

As a schoolboy, Bertie Dwyer was a champion on the St Moritz Cresta Run. Born in 1872 in Gravesend, he was staying in St Moritz with his uncle and mother. His father, Captain Robert Dwyer was born on Ascension Island but had died of heart disease in 1881, aged thirty-eight. At the time of the 1881 Census Bertie's parents were living apart. His uncle Major Lambert Dwyer was on the first committee of the St Moritz Toboggan Club. Bertie's grandfather was also a military man, Major General Thomas Pearl Dwyer of the Royal Marines who had been born in Ireland. Bertie's mother was Beryl Gillman who the census of 1881 says was born in Canada but her descendants believe she was probably from Scotland. After her husband's death, Beryl seems to have become very close to her brother-in-law Lambert and they may have been cohabiting. In 1891 she was head of the household at their home in Portsea, with Lambert Dwyer staying there listed as a visitor. In 1901 Beryl was said to be boarding with her brother-in-law. Young Bertie grew up to be Lieutenant Colonel Bertie Cunningham Dwyer DSO but he later changed his name to Dwyer-Hampton. Bertie died aged ninety-five in 1967 so doesn't seem to have been greatly affected by his asthma. The family had aristocratic connections through kinship and friendship.[37]

The Wroughton brothers, founder members of the Davos ski club, like many other young Victorians, seem to have had an unsettled life as children. In 1881 E.H. and J.C., that is five-year-old Edward and seven-year-old John, were staying with their grandmother Ellen Farran at Bonny Bank, Larkhill Rise in Clapham. Also in the household were their older brother Charles and their cousins Henry and Joseph Sontar. In 1891 Edward H. Wroughton was fifteen and a boarder at a small school in Eastbourne. The brothers were born in Aylesbury but as they were not staying with their parents who cannot be located in the census it is not possible to use this data to discover the exact class or occupational background of the family although it seems to have been middle class as Edward was at a boarding school at an age when lower-class young people were aleady working. Army records from World War One reveal that John rose to the rank of brigadier.[38] The absence of the parents was probably because they were working abroad.

Leslie C. Coventry was the son of an officer in the Seventh Fusilier Rifles and so he probably travelled with his father unless he was sent to a boarding school in England as were many such children. He too would have an awareness of life abroad or at least a familiarity with the idea of travel.

Frank V. Arbuckle was not found in the 1891 or 1901 Census, possibly because he too spent much of his time abroad. The Vaughan Arbuckle family lived in the Military Barracks Garrison at Sheerness, Kent. In 1851 Frank was a gentleman cadet at Alliscombe College in Croydon. By 1871 he was a captain in the Royal Artillery and then in 1881 was a lieutenant colonel on the active list and so was probably posted somewhere overseas.

A Davoser who became known as the father of British skiing was E.C. Richardson, born in 1871 and educated at Harrow and Trinity Hall, Cambridge. He was called to the Bar in 1898 but never practised as a barrister.[39] He and his brother C.W. Richardson had learnt to ski in Norway before their first trip to Davos in 1901 where they found the snow every bit as good as in Norway. They too were used to foreign travel and taking extended holidays before they went to Davos for the first time.

Some families included foreign governesses and servants in their household, showing that they wanted their children to learn other languages. John Crewdson, born in 1870, had been on the committee of Davos ice-skating club in 1889.[40] John's father was Theodore Crewdson, a fifty-six-year-old widower who was a cotton cloth commission agent, manufacturer and an East India merchant. Obviously prosperous, the family lived at Norecliffe Hall near Manchester. John had three younger sisters and an older brother, Theodore junior. In the household were a German and an English governess, implying that the family felt the need for the younger members to be multilingual. Young Theodore went to Trinity Hall, Cambridge in 1885. His health was not good, it seems, and he was the reason that the male members of the family stayed in St Moritz and in Davos in the *Belvedere*. Theodore Crewdson placed an advertisement in the *Davos Courier* to try to find a new position for a man servant, skilled in sick nursing and Swedish massage who had worked in St Moritz and Davos. John had to resign from the Skating Club Committee as his family were not returning to Switzerland. A search of the Birth, Marriage and Death indices reveals the sad reason. Theodore junior died in the final quarter of 1889 in Bangor.

In 1891 Charles Ralph Borlase Wingfield was a seventeen-year-old scholar living with his father Charles G. Wingfield at Onslow Hall in Oswestry, Shropshire. His father lived on his own means, was a magistrate and proprietor of land and houses. There was a resident French tutor in the household so the young Wingfields would have known foreign languages, or at least French. In 1904 Charles became secretary of St Moritz Ski Club. In 1917 he was, according to *Kelly's Directory*, an army major and Lord of the Manor of Yockleton.

A member of an aristocratic family was Hon. Francis C. Brownlow who entered the Chelsea Cup for clay-pigeon shooting in Davos in 1903 when he was about thirty-two years old. His occupation was stockbroker's clerk. As the eighth child of Lord Lurgan, he was from a privileged aristocratic background. Lord Lurgan was a Lord in Waiting to Queen Victoria and Lord Lieutenant of County Armagh. As a baby in 1871, Francis lived with his family at 70 Eaton Square. In the household there were a German governess and a Swiss servant so the children probably had an international awareness and learnt foreign languages. Francis is not on the censuses of either 1881 or 1901 so perhaps he was out of the country but in 1891 he was living with his widowed mother, Lady Lurgan, in Knightsbridge. He married in 1909 at St George's Church, Hanover Square.

Mr Assheton was either Richard Assheton of Downham Hall, Clitheroe, Lancashire or his elder brother Ralph. The 1881 Census shows that Richard was seventeen years old and at Eton. Ralph was aged twenty and a student at Jesus College, Cambridge where he lodged on Jesus Lane with a municipal rate collector and his family. Also in 1881, their three sisters were living in London, with a governess born in the East Indies for company. The oldest of the sisters was twenty-five and head of the household. By 1901 the aging parents, Ralph and Emily Assheton, were resident at Downham Hall, Ralph was living on his own means at Worston and Richard was married with a six-year-old son and living in Grantchester where his occupation is given as 'scientific investigation, biology – living on own means'. As a zoologist, Richard Assheton was a Fellow of the Royal Society and a Doctor of Science. Older brother Ralph lived until 1955; he had become a baronet in the same year.[41]

Another aristocratic visitor to St Moritz was Lady Katherine Coke, wife of Henry Coke of Holkham Hall. Their respective occupations were given in the census as 'lady' and 'honourable'. Lady Katherine was the daughter of Thomas Grosvenor Egerton, second Earl of Wilton, and Lady Mary Stanley.

John Moore-Brabazon was an aristocrat who braved the Cresta Run in

St Moritz every year from 1907 until he was in his eighties, except during the wars. He was first Baron Brabazon of Tara. He won the Curzon Cup for tobogganing in St Moritz three times. He had been at Harrow and then Trinity College, Cambridge but he did not graduate. As a lover of speed and mechanics, Brabazon worked unpaid as a mechanic for Charles S. Rolls, the motor car pioneer, during his holidays. He then became an apprentice at Darraccq in Paris, where he became a racing driver. His adventurous spirit led him to flying and Brabazon became the first Englishman to pilot a powered machine in England, flying for just over a minute over the Isle of Sheppey. He then became the first Englishman to fly for over a whole mile. In the First World War he served with the Royal Flying Corps where he developed aerial reconnaissance photography. In the 1920s he entered parliament as a conservative. In the Second World War he became minister of aviation production.[42]

Mrs Elizabeth le Blond was the only child of a baronet, Sir St Vincent Bentinck Hawkins-Whitshed of County Wicklow. Her father died when she was only eleven, leaving her as a very wealthy ward in chancery. She lived with her mother, a clergyman's daughter. Before the end of her first season, the teenage Elizabeth was engaged to Colonel Frederick Gustavus Burnaby and they were married in 1879. The following year she had a son. Her health was not entirely sound and in 1881 she travelled 'on the borders of consumption' to Algiers, Hyeres, Menton, Chamonix and Switzerland, where she was sent by her doctors. In the mountains she learnt to be independent of servants; she found she could put her own boots on and soon realised she could do without a maid. Around Chamonix she made many winter climbs with a guide.

Elizabeth's husband was killed in 1885 near Khartoum. A year later she was married again to Dr John Main, a professor of engineering at University College, Bristol and the Royal College of Science in London. Her husband became a banker, moved to Colorado and died in 1892. Elizabeth married for a third time in 1900 to Aubrey le Blond.

Independent by nature, Elizabeth lived apart from all her husbands for long periods, almost entirely in St Moritz. She loved mountaineering, becoming one of the first women to indulge in 'manless' climbing, and winter sports, such as tobogganing and skating. She was the first woman to pass the men's skating test, resulting in the abolition of separate tests for men and women in St Moritz. She made bicycle tours through the Alps and raced motor cars in hill-climbing competitions. She was such a believer in the beneficial qualities of the alpine air that she founded the St Moritz Aid Fund to enable people to convalesce in St Moritz who could not otherwise afford to do so. Founder of the Ladies' Alpine Club in 1907, she was also a skilful photographer and contributed pictures to many books and articles. In addition to all this she was an author herself, of both fiction and non-fiction works. During the First World War she volunteered to work in a hospital in Dieppe until in 1916 she took charge of the British Ambulance Committee's fundraising. Elizabeth travelled in the Far East, North Africa and America. She died in 1934.[43]

William Douglas Knox was the son of William Henry Worsley Knox. He went to Harrow and then to Trinity Hall, Cambridge where he graduated as a Bachelor of Arts in 1889. He became a Member of Lloyds so was obviously very wealthy. He served as a captain in the Royal Scots Grenadier Guards in World War One. William Knox died in 1947.[44]

Charles Digby Jones was another regular to St Moritz who staked out the original Cresta Run. His British home was in Edinburgh. His two sons Robert and Owen were also winter sportsmen. The eldest, Robert Digby Jones was a lieutenant in the Royal Engineers, who was killed in action during the battle of Ladysmith in 1900 when he was only twenty-three. He was awarded the Victoria Cross for his valour in the defence of Waggon Hill West where he met his death on the same day that his brother Owen was commissioned into the Royal Engineers.[45] Owen, the younger son, was eleven years old in the census of 1891 and a boarder at Sea Bank House, Alnwick. Ten years later he was a lieutenant and the superintending officer at Crown Hill Huts at Egg Buckland in Devon. He was later promoted to the rank of captain.[46] In 1907 Owen married Gwenllian Cecil, the daughter of Revd. George Phillips. Listed as Plantaganets of the Blood Royal, the Digby Jones upper-class credentials were impeccable.[47]

The newspaper in St Moritz in its ice-skating reports mentions a G.N.E. Hall-Say. In 1891, the census tells us that Norfolk born Geoffrey Norman E. Hall-Say was a single man of twenty-six with no given occupation. He was living at 14 Finchley Road, St. Marylebone, London.[48] His father Sir Richard was justice of the peace for Berkshire and Norfolk who was living on his own means; he was married but his wife was away from home. Their home had three servants: a maid, a cook and a butler so the Hall-Says were obviously well off. In 1908 G.N.E. Hall-Say came third in the St Moritz special figure skating contest and won a bronze medal for the same event at the London Olympics of that year.[49] By 1921 Geoffrey Hall-Say was chairman of the *Billiards Association and Control Council*, showing an enthusiasm for sport other than skating.[50]

Another group of guests represented in the Swiss resorts were those in the medical profession and their families. The commitment of physicians to the mountains demonstrates the widespread support in medical circles of the theories associated with climatology and the benefits of fresh air. They show that within the medical profession in general, these ideas were not regarded as mere quackery. Born in about 1862, Davoser guest Frederick Butler was a medical student in 1881. His home was in St Thomas Street, Winchester where his father was himself a general practitioner. Frederick had a sister, Edith, who was twenty-two in 1881. The household was affluent, with a lady's maid, a cook, a parlour maid and a fifteen-year-old page.[51] Another medical practitioner was Louis Robinson of Lewisham who in 1891 lived there with his wife Edith and two infant children when he was thirty-three years old.[52]

A leading St Moritz bobsleigher was Nugent Smyth who was thirty-seven in 1901 and a medical practitioner in Malvern where he lived with Jessie, his wife. Smyth was part of the same St Moritz bobsleigh team as Gordon Duff. In the 1891 Census his occupation was recorded as a physician and surgeon. His household had just one live-in servant in the house. Within the middle class was a range of incomes and status; in the 1880s two thirds of their households had incomes of between £200 and £300 pounds. For these families the choice might have been between a second servant and sporting participation and paraphernalia or even going to Switzerland.[53]

Continuing to demonstrate the commitment of physicians' families to the benefits of the Alps were general practitioners' daughters Georgina Savile, whose father was in practice in Retford, Nottinghamshire,[54] and Mary Mudge, who was seventeen in 1881, and lived with her father in Phillack, near Hayle in Cornwall.[55] Another medic was William Page May who was in Davos in 1903 when he was thirty-nine years of age. He does not appear in the 1901 Census, which probably shows he was abroad at that time too. In 1881 he was seventeen and an undergraduate staying at Gantsburn House School in Lewisham where his aunt was head and schoolmistress. In the school were five governesses and forty female scholars. Ten years later William was a physician at the *National Hospital for the Paralyzed or Epileptic* in Holburn.

Godfrey Wakefield was an engineer who in 1881 was twenty-six and living with his retired parents in Islington. Though Godfrey himself was not involved in medicine, his father, Thomas, had been a surgeon until his retirement. He was part of a large family of about fourteen children. Two brothers were dentists, one a commercial clerk; others included an architect, a banker's clerk and a tea salesman. The family had two or three servants. Their Islington neighbours were a cap manufacturer, a hat exporter and a merchant clerk. The family were therefore middle-class professionals but not necessarily wealthy when Godfrey stayed in Davos.

One of the most unusual stories of an alpine winter regular is that of Laurence G. Linnell of Leicester. Laurence frequented Davos between 1898 and the mid-1900s. In 1898 he stayed at the expensive *Hotel d'Angleterre* in the winter of 1898–99 but in the five subsequent winters his name appears on the guest list of the small English boarding house, *Pension Villa Freitag*. In 1906 he was back at the *Hotel d'Angleterre*, perhaps reflecting changes in his circumstances. Every winter he arrived in November and remained until April. While he was at the *Villa Freitag* in 1903, among his companions were other people there from his home town of Leicester, Mr and Miss Anderson. The pair could have been father and daughter or brother and sister. Mr Anderson left the *Villa Freitag* in the week before 1 March but Miss Anderson remained until 5 April. Laurence was there even longer, until 12 April.

In order to discover whether there was any connection between the visitors who came from Leicester, the background of these people was investigated further. During that winter of 1903, Laurence had been the first winner of the Manchester Cup for bobsleighing. The wooden bob he steered was called 'Trilby'. Newspaper reports of this victory described Linnell as an artist.[56] He painted watercolour landscapes and alpine scenes. Laurence was not just a champion on the bobsleigh, he was also an expert skater. During the 1899 to 1900 season, only his second winter in Davos, when he was nineteen years old,

Bobsleigh race in Davos Platz, about 1900   12

Laurence was one of only three members of the English Skating Club to gain the first class badge for his skill on ice.[57]

At home in England, Laurence lived at 22 Upper King Street, Leicester, a modest terraced villa. He lived there with his parents, William, a sixty-five-year-old retired farmer born in Cranford, Northamptonshire, and his mother Ann born in Kettering. Also living in the house were his sisters Susan and Mary. At the age of thirty-two, Susan was still single and recorded in the census of 1891 as a 'Morning Governess', although the enumerator added the note 'school' in brackets beside the entry. Mary, aged twenty-nine, was also single but she had no occupation recorded. Two brothers were residents in the house as well; John was twenty-six and a manager in a stay factory and seventeen-year-old Bernard was a shoe clicker. A shoe clicker is a semi-skilled occupation in a footwear factory, an industry that attracted many migrants from Northamptonshire to Leicester in the late nineteenth century, perhaps because it was perceived as familiar by them because of the home-based hand manufacture of shoes in the former county. Laurence himself was twenty and listed as a lithographic artist, a maker of illustration plates for printing, not yet the painter he would become. The family had just one general domestic servant so the women of the family would have had to do some domestic tasks themselves. All the children were born in Arthingworth in Northamptonshire.

This family background is not what would be expected of a typical Davoser. The Linnell family seem to have straddled the lower middle class and working class, not the sort of people who would normally have been able to afford to send an adult son, who does not appear to have been ill, to stay in Switzerland for five months every year when he could contribute nothing to the family while a daughter had to go out to work in a school. As Laurence is remembered as a painter of alpine scenes, he possibly helped finance his own trips by painting and selling his pictures of local landscapes.

Earlier census records show the changes in circumstances of the Linnell family beginning in 1861 when William Linnell, the father, was a farmer and grazier of 330 acres at Arthingworth Farm Lodge where he employed six men and five boys. He and his wife Ann at that time had four children: William, five; Robert, one; Frances, three and Susan, two. As well as the farm workers there were four household servants, a nursery governess, a housemaid, a general servant and a groom. Another family shared the address. William seniors' father was also a farmer of 160 acres, employing five labourers and three boys, at Cranford where he was born. He had a daughter, Susan, aged thirty-one and a son, Charles, aged thirty-seven, who was his father's assistant, showing William born in 1826 was the younger son.

William's fortunes prospered over the next decade and the size of his farm doubled. In the 1871 Census he was a farmer of 700 acres employing fourteen men and seven boys. There were now eight children living at home, Frances, Susan, Mary, Annie, Margaret, John, Joseph and baby Laurence. There was a resident governess, a cook, a housemaid, a nursemaid and a groom. The elder son, William, born in 1856, was away from home, one of sixteen pupils of William Anthony in Belper.

During the Great Depression of the 1870s this well-off family's fortunes declined as rapidly as they had risen. By the time of the 1881 Census, William Linnell was still living at Farm House but was unemployed. None of his at least eleven children were living at home even though Laurence was only ten years old and Bernard just seven. Also in the house with them were farm waggoner George Wilford aged twenty-nine, George's wife Emma, who was a servant, and their three young children. There was a visitor too, Ann Wilford, possibly George's younger sister. A decade earlier, Clara Wilford had been the nursemaid in the household. Everything seemed to be lost to the Linnell family, not just land and wealth but status and family life. Former servants seemed to be ruling the roost, with their own relatives being installed in the family home.

It was soon after this that the family took the drastic step of moving to Leicester where William could style himself as a retired farmer rather than unemployed. His children could help maintain the household by entering trades in the town. The education they had received at boarding schools during the time of plenty in the 1860s and early 1870s stood them in good stead and the younger William became manager at Faire Brothers, one of Leicester's largest and most prestigious factories, making elastic products such as braces and suspenders. He had a home in the affluent middle-class suburb of Stoneygate by 1906.[58] His mother Ann was by then a widow and lived on St Stephen's Road, in the developing lower-middle-class Highfields area of the town.

The rise and decline in the fortunes of the Linnell family could indicate that Laurence may not have felt comfortable living on the edge of the working class in industrial Leicester. He was well educated and had spent his early years in the country with servants, a nursemaid and governess. In Davos, if he had a middle-class accent and education he may have fitted in better than he would in Leicester. No one in Davos would have been aware that he lived in a modest terraced villa with a working sister and brothers employed in factories. He went on to consolidate his restored position in the middle class by marrying

Marjorie Scruton, the daughter of a Staffordshire tailor and textile merchant in 1912. Their son attended public school and became a clergyman in Norfolk.

Investigating Laurence Linnell's story revealed another interesting feature of the Davos community members who were from Leicester. They all lived in a small area of the town, within about a quarter of a mile radius and so probably knew each other. This leads to the conclusion that perhaps many of those who went to Switzerland learnt of its charms through word of mouth and personal recommendations. In the winter of 1902 to 1903 Mr and Mrs J.D. Johnson of Leicester were staying at the *Hotel d'Angleterre*. In *Wright's Directory* of 1906 John David Johnson is living on St. Peter's Road, around the corner from Linnell's widowed mother. His occupation is given as estate agent of H. Johnson & Son of Leicester, presumably his family business.

Another near neighbour of the Linnell's at their earlier address on Upper King Street was John Adam Morton, a leather merchant whose business was around the corner on Welford Place although his home was a mile away on Clarendon Park Road. These addresses show that these Davosers lived in modest terraced villas. Morton was also staying in Davos at the same time as Linnell.

Even closer neighbours from Leicester were staying in Davos too. Miss Louise and Miss Gussie Britten were staying at the *Belvedere* with Miss Beatrice Broadbent. Directories and census records reveal that Beatrice Broadbent was only about eight years old at the time of her visit in 1903. Her two companions appear to be daughters of Mrs Jane Britten, a deaf widow, living on her own means on New Walk in Leicester in 1891. A connection between the Britten and Broadbent families was found in the census record of 1901 that shows that the Broadbent family home was in Whetstone, a village near Leicester. With six-year-old Beatrice and her parents and younger sister lived Charles Britten, aged thirty-one, who was born in Yorkshire, living on his own means and a rather mature undergraduate scholar, the brother-in-law of the head of the household. The two Miss Brittens, therefore, were likely to have been Beatrice's aunts.

Beatrice's father Stanley was proprietor of a slate, tiling and chimney merchants established by his father in 1840. With the urban expansion in Leicester, this business would have been extremely prosperous, hence Broadbent's move from his parent's modest villa on Hinckley Road to smart New Walk and then to a large house in the country. An initial explanation of Beatrice Broadbent's trip to Davos was that she was ill but whatever the reason it did not adversely affect her longevity. Beatrice married, had at least one daughter of her own and lived to the ripe old age of ninety.[59]

The connection with the Britten family of New Walk is that the older children of the six daughters and a son were, like Charles, born in Yorkshire. Mary Britten the mother of the family was the widow of the vicar of Somerby. He had been born in Nevis in the West Indies. It seems the Broadbent's had only recently moved to the country house in Whetstone; previously they had also lived on New Walk.

These were not the only people with Davos connections on New Walk. A member of the Faire family, the employers of Laurence Linnell's older brother William, also lived on New Walk, as did the Viccars family, the widow and children of a wool merchant.[60] Their relatives, John E. Viccars and Miss Viccars, were staying at the *Sport Hotel* in 1903. John Viccars lived in the country at Anstey Pastures but moved to the stately Ingarsby Hall.

Another Davoser living in the same neighbourhood of Leicester was Dr Charles Coles, a physician, who lived on Saint James Road there. He and his wife were staying at the *Hotel d'Angleterre* at the same time as Linnell in 1898 when Charles was aged about thirty.[61] No positive identification of Mr and Miss Anderson who were Linnell's companions at the *Villa Freitag* has yet been made but they too were from Leicester. What this discussion of Leicester Davosers has perhaps served in highlighting is that these people were probably known to each other before they went to Switzerland and personal recommendation is likely to have been a factor in their decision to go to Davos. All of them were in trade or minor professions rather than gentlemen. This is unlike many of the other members of more elite groups who went to Switzerland at the turn of the century. There were other people in trade in Switzerland, who could have had similar unusual backgrounds showing rapid mobility up or down the social scale. Other groups of people may have been influenced to visit the Alps by social networks within their home community.

As demonstrated above, not everyone who went to the Alps was from an aristocratic or necessarily wealthy background, although most of them were. The example of the Leicester Davosers shows that there were some from the lower middle class, in trade and in socially ambiguous positions. Just how socially acceptable this group were to the more upper-class people in the resorts it is impossible to tell. In the *Davos Courier* at the time Laurence Linnell was there and being celebrated for his sporting achievements a list of guests attending a ball at the *Hotel Buol* appears. Laurence's name does not appear on the list so perhaps he did not move in the social circle that went to such functions.[62] In her novel *Story of an Alpine Winter*, one of Mrs Aubrey le Blond's upper-class lady characters makes condescending comments about the low background and accent of another couple. This is despite the couple being obviously wealthy and having titles due to the husband having received a knighthood.[63] The woman who could not accept these social climbers as equals was Lady Livingstone, who according to the story, was in St Moritz because of a slight delicacy brought on by too long a residence in the tropical climate when her husband had held an appointment. This work of fiction cannot be used as proof but as Mrs le Blond's story is based on her own long experience of winter life in St Moritz, it would seem that at least some of the upper class looked down on those 'in trade' or the *nouveau riche*. How prevalent this snobbery was cannot be accurately judged, though. Other evidence shows that some people liked life in the Alps as it was less socially constrained than life in Britain.

Someone else with an unusual background for a visitor to Switzerland was Madge Syers. She was born Florence Madeline Cave in 1881, though her birth was registered with the first name Mabel. Her father was a builder living in Kensington who also traded as a hosier, farmer and property developer. However he went bankrupt in 1900 and Madge's trips to Davos and other ice-skating centres were made possible due to her own talent. Madge Cave became famous as an ice skater on the Prince's Club ice rink in Knightsbridge. She excelled at the formal English style of skating. Through skating she met her husband Edgar Syers who induced her to give up the English style in favour of the more flamboyant continental style. With him as her partner they won the first British pairs event in Brighton in 1899 and in January 1900 came second in Berlin in one of the first international pairs events. The couple were married in June 1900. Madge entered the figure skating world championships in London in 1902, coming second. The International Skating Union, who organised the event, was disconcerted by this as until then it had been an exclusively male event, even though there was nothing in the rules to exclude women. She also won the pairs championship with Edgar.

As a result of her success, the ISU banned women from entering future championships, but not before Madge had won the British championship that year. She also managed to win fourth place in the European championships in Davos in 1904 where she became a regular contestant and also an attraction for spectators. She had proved that women could be just as good at skating as men and in 1905 the ban was lifted before a separate ladies' event was introduced in 1906. Madge won the first women's championship in Davos that year. She became the first woman Olympic gold medallist for ice-skating in London in 1908 and won a bronze medal in the pairs with Edgar. Sadly, Madge died of heart failure in 1917 when she was still only in her mid-thirties.

Edgar Syers himself had also been an important figure in the development of winter sports in Britain. He helped found the national figure skating club in 1901 and was also a founder member of the Ski Club of Great Britain in 1903. Unlike Madge, Edgar was a relatively wealthy man of independent means, provided for by his merchant father.[64]

Other people from professional family backgrounds were Davosers Louis Robinson and Harold Vacher. Robinson was recorded as an accountant living in Lambeth in the census of 1901. He was born in London in about 1867 and went to Harrow school, showing his family were part of the wealthy elite.[65] Also from a financial background Vacher was born in 1880. His father was a bank manager, his family lived in Camberwell and they had six servants to look after the household.[66]

The Dod family were visitors to St Moritz in the 1890s. Their father Joseph Dod was a Liverpool cotton broker and banker who left his four children with a large private income when he died in 1879. The children were educated at home in Bebington by governesses. The young Dods loved the new sports that were becoming popular in late Victorian times, such as skating, croquet, archery, bowls, golf and billiards. Ann Dods was an accomplished skater and expert billiards player. William Dod won a gold medal for archery at the 1908 Olympics, Anthony was chess champion of Cheshire and Lancashire and Charlotte (Lottie) was a golfer and cyclist. In St Moritz, in the winter of 1895 to 1896, Lottie took part in winter sports, including the Cresta Run and mountaineering.[67]

Another Davoser who was a professional person, a solicitor who was there in 1903, was John Verity Watson of Southport. His father was a hotel keeper and town councillor. On the night of the 1901 Census John was not at home, his wife and son were alone.

Another person supported by a profession though not her own was solicitor's daughter Ellen Maples born in 1855 and living in Cleveland Gardens, Paddington.[68] Clive Leese came second in a clay-pigeon shooting contest in Davos in 1903. Clive, born in Woking in about 1886, was the fourth son of Joseph Leese QC.[69]

Staying at the *Pension Villa Freitag*, the English boarding house in Davos, was Mr Lulham of Brighton, who was probably one of the two sons, Sidney or Cecil, of leather merchant, Horace Lulham. The family lived in the village of Keymer just outside Brighton and had four servants.[70] William J. Urquart was also a guest at the *Pension Villa Freitag* in 1903. In the 1891 Census he was living with his father, also called William, who was an auctioneer. William the son was born in 1877 and was about twenty-six years old when he was in Davos. Living in Upper Holloway, Islington the household had only one general servant showing that William was not part of the upper class nor even wealthy.[71] Another guest at the *Villa Freitag* was a Miss Habbyam of Cheffield (*sic*). A Mary Ellen Habbyam was aged twenty at the time of the 1901 Census and was living with her widowed grandmother in Sheffield. The grandmother, whom she was named after, Mary Ellen Richardson was living on her own means. A twenty-year-old male cousin was also part of the household. His occupation was technical college superintendent. Again, hardly part of a ruling or wealthy elite.[72] The *Pension Villa Freitag,* offering moderate prices in its advertisements, appears to have been a small establishment catering for the needs of the less affluent English travellers from the lower middle class, such as Laurence Linnell, already discussed above.

Edward Allcock was born in Nottinghamshire in 1879, he was the son of a prosperous farmer of 475 acres, who employed six men and five boys at East Retford. At the *Hotel Victoria* in Davos, he registered as being a resident of Nottingham. Edward was one of eight children who had a governess and six servants to help care for them.

Arosa regular John A. Peppercorn was a prize-winning bobsleigher and curling player. He was seventeen in 1891, the son of a Bedfordshire land agent. His family home had four servants including a governess and so was quite affluent.[73]

Grindelwald guest Joseph Hoyland Fox, the father of Gerald Fox, the first skier in Grindelwald, was justice of the peace for Somerset. He was a woollen manufacturer who in 1914 published *Woollen Manufacture at Wellington Somerset compiled from the Records of an Old Family Firm,* presumably his own. His son Gerald who was born in Wellington in 1866, was at boarding school in 1881 at Cotton House, Preshute, Wiltshire.[74] Again, this was a very affluent family whose wealth derived from the textile industry.

Another guest deriving his income from industry was F.E. Andrews of Loughborough, staying at the *Hotel Buol* in 1903. Frederick Ernest Andrews was born in Lambeth in 1862 and was a mechanical engineer. He was married to Annie born in Surrey and in 1901 they had one child, Eveline. The household included two servants.[75]

A guest from another family in trade, Henry Palmer, was born in Bromley, the son of a Great Yarmouth maltster. His grandmother was an annuitant but from this information we can't tell whether the family was wealthy or just comfortably off.[76]

A further guest, Franklin Adams, was born in 1881, the son of a commercial traveller and so not part of a ruling elite or particularly privileged background. This Walsall family had six children and just two servants to run the house so they were better off than most Victorian households.

In 1891 John J. Dodgshon was thirty-seven years old. In February 1904 he became president of the St Moritz Ski Club following the resignation of Clarence Martin.[77] He had been born in 1853 in Hazelgrove and later moved to Higher Broughton in Lancashire. He lived with his widowed mother, Sarah, born in 1824 who by 1871, was in receipt of an annuity. Both John Julius and his mother were living on their own means in 1891. Another family member, possibly John's grandfather, was a cotton spinner and manufacturer living in Lower Broughton with his son Edmund born in 1833 who was in the same business, employing 280 hands. A younger Edmund Dodgshon, also born in Upper Broughton in 1866, was running The Cock Hotel in Sutton, Surrey in 1891. In 1881 John was a lodger in St Pancras, London where he was a medical student. His wife was Ada Dundas the daughter of a captain. He later became a justice of the peace. John Julius died in England in 1931.

The winter season visitors to Switzerland discussed above were chosen from a sample of names and places of residence given on guest lists for hotels published in the resorts' newspapers and other publications. What is most unusual is that so many of them could not be located on census records in the preceding and subsequent decades, which may show that they were abroad at the time of the census taken in the spring, implying an even greater number of travelling families than those noted. Of those where information was found, it was also remarkable how many had been born or been living abroad or had family members that had done so. About forty out of a hundred guests had such overseas connections. This could indicate that they were familiar with an émigré lifestyle, were comfortable with other cultures and perhaps spoke more than one language. Another group is of clergymen or clergymen's families, twenty out of about a hundred people. It could also indicate ill health in the case of those with a vocation who were not following it. Growing English colonies in the Alps required their own ministers of religion so there would have been opportunities to officiate at services and perhaps earn a small income for some of them. Another group is of people in unusual circumstances, such as Laurence Linnell and the Dwyers. Perhaps something all these British people who chose to spend months at a time colonising the Alps and indulging in winter sports was that they did not fit comfortably into society in England. The alpine resort colonies tolerated a kind of counter-hegemony – the relaxation or overturning of normal means of social control in liminal places.[78] This may explain why some openly gay people felt comfortable enough there to make the places home or at least second homes. Possibly even that other big social taboo, heterosexual relationships between unmarried couples, was less frowned upon there or at least more easily hidden. The resorts also offered at least limited social inclusion for the newly rich or even aspirational social climbers, at least temporary ones, who could live in those bourgeois palaces, the grand hotels.

Social networks probably played an important role in encouraging people to go to Switzerland; word of mouth was an important factor in recommending particular accommodation in English resorts and so this is likely to have been the case in the alpine resorts. The information revealed about the connections between Leicester Davos visitors illuminates this hypothesis although it does not provide definite proof. Other social networks were based on education. Looking at the educational background of alpine enthusiasts, not only did many go to Oxbridge and public schools but a high proportion of these went to Harrow or to Trinity College or its neighbour Trinity Hall in Cambridge. These social networks were also continuations of the English sporting ethos and values promoted in these institutions.

Politically, most of the English, despite their unconventionality, were seen by outsiders as conservative. 'In a month every hotel in Switzerland will teem with English people who take Mr F. E. Smith seriously and who would be genuinely ashamed to be caught reading a Radical newspaper. Now there are about a thousand "grand hotels" in Switzerland and they all live on British Toryism.[79] The writer obviously knew nothing of the unusual way of living and outlook of some of the English guests or even the avowed socialism or radicalism of at least a few of them such as Dr Aked or even the idealism and benevolence of Sir Henry Lunn. As Mike Huggins has noted 'middle class respectability was never strong even among the middle classes'.[80] Away from the restrictions of English life, albeit under the scrutiny of many of their peers, respectability could fade a little into the background. For instance, young men and women might call each other by their Christian names while on the slopes and rinks, situations that lent themselves to informality. This leads to a comparison between the Swiss resorts and the British seaside which gave opportunities for middle-class female participation, mixing between the sexes and courtship in a sporting context. 'Resorts all provided fertile grounds for many of the earlier middle-class women's sports clubs'; the remote mountains were another such context.

'Upper middle-class climbers in the Alps from the 1850s often exhibited a fairly wild informality at odds with their respectable lives as did the professors, teachers, businessmen, doctors and lawyers who developed the sport of rock climbing…'.[81] Lowerson's observation here referred to climbers in North Wales and the Lake District but applies equally to climbers in Switzerland and later in the nineteenth century to those in other mountain sports, sledging, skating and skiing.

As the mountain sports were new they had not yet developed any gender traditions, as was shown in the case of Madge Syers, the ice skater. In the women's colleges and private schools, girls took part in sports in the shelter of college or private grounds and were invisible to the public. In educational institutions this was given legitimacy by its acknowledged value as a curative for the physical and mental defects supposedly caused to females by higher learning. Sporting activity always took place in modest attire and carefully avoided flagrant violations of behavioural codes.[82] What could be more out of site than a remote mountain side and more modest than the layers of clothing necessary not to freeze in the extreme cold and the veils that protected the face from sunburn? Even so, many women were frowned upon because in the early twentieth century they wore trousers to take part in sport, deemed to be immodest, indecent and unfeminine.

The English who settled in the Swiss resorts created communities living like small British colonies in the Empire. When the English referred to 'foreigners' in the resorts this did not mean the non-Swiss but all of the non-English. Some of them referred to Swiss people as 'natives'. When an Austrian bobsleigh team came to St Moritz determined to beat the English competitors, a letter appeared in *Alpinismus und Wintersport* in 1907 claiming that the English had said that they had been beaten on their home ground.[83] For the English colonists, Switzerland was their home territory! An article in the journal *The New Age* shows its author's contempt for the imperialist attitudes or chauvinism and way of life of the British staying in the Alps: 'I must say here that no intelligent Englishman can quite understand the forces which are opposed to English progress until he has made a prolonged sojourn in a Swiss grand hotel.'[84]

This was not the type of attitude expressed by those who went to the Alps for sport. Mountaineers and then early skiers had a great respect for the guides they employed. For instance, Arnold Lunn's numerous autobiographical books about his experiences in the mountains show not just respect but affection and friendship towards the guides that accompanied him on many of his mountain tours, both on ski or on foot.[85] John Addington Symonds also made many friendships among local Davos people. While some English visitors probably did have condescending attitudes, this was by no means universal nor confined solely to them. In 1850 a travel writer from Geneva referred to the primitive people of Grisons and Engadine; the guide to the area he produced was both voyeuristic and patronising, not to say sexist, towards the writer's Swiss countrymen and women, emphasising the 'otherness' of the inhabitants of this remote region, even to those who shared the same nationality. A pastime he recommended was to sit on a bench and listen to the conversation in Romansch of women and young girls. An indiscrete manoeuvre for a foreigner, he admitted, but he concluded that it had a great charm.[86]

Sport allowed those with unearned income to use time to develop their physical prowess. This reflected the public school games ethos. Sport developed a character to be looked up to and good physical health was vital for this.[87] These characteristics were precisely those valued in imperial officers, of which there were a high number in the pseudo-colonies of Davos and St Moritz in particular. In this context, the creation of clubs and the development of rules and regulations for the new snow sports reflected this civilising mission of the English, to tame the untamed. The public schools sports ethos had its roots in the need for reform in the upper middle-class education system where boys could be unruly, rebellious, brutal and brutalised. The house system, team games, playing fields, cups and cup ties, leagues and league tables were, according to Huggins, a reaction to this. 'The ornate trappings of athletic success, blazers, badges and strips were often carried to new sports clubs, transferred with mannerisms and expectations, the potent symbols of a corporate class culture.'[88] Bobsleigh teams, skating and skiing clubs all adopted these trappings, indicating affiliations and tests successfully passed. For John Mangan, discussing Cambridge University, 'it was this muscular morality above all else which the British product of public school and ancient university took to every corner of the Empire. It served teachers, missionaries and colonial administrators well in their efforts to train the child at home in Britain and the child-like nature in the colonies.'[89]

Analysis has shown that a large proportion of men in St Moritz and Davos had been to Trinity Hall and Trinity College in Cambridge, although there were plenty of people from other Oxbridge colleges in Switzerland. Almost all the British young men and some of the women in the Alps, or if not their brothers, had been raised within this culture. The adaptation of the norms of public school life was part of the creation of English colonies in the mountains. Tobogganing, skating, curling, bandy and later skiing and ice hockey clubs all had their own rules, regalia, badges, tests of skill for members, uniforms and sashes for members of teams, which promoted camaraderie. All of these things created a sense of identity beyond that of nationality or social status, or even sick or healthy. This reinforces Patrick Joyce's argument that people possessed a spectrum of collective identities not only class, but also of neighbourhood, workplace, town, region, religion and nation and that these can involve shared values and perspectives which cut across class.[90] The different alpine communities developed identities of their own, as Davosers or St Moritzers and later Murrenites and Wengenites. These groupings could include people who were not English provided they had the qualification of staying in one of the resorts, having time to practise and money to buy equipment as well as sufficient class status in their homelands. As the resorts grew, class was more important than nationality in the formation of communities.

Notes

1 Lunn, p. 32.
2 *Oxford Dictionary of National Biography*, 2004–2007 (*ODNB*) (online).
3 Tonson, Jacob, 'Books and persons (an occasional causerie)', *The New Age, a Weekly Review of Politics, Literature and Art*, 5 January 1911, p. 231.
4 *Davoser Blätter*, 3 June 1916.
5 UK Censuses 1861 and 1901.
6 Foss, P.J., *ODNB*.
7 Census 1901.
8 Censuses 1891 and 1901.
9 Census 1881.
10 *ODNB*.
11 Basu, Sayoni, *ODNB*.
12 Norton, Rictor, *ODNB*.
13 Lubenow, William C., *ODNB*.
14 McConkey, Kenneth, *ODNB*.
15 Burns, T.F., *ODNB*.
16 Lambert, J.W. (ed.) Introduction to *The Bodley Head Saki*, London, 1963, p. 18.
17 Lambert, p. 19.
18 Saki, 'The unbearable Bassington' (1912), in *The Bodley Head Saki*, London, 1963, p. 447.
19 Saki, p. 356.
20 Saki, p. 435.
21 Saki, p. 455.
22 Wood, Stella, *ODNB*.
23 Ring, Jim, *ODNB*.
24 *The Davos Courier*, 8 March 1890.

25 Ibid.

26 *The Alpine Post and Engadine Express*, 13 February 1904.

27 Rugby Football Union Museum, Twickenham.

28 Censuses 1871 and 1881.

29 Census 1881.

30 Census 1881.

31 Census 1881.

32 Allen, Kevin, *ODNB*.

33 Jaeger, A.J., Letter to Sir Hubert Parry, from Hotel Buol, 25 March 1906.

34 Allen, Kevin, *August Jaeger, portrait of Nimrod, a life in letters and other writings*, Ashgate, 2000.

35 Russell, Colin A., *ODNB*.

36 Fryer, S.E. revd. Roger Morriss, *ODNB*.

37 Dwyer family history website, www.Geocities/layedwyer/bertiedwyer.htm.

38 Census, 1881, 1891 and 1901.

39 Lunn, p. 32.

40 *The Davos Courier*, 9 February 1889.

41 Censuses 1881 and 1891.

42 Rose, Kenneth, *ODNB*.

43 Hansen, Peter H., *ODNB*.

44 www.Ancestry.co.uk.

45 www.northeastmedals.co.uk/vc_victoria_cross/robert_james_digby_jones.htm.

46 Censuses 1891 and 1901.

47 www.Ancestry.co.uk.

48 Census 1891.

49 www.gbrathletics.com/olympic/figure.htm.

50 *The Billiard Player*, 15 July 1921.

51 Census 1881.

52 Census 1891.

53 Huggins, Mike, 'Second-class citizens? English middle-class culture and sport, 1850–1910: a reconsideration', in Mangan, John (ed.), *A sport loving society: Victorian and Edwardian middle-class England at play*, London, 2006, pp. 11–42, especially p. 23.

54 Censuses 1871 and 1881.

55 Census 1881.

56 *The Davos Courier*, 13 February 1925.

57 *The Davos Courier*, 22 March 1900.

58 *Wright's Directory of Leicester*, 1906.

59 Inscription on Broadbent family grave memorial, Welford Road Cemetry, Leicester.

60 Census 1881, *Wright's Directory of Leicester*, 1898.

61 *Kelly's Directory of Leicester*, 1900, Census 1901.

62 *The Davos Courier*, 4 January 1900.

63 le Blond.

64 Wilson, Judith, *ODNB*.

65 Censuses 1881 and 1901.

66 Census 1891.

67 Jeremy Miles, *ODNB*.

68 Census 1881.

69 Census 1891.

70 Census 1881.

71 Census 1891.

72 Census 1901.

73 Census 1891.

74 Census 1881.

75 Census 1901.

76 Census 1881.

77 *The Alpine Post and Engadine Express,* 13 February 1904.

78 Stanely, Jo, 'And after the cross-dressed cabin boys and whaling wives? Possible futures for somen's maritime historiography', *Journal of Transport History,* 2002.

79 Tonson, p. 231.

80 Huggins, p. 15.

81 Lowerson, John, *Sport and the middle classes, 1850–1914,* Manchester, 1993, p. 55.

82 McCrone, Kathleen E., 'The "lady blue" – sport at the Oxbridge women's colleges from their foundation to 1914', in Mangan (ed.), p. 169.

83 Letter appearing in *Alpinismus und Wintersport,* 14, 10 May 1907, quoted in German by Busset and Marcacci, pp. 5–33, especially p. 25.

84 Tonson, p. 231.

85 E.g. Lunn, Arnold, *The mountains of youth,* London, 1925, pp. 120–131.

86 Rey, W., *Les Grisons et la haute Engadine,* Geneva, 1850, p. 54.

87 Cain, Peter, 'Sport and British imperialism, 1880–1914', Historians on sport conference, de Montfort University, 27 October 2007.

88 Huggins, pp. 17–19.

89 Mangan, J.A., '"Oars and the man", pleasure and purpose in Victorian and Edwardian Cambridge', in Mangan (ed.), pp. 93–118, especially pp. 110–111.

90 Joyce, Patrick, *Visions of the people: industrial England and the question of class 1848–1914,* Cambridge, 1991, quoted by Huggins, p. 25.

Conclusion

Before concluding this work an apology is due for the potential overplaying of the role of the English in the development of Swiss tourism in comparison with the input of the Swiss themselves, German medics and also travellers of other nationalities. These have all played a significant and major part in this development. Although the English played an important role, there has been a tendency to underestimate that of hoteliers and local promoters in the development of alpine winter tourism.[1] I have tried to use a variety of sources written in English, German and French in this study. However, for the section looking at the biographical background of travellers, the main sources consulted were the *Census of the United Kingdom* taken between 1851 and 1901 which included details of birth place as well as occupation, and the online version of the *Oxford Dictionary of National Biography*(the 'national' referred to here is British). The names used as keys in this search were obtained from hotel guest lists where I selected entries with United Kingdom addresses for the purposes of further research. The tourist press published in English, German and French by long-stay visitors to the resorts carried similar news items, features and reports in all three languages and I have drawn on all of them. Further research in France, Germany and other countries whence tourists came would be useful so that the backgrounds of those of different nationalities can be compared.

I hope that when discussing innovation and other developments in Switzerland I have used a much less ethnocentric range of resources and so I trust I have done justice to the entrepreneurship of the Swiss involved in the tourism industry and to the pioneering work of those in the medical profession who worked there or influenced the development of altitude cures.

In all the Swiss resorts discussed, the infrastructure of an extended summer business, with a large number of health stations, was easily converted into winter use.[2] However, at the beginning of the twentieth century when Switzerland was poised to extend its reputation as the 'playground of Europe' to a wider middle-class clientele, there were only five moderate to large-sized resorts open in winter. Davos was by far the largest, followed by St Moritz, then Grindelwald, Arosa and Leysin. Of these, only Grindelwald was not a health centre. Three out of the remaining four were centres mainly for high-altitude tuberculosis cures, while St Moritz was a famous spa and summer resort that had diversified its tourist product to include a winter sports season. By 1907 there were so many winter sports enthusiasts that it was considered to pose a danger for the Riviera's long-established winter season.[3]

In the preceding discussions the five different Swiss resorts have been analysed and their origins and styles of subsequent development, particularly in winter, compared. Davos began its winter career with the arrival of two sick young German men in the closed-up village in February 1865 through the influence of the reports compiled by the German physician, Alexander Spengler. From the *Hotel Strela*, accommodation for health seekers soon progressed with the opening of the *Kurhaus*, followed soon by grand hotels like the *Buol, Belvedere* and their annexes before a new stage of development began with the opening of the first closed sanatorium by Dr Turban from Germany in 1888. Davos, however, had a duel development: first as a centre of healing but soon to be followed by the growth of winter sports among both the convalescent and their healthy companions. As awareness of the nature of tuberculosis as a bacillus infection spread, so the concerns of contagion from sick to healthy grew. This was soon followed by the appearance of dedicated sports hotels where no tuberculosis patients were allowed. The development of the sport-hotel in Davos was a response to the sports enthusiast in sound health who did not want to stay in an establishment associated with illness or with the risk of contagion. This dual parallel development as both a cure and sports centre in Davos meant that the decline in the number of tuberculosis patients visiting sanatoria after the discovery of penicillin in 1945 did not lead to a decline in the fortunes of the resort. The continued expansion of tourism among native Swiss as well as visitors from abroad made up for any loss in health seekers. The accommodation and infrastructure already existed, as did facilities for sports, including the *Schatzalpbahn,* ski lifts, toboggan and bobsleigh runs and ice rinks.

St Moritz has its own founding myth centred around Johannes Badrutt and the *Engadiner Kulm* with its first winter guests in late 1864, a couple of months before the arrival of the first winter visitors in Davos.[4] The beginnings of tourism in this resort had their origins in the village's reputation as a spa where summer guests went to have all manner of ailments treated. In St Moritz there is evidence that some of the earliest winter visitors were hoping to benefit their health but, unlike in Davos, there were no specialist buildings for the use of the sick in particular, in St Moritz development focused on grand hotels like the *Engadiner Kulm* and the *Palace*. By 1873 St Moritz was welcoming more winter visitors coming to the resort for health and sport than summer visitors. The history of St Moritz was determined by those with vested interests in the spa and hotels who decided to choose a different route to expansion than in Davos, by making tuberculosis sufferers unwelcome in all their establishments. This did not stop all those in a poor state of health from visiting but the resort lacked any special facilities for the sick and in its publicity made it clear that those with consumption would not be admitted to its hotels. Aspects of the resort relating to illness were suppressed and covered up in resort literature and its sporting and elite activities were emphasised. St Moritz therefore never had to make a transition from health to sporting centre but developed for elite sports tourism.

Arosa began its rise as a resort from a scattered farming community, with just a few summer visitors from the nearby city of Chur, to international renown through the initiative of physicians who wanted to begin their own careers in curative establishments. These medics were mostly German who had either been patients themselves in Davos, like Dr Herwig, or had been employed earlier in their careers in the sanatoria there, such as Dr Lichtenhahn. Among those Germans migrants in the medical profession were also Dr Jacobi, Dr Römisch and pharmacist Dr Schaeuble. Arosa initially focussed on promoting its reputation as a cure-centre but those with interests in the development of the resort were also involved in the initiation of sports facilities. Between 1915 and 1920, Felix Moeschlin, director of tourism at that time, increased the provision of sports facilities to prevent the resort becoming too dependent on health seekers alone and so that it could see itself as the smaller, less urbanised 'rival of Davos'.

Leysin's development was entirely devoted to the care and needs of invalids. All development was tightly controlled by the *société d'initiative* that turned the upper part of the village into an almost private concern. Winter sports were tolerated but only for those patients sufficiently recovered to take part in them and their healthy companions, sanatoria staff and villagers. The society actually tried to prevent any developments that would open up the resort to sporting visitors, as demonstrated by its opposition to the opening of the hotel *Mont Blanc*. Publicity focused on promoting the health benefits of the situation and the medical facilities available there.

Like in any other form of tourism, health resorts had to attract visitors to their sanatoria facilities rather than those of a competitor centre – similar centres elsewhere in the Alps, cheaper facilities in the lowlands of Europe, spas or the Riviera. For this reason, Leysin, whose medics wanted to develop a centre dedicated only to health seekers and those recovering from illness, had also to provide sporting facilities for both summer and winter. Confining its market to one single group meant that when the change in therapeutic methods to drug treatment using penicillin happened, Leysin suffered more than the other resorts discussed. Tuberculosis no longer took months or years to cure in the mountains but could be eradicated in a few weeks through the administration of antibiotics. This led to a dramatic decline in the number of health seekers without there being a corresponding number of healthy sports tourists to replace them. Sanatoria stood empty until in the middle of the 1950s when the resort began its conversion from a health to a sports centre. Many of the now-deserted sanatoria were converted into large hotels. *Club Méditerranée* was one of the largest of those that took over and turned Leysin into an alpine holiday village.

Grindelwald's origins as a resort were older than the others due to its accessibility from the industrialised areas of Western Europe. It first rose to fame as a centre of sublime and majestic beauty and amazing natural, scientific phenomena, which appealed initially to the ideals of the Romantic Movement. Its earliest winter visitors probably arrived in 1860, which would make it the first of the resorts in this study to welcome guests at that time of year. Right from the start, the hotels promoted sport in winter (skating and sledging), as well as mountaineering in summer. Accommodation was in hotels that became more luxurious as prosperity increased with visitor numbers. A couple of attempts to induce health-seeking visitors to Grindelwald ended in failure, despite medical endorsements. The situation of the village at a lower height above sea level than the other high alpine resorts in the study meant it could not compete based on the theories of the altitude cure. Grindelwald was free to focus on sport and outdoor leisure activities as it had no market of health seekers to satisfy or lose as fashions in therapies changed. It therefore did not have to adjust the orientation of its product to meet changes in demand from those seeking treatment for illnesses that could now be cured with medication.

In Davos, St Moritz and Arosa it is remarkable that those who took an early lead in initiatives to develop and improve the resorts were often former patients themselves, who had initially gone to the Alps for the sake of the health of themselves or of loved ones. Those with an interest in sanatoria were able to influence the nature and amount of development in the resorts. These entrepreneurs were frequently outsiders themselves, such as Holsboer in Davos and Bohren in Grindelwald. Those in the medical professions often came from Germany, for example Alexander Spengler, Felix Unger in Davos, Dr Herwig and Fritz Lichtenhahn in Arosa. Lists of members and subscribers to infrastructure and sporting projects show that those with a professional or financial interest in sanatoria or hotels were the key investors. Those who developed the pastimes of skating and tobogganing into organised sports were also part of this group together with patients and their visitors. The early pioneers of skiing in these centres were disproportionately represented by those in the medical profession employed in sanatoria, many of whom had come to the Alps because of their own respiratory illnesses. As therapeutic cures and antibiotics that could be administered in lowland hospitals were developed, it meant that there was no longer any need for tuberculosis sufferers to spend years and large amounts of money staying in sanatoria in the high Alps. The former sanatoria, with private rooms, south-facing sunny balconies, large dining rooms and communal areas were perfect for conversion into hotels to meet the growing demand for mountain and winter sports holidays. Compared with other mountain villages, they were easily accessible and had good communications with major rail hub towns. The infrastructure of these resorts was readily adapted for a new, healthy clientele.

Many of the British guests investigated were part of a wealthy elite but there were many from the middle classes who were less well-off. Nearly half, at least 40 per cent, and perhaps more, had connections overseas: perhaps they were born in the colonies or were part of army families that served abroad in the British Empire. Others were members of civilian families who travelled either for business or pleasure. Twenty per cent were either clergy or members of clergymen's families. Some of them had unconventional lifestyles, such as homosexuality, unmarried heterosexual cohabiting couple, those who were creative in art or literature or occupied ambiguous class positions after mobility up or down the social scale. This suggests that perhaps many guests did not feel comfortable living in England as they were happy to spend so long away, for up to at least four months a year or even almost permanently.

A sign of English cultural hegemony is shown in the nomenclature related to the industry. There were changes in semantics. Before the First World War, the Swiss called visitors *hôtes* or *étrangers* or *Fremde*. The first tourists took part in *l'industrie des étrangers*. Soon the word used in most languages was 'tourism' or a linguistic variation of that word such as *Turismus* and *tourisme*. The accent was not only on the stay but on the movement of people. Tourism implied a network of cultural and economic things. It was not confined to foreigners but could include urban Swiss travellers.[5]

Winter sports spread through the influence of Sir Henry Lunn's *Public Schools Alpine Sports Club* that opened up more resorts for winter sports such as Mürren, Wengen and Adelboden. His son Arnold promoted downhill skiing and slalom and pushed for their acceptance as events in the Winter Olympics. Arnold Lunn wrote in *The Story of Skiing*, 'Davos was the cradle of British ski-ing, and the group of British skiers who made Davos their headquarters ran British ski-ing in the early years of the century, but the division of control really began when Adelboden was opened up for winter sports in 1902–3, by the *Public Schools Alpine Sports Club*.'[6]

In those days there was still some social stigma attached to the 'personally conducted' party and Henry Lunn decided to reserve certain hotels in winter for the exclusive use of members of a 'club'. By calling his organisation a club for former public school pupils, university graduates or their sisters and wives, Henry managed to entice a select group of young people away on winter sports holidays who would not otherwise have dreamt of going with an inclusive tour operator. Lunn persuaded a master at Harrow, John Stogden, to sign a letter circulated to Etonians and Harrovians announcing Lunn's discovery of Adelboden as a winter sports centre. The proprietor of the *Grand Hotel* there opened his hotel for the first time in winter and at Christmas it was filled to overflowing. More than 440 members booked with the club in its first year. Soon more than five thousand clients travelled with the club every winter and it had contracts with over thirty hotels for the exclusive use of club members.[7]

Other new centres were opened up by Lunn in the early twentieth century in addition to Adelboden, Mürren, Wengen; they were Kandersteg, Grimmisalp, Montana, Villars, Ballaigues, Beatenberg, Morgins, Montana, Sils-Maria, Pontresina, Maloja, Lenzerheide and Klosters. The 'club' gained credibility when Henry Lunn persuaded Lord Roberts of Kandahar to become its vice-president. As the English colonies of Davos and St Moritz had done, the *Public Schools Alpine Sporting Club* continued to cater for people who liked to preserve their social environment while changing their physical environment.[8]

The first British ski race, the *Public Schools Alpine Sports Club Challenge Cup*, was held in Adelboden in January 1903. The trophy was awarded on the combined result of a ski race, a skating competition and a toboggan race.[9] By the end of the decade, winter sports became more specialised and separate trophies were introduced for the different sports. The skating prize was named the Lytton Cup after the Earl of Lytton and the skiing trophy was named after Lord Roberts. The latter was the first challenge trophy for downhill racing and it became known as the *'Kandahar' Cup*. Ten competitors took part in this event at Montana in 1911. They climbed up to the Wildstrubel Hut where they spent the night, before racing down again the following morning. There was a group start and the competitors raced down natural snow; there was no prepared slope or *piste*. The next year the competition was transferred to Mürren in the Bernese Oberland.[10]

The rules for downhill ski racing were not published until they appeared in the *British Ski Year Book* in 1921. In 1922 Henry Lunn's son Arnold devised a new kind of ski race, the slalom. The first slalom was held at Mürren on 6 January that year and was won by J.A. Joannides. Katherine Furse, a daughter of John Addington Symonds and now a widow, was still a keen skier and came third. In this new event the 'gates' or pairs of flags were placed at points that would force the racer to make every variety of turn, long and sweeping, short and abrupt. The rules for this new type of contest were first published in the club's year book in 1922. The slalom was introduced into the British Championship in 1923.

Together with the enthusiasm of Walter Amstutz, son of the owner of the *Pension Alpina* in Murren, Arnold Lunn promoted downhill and slalom skiing. Amstutz was a founder member of the *Schweitzerische Akademische Ski-Club*. The slopes of the Scheidegg in Grindelwald hosted the first skiing event to be decided solely by a downhill race in January 1925, with Amstutz as the victor of both downhill and combined competitions. Mackintosh won the slalom held at Mürren for England and other races were won by Swiss racers. Amstutz went on to promote downhill skiing to the Germans and Austrians by organising ski tournaments against university teams from those countries.[11] Previously all ski competitions had been based on cross-country and jumping contests so these new disciplines were a major change. It wasn't until the 1936 Winter Olympics at Garmisch-Partenkirchen in Germany that upstart downhill-slalom racing was accepted as part of the competitive programme.[12]

Both winter sports and health tourism continued to grow, reaching a peak in 1913 and were set for another bumper year in 1914 when the First World War cut off the source of sporting tourists, although there still remained health seekers and the rudiments of a much reduced winter season in the resorts. For instance, in Davos in 1913 there had been 31,632 visitors. This total fell to 20,523 in 1914 and to 12,474 in 1915. Despite a smaller number of visitors, those who actually went to the resort stayed longer, the mean length of stay had risen from 59 days in 1913, to 70 in 1914, rising to 80 in 1915.[13] Many visitors were new to Davos and so did not miss the social scene of the pre-war resort.[14] The war dwindled the British colony to just 62 in 1916. However, newspaper reports say that there were actually more visitors in Davos than there had been ten years earlier.[15] Prisoners of war from Britain, France and Germany were interned in Switzerland and housed in some of the hotels, including those in Leysin and Davos.

After the war it did not take long for Switzerland to regain and increase its quantity of winter tourists. By the 1930s skiing had became the premier winter sport in the Alps and to satisfy the demand of skiers who wanted to slide down the slopes without spending hours of hard work walking up them carrying or dragging or even wearing skis, more and more ski lifts were built of various kinds. Davos had two funiculars by 1934 when the *Schatzalpbahn* was joined by the *Parsennbahn*. In St Moritz the *Chantarellabahn* had been extended up to Corviglia in 1928. Cable cars were becoming more common, Arosa had one up the Weisshorn and Hornli. Grindelwald had lifts of various types such as that dragged up Bodmi. The *Jungfraubahn* began to open in winter in 1933 taking skiers up to the Kleine Scheidegg. However, in Leysin there was no cable car until the one up the Berneuse opened in 1955 as part of the resort's conversion from a health resort into a sports centre.

Tourism statistics were again adversely affected by the economic depression of the 1930s. This followed by the Second World War and another decline in the number of pleasure seekers masked the fall in demand for sanatoria treatment as this was sometimes seen as a consequence of the general depletion in visitor numbers rather than a permanent change in the composition of the tourist market which now had to attract a new, less well-off, shorter staying kind of guest to replace those it had lost.

Notes

1 Busset and Marco, pp. 5–33, especially p. 9.
2 Allen, E. John B., 'The British moment in ski history', in *Europäische Perspektiven zur Geschichte von Sport, Kultur und Toourismus*, Berlin, 2000, p. 2.
3 Allen, 'The British moment', p. 3.
4 Wraight, p. 254.
5 Desponds, p. 49.
6 Lunn, *The story of ski-ing*, p. 33.
7 Lunn, *Switzerland and the English*, p. 190.

8 Ibid., p. 192.
9 Lunn, *The story of ski-ing*, p. 45.
10 Ibid., p. 46.
11 Ibid., pp. 56–59.
12 Ibid., p. 121.
13 *Davoser Blätter*, 25 March 1916.
14 *Davoser Blätter*, 8 April 1916.
15 *Davoser Blätter*, 13 May 1916.

Select bibliography

Manuscript sources

Festschrift zur 40 Generalversammlung des Schweizischen Ingenieur und Architektenv-ereins, Chur, 1903
The Grindelwald Conference 1894, Swiss National Library
Jaeger, A.J., Letters to Sir Hubert Parry, from Hotel Buol, 9 March, 25 March 1906, Documentazions Bibliotek Davos (DDB), Ref: 01.11.125
Pfarrhaus-Gastebuch, 1805–1817, Grindelwald Museum

Oral reminiscences

Reminiscence of Maurice André, former patient, interviewed in Leysin, 2003.

Newspapers

The Alpine Post and Engadine Express
Berner Taschenbuch
The Billiard Player
Le Courrier de Davos
The Davos Courier
Davoser Revue
Echo von Grindelwald
Freien Oberlander
Neue Zürcher Zeitung
The New Age, a weekly review of politics, literature and art
St Moritz Post, Davos and Maloja News

Printed primary sources

Badrutt, Johannes, *Fremden-Liste vom Engadiner-Kulm*, St Moritz, 1842–79, St Moritz, 1880

Baedeker, Karl, *Switzerland, and the adjacent portions of Italy, Savoy, and the Tyrol, handbook for travellers*, sixteenth edition, Leipzig and London, 1895

Baedeker, Karl, *Switzerland, and the adjacent portions of Italy, Savoy, and Tyrol, handbook for travellers*, twenty-second edition, 1907

Baedeker, Karl, *Switzerland and the adjacent portions of Italy, Savoy, and Tyrol, handbook for travellers*, twenty-third edition, 1909

Bandlin, Dr A., *Grindelwald als Winterkurort*, Bern, 1875

Behrman, H., translated by Cayley Mann, J., *Summer Days in St Moritz – letters from the pearl of the Engadine with a short guide, published by the Kurverein*, St Moritz, 1911 (German version, 1910)

Burney Yeo, J, *Notes of a Season at St. Moritz in the Upper Engadine and a Visit to the Baths at Tarasp*, London, 1870

Conan Doyle, Sir Arthur, *Memoirs and Adventures*, New York, 2002

Coxe, Henry, *The Traveller's Guide in Switzerland; being a complete picture of that interesting country*, London, 1816

de Beauzemont, Henri, *Comment j'ai gueri une Tuberculose Pulmonaire au 3e Degré sans Médicaments, sans Drogues et sans Operation.* Leysin, 1902

Domville-Fife, C.W. *Things seen in Switzerland in winter*, London, c. 1925

The Grindelwald Conference 1894, Swiss National Library

Hen, Henri, 'Souvenirs d'Hivernage, 'A l'ouvre! Quelques pages vendues au profit de l'Asile de Leysin'*, Neuchatel, 1894

Hückstaedt, Hans, *Der Winterkurort Grindelwald zur Winterzeit*, Zurich, 1892

Jakober-Peter, J. *Grindelwald im Winter*, Kur und verkehrsverein Grindelwald, 1913

Jungfrau Railway, Bernese Oberland, Swittzerland, third edition, Zurich, oJ, c. 1907

Just, Robert, *Alpdorf und Kurort Arosa,* Zurich, 1908

Kelly's Directory of Leicester, 1900

Le Sanatorium Universitaire International, Leysin, Suisse, c. 1930

Lunn, Henry S. and Lunn, W. Holdsworth, *How to Visit Switzerland*, London, 1898

MacMorland, Mrs, *Davos Platz: A New Alpine Resort for Sick and Sound by One Who Knows It Well*, London, 1878

Maran, Fritz, *40 Jahre Ski-Club Arosa, 1903–1943*, Arosa, 1903

Matthews, Henry, Esq, *The Diary of an Invalid being the Journal of a Tour in Pursuit of Health in Portugal, Italy, Switzerland and France in the Years 1817, 1818 and 1819*, London, 1820

Murray's Handbook, Switzerland, Savoy and Piedmont, 1856

Le nouvel ebel manuel du voyageur en Suisse par Richard, Paris, undated, c. 1835

Poster advertisement for Hotels Bear and Adler, c. 1890s

Prospectus, *Home les Esserts sur Leysin Suisse*, by M. et Mme E. Zitting, undated, c. 1925

Rey, W. *Les Grisons et la haute Engadine*, Geneva, 1850

Robertson, Hans, *St Moritz – seine Fremdenindustrie und sein Gemeinwesen, eine Kultur-historische und Volkswirtschaftliche Studie*, Samaden, 1909

Schlaefli, Otto, *Winter Life in Grindelwald*, Interlaken, 1903
Schweizer Badekurorte und ihre Heilquellen, c. 1920
Sleighbells, Davos, December 1889
The Sulphur Baths of Alveneu, Grisons, Switzerland (3150 feet above the sea) with the neighbouring mineral springs of Tiefenkasten and Solis. Medicinally and topographically described by Dr Victor Weber, resident physician, second edition, Zurich, 1883
Tarnuzzer, Dr Chr., *St Moritz. Engadin, Neuer Führer für Kurgäste*, undated, c. 1908
Travels in Switzerland, Compiled from the Most Recent Authorities, London, 1831
Tucker Wise A., M.D., *Contra-indications for visiting the High Altitudes with a description of the environs of Maloja, Upper Engadine*, London, 1886
Weber, J. *Illustrated Europe – Davos*, London, Zurich and Paris, 1876
Wright's Directory of Leicester, 1898, 1906
Zdarsky, Matthias, *Lilienfelder Skilauftechnik,* Vienna, 1896

Secondary sources: books

100 Jahre Skiclub Alpina St Moritz (und Kein Bisschen alt), St Moritz, 2004
A century of Swiss alpine postal coaches, Geneva, 1932
Abbott, Jacob, *Rollo in Switzerland*, Boston, USA, 1854
Allen, Kevin, *August Jaeger, portrait of Nimrod, a life in letters and other writings*, Ashgate, 2000
André, Maurice, *Leysin, station médicale*, Pully, 1993
Aubrey le Blond, Mrs, *The story of an alpine winter*, London, 1907
Bachmann, Stefan, *Zwischen Patriotismus und Wissenschaft – die Schweitzerischen Naturschutzpioniere*, Zurich, 1999
Badrutt, Anton R., *Mein Wegweiser. Errinerungen eines St Moritzer Hoteliers*, Sameden, oJ
Bazalka, Erich, *Skigeschichte Niedrosterreichs*, Verfasst im Auftrag des Landesskiverbandes Niederosterreich Waidhofen/Ybbs, 1977
Berger, Anton, *Histoire Economique de la Suisse*, Lausanne, 1983
Danuser, Hans, *100 Jahre Ski Club Arosa 1903–2003*, Arosa, 2003
Danuser, Hans, *Arosa, wie es damals war, Band 1, 1850–1907*, Arosa, 1997
Danuser, Hans, *Arosa, wie es damals war, Band 2, 1907–1928*, Arosa, 1998
Desponds, Liliane, *Leysin, histoire et renconversion d'une ville a la montagne*, Yens-sur-Morges, 1999
Donzé, Pierre Yves, *Bâtir gérer soigner, histoire des établissements hospitaliers de Suisse romande*, Geneva, 2003
Dormandy, Thomas, *The white death – a history of tuberculosis*, London and Rio Grande, 1999
Dubos, Rene and Jean Dubos, *The white plague – tuberculosis, man and society*, New Brunswick and London, 1952
Ferdmann, Jules, *Der Aufstieg von Davos*, Davos, 1945, second edition, 1990

Fox, Hubert, *An English family and the mountains of Grindelwald and how in 1891 the first ski came to Grindelwald*, Grindelwald, 1991, second edition, 2001

Gartmann, Johannes Chr., *Altein – Arosa, Erlebnisse und Gedanklen um eine Höhenklinik und eine Epoche*, Arosa, 1979

Gibbs, Roger, *The Cresta Run 1885–1985*, London, 1985

Haldimann, Ueli, *Arosa, Texte und Bilder aus zwei Jahrhunderten*, Zurich, 2001

Hesse, Hermann, *Arosa, Beschreibung einer Landschaft*, Suhrkamp Taschenbuch, 1970

Hobday, Richard, *The healing sun: sunlight and health in the twenty-first century*, Scotland, 1999

Joyce, Patrick, *Visions of the people: industrial England and the question of class 1848–1914*, Cambridge, 1991

Lichtenhahn, Ernst, *Aus der Geschichte de 'Prasura'*, Basel, 2003

Liliane Desponds, *Leysin, Histoire et renconversion d'une ville á la montagne*, Yens-sur-Morges, 1993

Lockett, W.G., *Robert Louis Stevenson at Davos*, London, c. 1930s

Lowerson, John, *Sport and the English Middle Classes 1850–1914*, Manchester, 1993

Lunn, Arnold, *The Bernese Oberland*, London, 1958

Lunn, Arnold, *The mountains of youth*, London, 1925

Lunn, Arnold, *The story of ski-ing*, London, 1952

Lunn, Arnold, *Switzerland and the English*, London, 1944

Mann, Thomas, *The magic mountain*, Translated into English in 1927 by Alfred A. Knopf Inc. and published 1928 by Martin Secker & Warburg. Same translation published by Penguin 1960

Margadant, Silvio und Maier, Marcella, *St Moritz – Streiflichter auf eine Aussergewohnliche Entwicklung*, St Moritz, 1993

Mettier, P. und Egger, Dr, *Arosa – Ein Führer für die Fremden*, Chur, 1889

Michel, Hans, *Berner Heimatbücher, Grindelwald*, Berne, 1953

Michel, Hans, *Tresors de mon pays, Grindelwald*, Neuchatel, 1953

Pemble, John, *The Mediterranean passion: Victorians and Edwardians in the South*, Oxford, 1987

Pimlott, J.A.R., *The Englishman's holiday: a social history*, Hassocks, Sussex, 1945

Porter, Roy, *The greatest benefit to mankind, a medical history of humanity from antiquity to the present*, London, 1997

Rayner, Ranulf, *The story of skiing*, Newton Abbot and London, 1989

Rhodes, Daniel P., *A Pleasure Book of Grindelwald*, New York, 1903

Riess, Curt, *St Moritz – die Geschichte des mondanisten Dorfs der Welt*, Zurich, 1968

Rollier, Auguste, *La cure de soleil et de travail á la Clinique Militaire Suisse de Leysin*, Lausanne, 1916

Rollier, Auguste, *Quarante ans d'héliotherapie*, Leysin, 1944

Rollier, Auguste, *The International Factory Clinic for the treatment by sun and work of indigent cases of 'surgical' tuberculosis*, Lausanne, 1929

Rubi, Rudolf, *Im Tal von Grindelwald, Bilder aus seiner Geschichte, vom Bergbauerndorf zum Fremdenort, Gastgewerbe, Alpinusmus, Band II*, Grindelwald, 1986

Rubi, Rudolf, *Im Tal von Grindelwald, Der Sommer und Winterkurort, Band III*, Grindelwald, 1986

Saki, *The Bodley Head Saki*, London, 1963
Senancour, Etienne Pivert de, *Obermann*, Paris, 1804
Seth-Smith, Michael, *The Cresta Run – A History of St Moritz Tobogganing Club*, Slough, 1976
Spyri, Johanna, *Heidi*, Zurich, 1880
Symonds, John Addington, *Our Life in the Swiss Highlands*, 1892; first published in *The Fortnightly Review*, July 1878
Tissot, Laurent, *Naissance d'une industrie touristique – les Anglais et la Suisse au XIXe siècle*, Lausanne, 2000
Triet, Max (ed.), *A centenary of bobsleighing, Swiss Sport Museum*, Basel, 1990
Wraight, John, *The Swiss and the British*, Salisbury, 1987
Wyder, Margrit, *Kräuter, Kröpfe, Höhenkuren, die Alpen in der Medizin – die Medizin in der Alpen*, Zurich, 2003

Secondary sources: articles and chapters in edited collections

Allen, E. John B., '"With a minimum of fatigue": women's skiing before World War I', in Ulla Palmgren (ed.), *The 2nd FIS Ski Historical Conference*, Lahti, 2001
Allen, E. John B., 'The British moment in ski history', in *Europäische Perspektiven zur Geschichte von Sport, Kultur und Toourismus*, Berlin, 2000
Boyer, M., 'Les alpes et le tourisme', *Tourisme et Changements Culturels/Toursimus und Kultureller Wandel: Historie de Alpes/Geschichte der Alpen*, ed. Thomas Busset, Luigi Lorenzetti, Jon Mathieu, Zurich, 2004
Hagel, Jürgen (Schriftleitung), 'Die Entwicklung eines Bergbauerndorfes zu einem internationalen Tourisenzentrum, Ein Beitrag zum Problem des Kulturgesgraphischen Wandels alpiner Siedlungen', *Stuttgarter Geographische Studien, Band 74*, Herausgeben von Wolfgang Meckelein und Christoph Borcherdt, Stuttgart, 1968
Heiss, Hans, 'Les grandes étapes de l'histoire du tourisme, 1830–2002', *Tourisme et Changements Culturels*, pp. 45–59
Huggins, Mike, 'Second-class citizens? English middle-class culture and sport 1850–1910: a reconsideration', in Mangan, John (ed.), *A sport-loving society: Victorian and Edwardian middle-class England at play*, London, 2006
Kittle, Fredereick C., 'Down the slopes with Conan Doyle at Davos', *Journal of the Arthur Conan Doyle Society*, Vol. 4, Chester, 1993
Kröner, Arlinde, 'Die Entwicklung eines Bergbauerndorfes zu einem internationalen Tourisenzentrum. Ein Beitrag zum Problem des Kulturgeographischen Wandelsalpinen Siedlungen', *Stuttgarter Geographische Studien*, Herausgegeben, von Wolfgang Meckelein und Christoph Borcherdt. Schrifterleitung: Jürgen Hagel, *Band 74*
McCrone, Kathleen E., 'The "lady blue" – sport at the Oxbridge women's colleges from their foundation to 1914', in Mangan (ed.), *A sport loving society: Victorian and Edwardian middle-class England at play*, London, 2006, pp. 153–176
Mangan, J.A., '"Oars and the man", pleasure and purpose in Victorian and Edwardian Cambridge', in Mangan (ed.), *A sport loving society: Victorian and Edwardian middle-class England at play*, London, 2006

Morgenegg, Hans, 'Der Skilift auf Bolgen', *Davoser Revue*, 78 Jahrgang, Nr 1, March 2003

Stanely, Jo, 'And after the cross-dressed cabin boys and whaling wives? Possible futures for women's maritime historiography', *Journal of Transport History*, 2002, pp. 99–22

Online sources

www.Ancestry.co.uk (United Kingdom Censuses 1861, 1871, 1881, 1891 and 1901)

www.gbrathletics.com/olympic/figure.htm

Dwyer family history website, www.Geocities/layedwyer/bertiedwyer.htm

www.northeastmedals.co.uk/vc_victoria_cross/robert_james_digby_jones.htm

Oxford Dictionary of National Biography (online), 2004–2007

Index